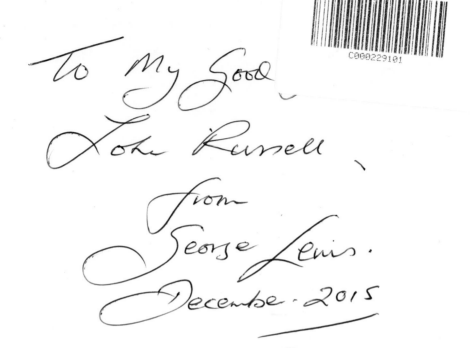

To My Good—

John Russell

from

George Lewis.

December · 2015

# Pathfinder Cranswick

50TH
ANNIVERSARY EDITION

# PATHFINDER CRANSWICK

THE RAF BOMBER COMMAND PILOT WHO FLEW THE MOST
BOMBING OPERATIONS IN THE SECOND WORLD WAR

## MICHAEL CUMMING

FOREWORD BY

AIR VICE-MARSHAL D. C. T. BENNETT
CB, CBE, DSO (RETD)

**By the Same Author**

*The Powerless Ones: Gliding in Peace and War*
*The Starkey Sacrifice: The Allied Bombing of Le Portel, 1943*
*Beam Bombers: The Secret War of No. 109 Squadron*
*Radar Reflections: The Secret Life of Air Force Radar Mechanics*
*in World War Two*

*Pathfinder Cranswick* was first published in 1962
by William Kimber and Co. Ltd.
Condensed as a Fleetway Colourback in 1963
by arrangement with the publishers of the original edition.
Paperback edition first published in 2006
by Exposure Publishing, an imprint of Meadow Books
of Burgess Hill, West Sussex, with a revised second edition
in March 2008.

Published in 2012 by Fighting High Ltd,
23 Hitchin Road, Stotfold, Hitchin, Herts, SG5 4HP
www.fightinghigh.com

British Library Cataloguing-in-Publication data.
A CIP record for this title is available from the
British Library.

ISBN – 13: 978-0956269676

Designed and typeset in Monotype Baskerville
11/14pt by Michael Lindley www.truthstudio.co.uk

Printed and bound by Toppan Printing Co. (UK) Ltd.
Front cover design by Michael Lindley

Dedicated to
Alexander Parr Cranswick
*So that he may
know his father better*

# Contents

# Foreword to the Original Book
## Air Vice-Marshal D. C. T. Bennett CB, CBE, DSO (RETD)

To look back at a boy-man so simply courageous and so selfless in his sacrifice as was Squadron Leader Cranswick is an inspiration which, in this bitter stupid world of early 1962, is both rare and elevating. He fought for the country and the people he loved and for their principles of freedom and justice.

He was not a flamboyant roistering character but simply a quiet honest Englishman. He hated war, but more he hated the tyranny and injustice which was Germany itself and he fought them with his all. He was not one of the lucky fearless ones – his courage was far greater, for he overcame real fear, as many did – and his sacrifice was therefore a thousand deaths before death itself.

Freedom and justice are not vague or empty ideals. They are real and practical – but we have lost a great deal of freedom, and justice is impoverished and fitful. Have the Cranswicks who saved us in war, lost in fact in peace? We who live on have a duty to see that the petty tyrants who have arisen in our community are denounced and removed.

Alec Cranswick paid the supreme sacrifice for us; to honour him, we can do nothing less than to work to make the country he loved a truly great and noble one.

*Don Bennett (1962)*

# Preface

It was back in the late 1950s when I first came across the name of Alec Cranswick and, urged on by curiosity – being a journalist on a London evening newspaper at the time – I launched into absorbing research that produced two entirely unexpected results. One was that I became so engrossed in Cranswick's story that I was able to turn it first into a feature series for my paper, *The Star*, then into a hardback book; the other was that it fostered an increasing interest in wartime aviation to such an extent that four more titles have followed *Pathfinder Cranswick* onto the specialist bookshelves.

Why was it that the initial awareness of Alec Cranswick's name set me off on such a route? In truth, it really was curiosity (though I prefer to

Newspaper cutting where Cranswick's name appears in print for the first time. He is dubbed the 'Quiet Hero'. (Author's Collection)

call it a finely tuned 'news sense'!) that prompted me to contact Air Vice-Marshal Don Bennett, the founder of RAF Bomber Command's Path Finder Force, and to ask him why it was to Squadron Leader A. P. Cranswick, DSO, DFC, that he had dedicated his own book, *Pathfinder*, which I had just been reviewing for my paper. It turned out that Cranswick was a pilot – a member of PFF from its early days – whose career distinction was that, as a bomber pilot, he apparently flew the largest number of operations. The use of 'apparently' is mine, despite Bennett's own enquiries having reached that landmark conclusion and my own subsequent research echoing it. Many years on, with no one having ever challenged this contention with me (or even, to my knowledge, queried it), I am confident we can regard the publication of this 50th Anniversary Edition of *Pathfinder Cranswick* as the defining moment when we can confirm that – certainly among ops crews flying the Blenheim, Hampden, Whitley, Wellington and Manchester twin-engined bombers and later the four-engined Stirlings, Halifaxes and Lancasters – Cranswick's record is no longer 'apparent': it has stood the test of time; it is beyond dispute.

In this present publication, by introducing an Appendix as follow-on pages to the original work, the 1962 biography has been extended and updated with significant new material. For instance, more about Cranswick's early brush with death on a dummy airfield in England and, after all these years, the definitive account of how his Lancaster was shot down over France on that final operation after backing-up the target indicators for Main Force bombers. Focus is also directed – too late now? – towards an inexplicable lack of formal recognition when Cranswick reached his 'century' as a bomber pilot, serving first with No. 214 Squadron and then successively with Nos 148, 419 and 35 Squadrons.

Apart from drawing upon German military documentation, which proved to be a surprising benefit in revealing how that 107th mission at the controls of a heavy bomber was hastened to its abrupt and tragic end, much of what is now included comes from being able to examine previously restricted documents within The National Archives at Kew – formerly the Public Record Office; so I am pleased to acknowledge the facilities offered and the assistance readily given by its staff.

Inevitably, 50 years on, the original text may sometimes seem at odds with studies published in the intervening period (having relied, at the time of writing, on contemporary accounts in the public domain or on personal recollections), though known discrepancies have been flagged –

and statistics updated – as Notes.

In the Acknowledgements section of the first publication of *Pathfinder Cranswick* I was pleased to note that without the complete cooperation of the two women in Alec Cranswick's life – namely, his mother and his wife – I could never have written this book. Their help was magnificent, and to them, above all others, I acknowledge my most sincere appreciation.

Many people, particularly those among Alec Cranswick's own aircrews, devoted much of their time so generously to assist me, and I express my grateful thanks to each one, especially Mr Ivor L. J. Howard, Mr Wilfred R. Horner, Squadron Leader H. Leslie Hulme, DFC, and Mr Harry H. Brown. My thanks are due, too, to Mr Frank Fisher, Warden of St Edward's, Oxford, and his staff, for guiding me throughout the chapter on this renowned school and the Old Boys who have distinguished themselves in the service of their country. A later incumbent and staff have continued this assistance in helping update it – most recently Mr Chris Nathan, Archivist, first by locating a Cranswick portrait unavailable in the original research and then enabling the inclusion of a range of illustrations depicting the school itself and its former pupils.

Also, I owe a debt to everyone who played a part in putting me in touch with the flying personnel whose exploits I am privileged to write about here for the first time.

It is very gratifying that Air Vice-Marshal D. C. T. Bennett, CB, CBE, DSO, (Retd), so kindly wrote the Foreword, because I first came across Alec Cranswick's name in his own book, *Pathfinder*. For permission to include extracts from this, as well as from other books as noted in the text, I acknowledge my thanks to him, to Frederick Muller Limited, to David Higham Associates Limited, and to the Controller of HM Stationery Office.

To Wing Commander C. W. Bromley, DFC, AFC, himself a Pathfinder, I offer my gratitude for his patience in going through the entire typescript and setting me on the right path towards ensuring the accuracy of such details as were within his wide personal knowledge.

In the original Acknowledgements, I ended by thanking all who encouraged me to place on record Alec Cranswick's story, foremost among them my wife, whose enthusiastic support in so many, many ways seemed to have known no bounds.

Rita and our son, Richard, have continued to be a driving force behind the updating of *Pathfinder Cranswick*, with the support of Alec Cranswick's son, Alex. The concept of this 50th Anniversary Edition owes much to Andy Wright, editor of the increasingly popular Aircrew Book Review website, to whom I am indebted for 'pushing' for this republishing with astonishing determination, and to Steve Darlow – incidentally the grandson of a Pathfinder – who made it happen. Steve's counsel has been so welcome at all stages.

I trust that this latest and most prestigious presentation of the Cranswick biography will come to be regarded as the worthy and prime source for generations of aviation enthusiasts, historians and others to learn more about the background and the achievements of one 'unknown hero' who made the supreme sacrifice.

*Michael Cumming*

Alexander Cranswick, wearing his father's medals, in a photograph included in Michael Cumming's feature series in *The Star* newspaper that led to the *Pathfinder Cranswick* biography, published originally in 1962. (Author's Collection)

# Prologue

Swiftly around the bedroom in a house in Oxford swept the inquisitive eyes of a prowling thief. In a moment his searching glances settled upon two jewellery cases on a dressing table. Time was short, but now the robber's quest was surely over.

In the cases were two medals, one the Distinguished Service Order, the other the Distinguished Flying Cross, medals not lightly bestowed at a time when bravery was a byword and courage almost universal. The thief snatched them and fled from the house. What did it matter to him that the medals were among someone else's most treasured possessions?

Those two medals had been won by a pilot named Squadron Leader Alec Panton Cranswick, one of the 110,000 men engaged on heavy bombing operations with the Royal Air Force in the Second World War.[1] But why should even that concern the sneak thief? He gave scarcely a thought to wondering about who had won them. To the thief, thrusting the medals quickly inside his pocket, they represented only a few shillings, which he knew he could collect from the nearest pawnshop.

In fact the name of Alec Cranswick would have meant nothing to the thief who stole his medals. Cranswick never made the headlines; he did not even attract the smallest paragraph during his long and brilliant career with Royal Air Force Bomber Command.

He was one of the forgotten heroes of the air in the Second World War; one of the many deserving flyers whom glory passed by.

Yet the Royal Air Force chiefs saluted his exceptional determination in carrying out every mission entrusted to him and declared that his excellent and sustained efforts were worthy of the highest praise. He flew on more than a hundred bombing raids, a staggering total that few men lived to equal and more even than the phenomenal Group Captain

Leonard Cheshire; it will be recalled that Group Captain Cheshire was nearing the end of his fourth tour of duty, with a total of 102 missions behind him, when he was withdrawn from operational duties and awarded the VC for outstanding personal achievement.

Everyone in the RAF bomber crews was a volunteer. They faced all manner of dangers, and the odds against surviving were among the heaviest of all branches of the fighting services. The statistics indicate that the overall average number of operational sorties flown by each man was about twenty, which means that Alec Cranswick actually participated in five raids to each one flown by the average member of a bomber crew.

Sir Archibald Sinclair, Secretary of State for Air, said of the crews who carried out these hazardous missions:

> Praise the men who are striking these hammer blows at German might, fearless young men flying through storm and cold and darkness above the height of Mont Blanc, through the flak, hunted by the night fighters, but coolly and skilfully identifying and bombing these targets. They are sustained by the knowledge of duty well done, and of high achievement, and they deserve our thanks and praise.

Alec Cranswick was one of those so-called fearless young men. When the bombing offensive was in its infancy, and success was hard to come by, Cranswick was one of the most zealous pilots. Later, as the campaign gained strength, with hundreds of planes streaming into each attack, he was in the forefront night after night with the highly skilled, trail-blazing Path Finder Force.

He had many opportunities to quit operational flying, yet he ignored all these chances. He had to be ordered to stop on more than one occasion – and even then he kept begging to be allowed to carry on.

Those who were close to him talk of the time when the late King George VI personally invited him to leave Path Finder Force and join the King's Flight, the handpicked team of pilots responsible for flying the Royal Family on almost all their journeys by air.

Alec Cranswick declined the invitation – he considered that his job was to continue bombing. So he went on flying his bomber against Germany when the raids were at their heaviest and the chances of personal survival were lessening with each attack.

He was one of the most experienced captains in Bomber Command as D-Day came nearer, flying in one of the most famous of all squadrons, No. 35 (Madras Presidency) Squadron, whose crews earned an astonishingly high number of gallantry awards.

When the war ended, No. 35 Squadron was chosen to represent all the RAF heavy bomber squadrons in the Victory Fly Past over Buckingham Palace on 8 June 1946. Two months later, No. 35 Squadron made an extensive tour of the United States – displaying some of their old Path Finder Force efficiency by never being more than fifteen seconds late on a tight cross-continent flying schedule.

Pathfinder Cranswick, DSO, DFC, was one of the war's unknown heroes. To the people of Britain in the Second World War, Alec Cranswick was just one of the nameless ones tensed at the controls of a huge bomber droning nightly towards a waiting enemy target.

This story of Alec Cranswick has been assembled with the same meticulous regard for accuracy as that with which Cranswick himself strived to ensure each one of his target-marking flares and bombs was dropped on every single mission.

It begins in a place he loved almost beyond all else – the cockpit of a Lancaster bomber illuminated by little more than the dim glow of the mass of dials in front of him as he checked the controls in the pressing moments before yet another raid.[2]

# Chapter 1

# Mission at Midnight

Tense in the pilot's seat of *J-Johnnie*, Squadron Leader Alec Panton Cranswick, DSO, DFC, waited with mild annoyance for the familiar winking of the Aldis signalling lamp that would stab the night gloom on the airfield at RAF Station, Graveley, Huntingdon. In those idle moments before take-off time on a bombing raid, Cranswick would toss an impatient glance towards the Aerodrome Control Post caravan drawn up beside the runway. He wondered if the signal would ever come.

It was the night of 4 July 1944, and he was to fly in a force of fourteen Lancaster bombers of No. 35 (Madras Presidency) Squadron from Path Finder Force chosen to spearhead an attack against the railway marshalling yards at Villeneuve-St.-Georges on the south-eastern outskirts of Paris – an attack in which RAF Bomber Command would be drawing upon some 126 four-engined planes in total and one of five separate raids taking place that night in which there would be as many as 500 bombers involved overall.

This important rail centre was one of the biggest in the French capital and, despite a series of well-intentioned bombing onslaughts, the yards were still functioning too well for the liking of the Allied invasion force, which had been swarming into Normandy for the past month. Trainload after trainload of German troops had been hustled through Villeneuve-St.-Georges and on towards the invasion area. Now, once and for all, the sprawling marshalling yards must be torn apart to check this flow before sufficient troops could be mustered to fling back the Allies from the threshold of Occupied Europe.

The waiting minutes are calculated to play havoc with the taut nerves of the bomber crews; they offer too much encouragement to the crews to start wondering if they will ever again see the green fields of England.

In Cranswick's case he did not suffer the tugging, nervous thoughts of a new crewman, for by now he had accumulated considerably more bombing experience than any of his comrades who waited with him in the great black, bomb-laden Lancasters lined up on the dark expanse of Graveley airfield. It was his 107th operational mission as an RAF bomber pilot flying against the enemy from dromes in Britain and the Middle East. Indeed, probably no other pilot had flown more heavy bomber ops at this stage of the war.

Even so, Cranswick was still only 24 years old – an eager, tireless veteran fighting with scant awareness of fear in a young man's war. He need not have flown so many times, but he had kept on volunteering. With as many as seventy or eighty bombers being lost in a single night, there was a pressing need for pilots of Cranswick's calibre.

In these bombing years Alec Cranswick had built up a remarkable reputation for enthusiasm and efficiency, which had made him an admired and popular figure. He had endeared himself particularly to his own crews and especially to those who had shared the hardships and hazards of as many operations with him, such as Flying Officer Ivor Howard, DFC. The two men had been together on a great many raids in the eighteen months since joining No. 35 Squadron from No. 6 (Canadian) Bomber Group in the East Riding of Yorkshire, and they had developed a firm respect for each other's capabilities during this time. Cranswick had been understandably shaken by Howard's news that morning.

Breezing into the office they both occupied on the airfield at Graveley, Cranswick announced with his customary brevity: 'We're aviating tonight!'

Instead of grinning amiably in agreement, Howard spun round in his chair and answered quietly: 'Sorry, old boy, you'll have to count me out. The doc won't let me fly. I've picked up a cold.'

Cranswick, caught by surprise, retorted: 'I'll damn well see about that. I'll phone the MO and get you on.'

But Cranswick's pleading was useless. The Medical Officer refused to let Howard fly, and for once Cranswick seemed unsure of what he should do. He had never made a raid without Howard in all their time together with the Pathfinders. Indeed, Cranswick's immediate reaction was not to go on the raid. In this respect he was in a position of privilege by virtue of his marathon service. He had more than done his quota of bombing trips long ago, so for this reason he knew he could drop out. With obvious irritation in his voice, Cranswick told his gunner: 'All right. If you can't come, I won't fly at all tonight.'

Half an hour later Cranswick returned to the office. Somehow he had
found out what the target was to be and knew, therefore, that the night's
mission would be only a quick job. He had discovered something else,
too. This was that Flight Sergeant E. M. Davies, the gunner allocated as
Howard's stand-in for the trip, needed to go on only one more raid to
complete his Path Finder Force tour of forty-five missions. When that
trip was over, Davies would be rested and in all probability he would
never again be called upon to do any more operational flying. The young
gunner was engaged to be married, and Cranswick was well aware how
much this must mean to him. He decided to do him a good turn.

Cranswick's mind was finally made up. He would fly tonight.

In *J-Johnnie*, out on the airfield, Squadron Leader Cranswick ran through
the pilot's vital cockpit drill and mouthed the letters T–M–P–F–F as he
checked Trimmers, Mixture, Propeller-pitch, Fuel and Flaps. His
bomber, numbered ND846 and bearing the squadron letters TL-J
(*J-Johnnie*) on the fuselage sides, was the one Cranswick had used for the
previous ten raids. He was growing more fond of the Lancaster with
each flight, although he said that he still preferred the Halifax, with
which the squadron had been equipped throughout his first Path Finder
Force tour of ops.

He called up each crew position over the internal microphone system
to make sure the sets were working efficiently and that the whole crew
was ready. One by one he heard their agreement as the successive voices
came through the earpieces inside his flying helmet: Wireless Operator,
Flight Sergeant W. R. Horner; Flight Engineer, Sergeant C. Erickson;
Air Bomber, Flight Lieutenant P. R. Burt, DFC; Second Air Bomber,
Flight Lieutenant A. C. M. Gibson Taylor; Navigator, Flying Officer
R. H. Kille. Flight Sergeant A. H. Wood, veteran of more than thirty
raids and normally Cranswick's mid-upper gunner, occupied the tail gun
turret, while in Wood's usual seat was Flight Sergeant Davies, Ivor
Howard's replacement. Outside, standing close by the bomber was
another crew member – Temporary Sergeant Kluva, Cranswick's
Alsatian, who had flown many times in training and even against the
enemy in his capacity as Assistant Engineer. In some four-and-a-half
hours' time Kluva would be back on the airfield, bright-eyed and
expectant at the dispersal point, ears cocked and straining to catch the
hum of the Lancaster's engines before the RAF Police NCO, in whose

care he had been left for the night.

In the queue for take-off, *J-Johnnie* was positioned near an intersection of the main east–west runway while Cranswick watched for his clearance signal to come from the Aerodrome Control Post caravan. Anxious to get on with the job, Cranswick glanced at his wristwatch and saw the hands edge up to 11.14 p.m. He was only waiting for that green signal lamp.

11.15 p.m. – no sign of the lamp yet. No one told him the reason for the delay, but he guessed that there was some hitch in making ready the Lancaster ahead of him in the queue.

11.16 p.m. – the signal at last. Instantly Cranswick set his bomber moving away along the broad ribbon of the dimly lit runway. He considered that he had had to idle away quite enough time already.

The four 1,280-horsepower Merlins shrieked beneath the strain of maximum revs as the bomb-heavy Lancaster gathered speed down the concrete strip. The wheels parted company with the ground, and *J-Johnnie* climbed above the village of Offord, set snugly in a valley, and on across the Ouse. The river stood out in the darkness of the night like a faint, silvery streak – its shimmering water perhaps the crew's last glimpse of England for a while, because the clouds hung low, stretching across the sky like a heavy blanket. The night was black, threatening and impenetrable.

As he eased back the control column to steepen the angle of climb, Cranswick's eyes fastened for a moment on a photograph fixed between the spectacle-shaped hand grips on the top of the column. It was a picture of Val Cranswick, his young blonde bride of eleven weeks.

As they climbed away from the airfield at Graveley, Cranswick's crew suddenly saw multicoloured rockets streaking high into the night sky. It took them completely unawares. In blacked-out, wartime Britain, one hardly expected to watch a fireworks display.

The RAF lads had forgotten the date: 4 July, American Independence Day. Not so the Yanks at one of the nearby air bases, however. They refused to allow a goddam nuisance like a war to louse up their annual celebrations. Rockets whooshed aloft, trailing a stream of tiny stars as if trying desperately to catch up with the climbing Lancaster. On the ground there were other brilliantly coloured fireworks, spurting and blazing brightly before fading abruptly. Shooting stars leapt into the RAF bomber's wake, and then for a moment darkness cloaked the base from which the fireworks were being set off.

Aboard *J-Johnnie*, Cranswick and his crew watched the display with child-like fascination. Perhaps the flyers viewed the fireworks as a bad omen; a suggestion, maybe, that fireworks of a more lethal sort awaited the bombers over France. Cranswick appeared to share this thought, for he reminded his crew grimly: 'Those blokes down there are having a good time while we go off. Probably we'll be shot to hell!'

Still, what did it matter if the Yanks wanted to have a little celebration this night of all nights: let them have their Fourth of July fun. As likely as not quite a lot of the Yanks from the firework-lit airfield near Huntingdon would not survive to see another Fourth of July, for these were the crews who manned the huge formations of planes that streamed over the Continent from dawn to dusk – the day shift of the bomber offensive into which was dovetailed the night shift worked by Bomber Command.

These were stirring days of courage.

In London a few hours earlier, Mr John Winant, American Ambassador to Britain, had told an Independence Day luncheon that in the past weeks the men of many countries, fighting their way forward on world battlefields in defence of freedom, had shown a courage and devotion that would become legendary. In recently liberated Rome there had been unfurled the actual Stars and Stripes that had been flown over the Capitol on the day the United States declared war. It had been taken to Italy for just that purpose at the suggestion of President Roosevelt. Handing over the flag to the Colour Party, General Johnson, Military Governor of Rome, brought a thrill to the heart of every American in the city when he said that in due course the same flag would fly in Berlin and Tokyo.

Throughout Western Europe this Fourth of July had been a day of intense air activity. American Flying Fortresses and Liberators under fighter cover had attacked enemy airfields in northern France; fighter bombers had been out strafing targets in support of the Allied Expeditionary Force. By now Allied troops had pushed forward to within 3 miles of Caen, the bastion that had blocked Montgomery's men for close on a month. And elsewhere on the Normandy battlefields the advance still continued with encouraging rapidity.

Now it was the turn of the night shift bombers. The attacks were already building up in strength as Cranswick left the fireworks of Huntingdon dimming far behind and set the Lancaster nosing up into the clouds on a course towards the south coast. Out over Beachy Head flew the great bomber with its powerful engines throb-throbbing through the night. Wave after wave of medium and heavy bombers droned above the coastal towns, for the assault force spread in a great arc across the night sky from Sussex to Lincolnshire and reached deep into France and Germany. Across the North Sea the tiny Mosquitos streaked towards the Ruhr to strike at one of the big oil plants. To the south, Lancasters were smashing the flying-bomb sites of northern France; between them and Cranswick's group of Pathfinders were the Second Tactical Air Force planes on the way to blast rail junctions, bridges and roads. Coastal Command aircraft were busy, too, attacking Channel shipping and laying mines.

Squadron Leader Cranswick, however, is not concerned with these multifarious operations. He is heading for Villeneuve-St.-Georges with the Pathfinders, the RAF's ace crews whose job is to fly ahead of the main bomber force, locating, illuminating and marking the target for them. Secure in the Lancaster's 33-foot-long bomb compartment, with the high explosives, are the special high-intensity coloured pinpointing flares known as target indicators, which must be planted among the railway lines of the giant marshalling yard with the methodical care of an expert gardener sowing a packet of choice seeds.

Flying at the head of the Pathfinders is the Master Bomber. It is his job to ensure the mission is pressed home with the maximum success. The men who fill this position are pilots of great experience and proven efficiency with Path Finder Force. The crews call him 'Master of Ceremonies' and the explanation is logical. It is he who sees that everyone sticks to the absolutely strict timetable of events in the aerial arena; it is he who introduces all the participants, encouraging and urging them on to give their best performance. In short, Master Bomber supervises the entire show from start to finish.

There is one Master Bomber in each Pathfinder mission, and he has to remain over the target area the whole time, from the placing of the first illuminating flares to the releasing of the last bomb. He must be satisfied that the targets are accurately marked by the Pathfinders; and when this has been done, he calls up the Main Force bombers with a code message on the radio telephone. Continuously circling, continually drawing the fire of the enemy guns, Master Bomber exercises a constant and rigid control of the operation. He instructs the Main Force aircraft when and where to bomb in relation to the markers. When smoke from the exploding bombs blots them out, he holds off the remaining bombers until fresh indicators can be dropped. He must always be ready to order instant changes in the plan of attack if circumstances require them. His is an anxious, dangerous role.

Cranswick's vigour and flair for leadership had won him graduation to Master Bomber during this, his second Pathfinder tour, but tonight the position was filled by another pilot from his squadron, Squadron Leader E. Keith Creswell, DSO, DFC, who had the advantage of having been to Villeneuve-St.-Georges once already as Master Bomber – his debut, in fact, in that role – when the squadron had led a force of about a hundred planes there on the night of 26 April 1944.

The inclusion of men as skilled as Creswell and Cranswick was necessitated because these rail yard assaults demanded an exceptional degree of accuracy. The pinpointing had to be exact so as to create the greatest dislocation to rail traffic with the minimum casualties among civilians.

Although leaflets were dropped warning the French and Belgians to keep clear of the danger spots, many died during this battering of the transport system, which formed an important and carefully prepared part of the Allied invasion plan.

The aerial onslaught had begun long before the first troops swarmed across the Normandy beaches, for there was faint hope of the Allied landings achieving much success if the enemy was able to rush adequate reinforcements and supplies easily and swiftly to the battle areas. Its means of communication, therefore, had to be pulverized into chaos.

From air reconnaissance and the observations of secret agents on the ground, Allied experts soon collected an immense stock of information about the currently existing transport facilities of Western Europe and particularly the railway network. For speed and ease of transport, the enemy was clearly going to rely upon its railways to carry the bulk of the troop and supply movements when the invasion came.

Obviously the rail system had to be quickly disorganized. The enemy would then switch to the roads and that would inevitably result in fatal delays. Attacks on the roads and bridges in their turn would further hamper the enemy. The greater the hindrances to the defenders, the better the chance of success for the invaders.

During the opening weeks of 1944 the relative importance of all the various rail centres was assessed, and close on eighty key servicing depots and repair shops in northern France and Belgium were ringed on the target maps as meriting special attention from the Allied heavy bombing forces in order to paralyse the entire rail network as a prelude to the invasion.

The crews were told during their briefings that the purpose of the aerial bombardment was to disrupt the enemy's system of rail communications by the time it was forced to bear the extra strain of movements towards the invasion battle areas. On the night of 6–7 March 1944, this series of Transportation Plan attacks began. More than 260 planes dropped 1,250 tons of bombs on the rail centre at Trappes, south-west of Paris, causing such severe damage that the centre was put out of action for over a month.

But the knowledge that friendly civilians would die or be maimed in these attacks weighed heavily on the minds of Britain's leaders. In the *History of the Second World War, United Kingdom Series, Grand Strategy, volume V,* John Ehrman records that there was a strong feeling in the War Cabinet that the loss of life and damage to property was likely to cause such intense and widespread anger among the French as to outweigh the military advantages. He goes on:

> The War Cabinet instructed the air commanders to select only such targets in territories occupied by the enemy as could be attacked with relatively little risk of injury to the civilian population.
>
> The Paymaster-General, Lord Cherwell, who was asked to examine the plan afresh as an independent authority, formed the conclusion that it was unlikely to achieve its object in the time available, even after a possible expenditure of 50,000 tons of bombs, and at the cost of perhaps 40,000 Frenchmen killed and a further 120,000 injured.
>
> The air authorities produced a revised list of targets and the estimate of casualties was drastically revised from a maximum of 160,000 to a mean of 16,000 – 10,500 killed and 5,500 seriously injured.
>
> By April 13, 1944, nine railway centres had been attacked and so far as could be discovered 1,103 civilians had been killed, compared with an estimate of 2,540 on the revised basis. . .
>
> With six weeks remaining before the Normandy landings were to start, 26,000 tons of bombs had been dropped on thirty-two targets and over one third of the Plan had been carried out. It seemed that at most 4,000 had been killed, and the casualties had therefore amounted so far, at the worst, to rather less than seventy-five per cent of the

number estimated. From photographic examination it seemed likely that this was due largely to the fact that bombing had been far more accurate than some authorities had anticipated.[1]

The controversy reached a point when the Prime Minister and the American President exchanged views in which each expressed distress over the loss of civilian life, but noted with satisfaction that all possible care was being taken to minimize it. The two leaders being in agreement, Britain's War Cabinet decided to let the matter drop. The railway bombing programme was allowed to go on.

By the dawn of D-Day, 6 June 1944, the aerial bombardment had slashed the volume of rail traffic between France and Germany by an estimated 70 per cent. British and American planes had flown almost 22,000 sorties to loose 66,000 tons of bombs on the selected rail targets. On the ground, French Resistance teams worked with stealthy cunning to disorganize the railway system still further, so that trains were having to crawl along, forced to make long detours and travelling mostly under cover of darkness.

On this night of 4 July 1944, flying confidently beneath a million twinkling stars on the way to devastate more of the railway network at Villeneuve-St.-Georges, Cranswick's bomber was a sombre lethal shape hidden now from the searching eyes of the enemy ground defence posts by a comforting protective cloud layer. The biggest menace ahead would come from the night-fighters.

'They'll be up tonight,' Cranswick warned his crew tersely.

A night such as this meant that everyone had to pay special attention for the wily night-fighters which prowled around waiting to pounce on any unsuspecting bomber. Ivor Howard was particularly adept at this job; he seemed to possess an extraordinary aptitude for dealing with all varieties of enemy opposition, whether fighters, searchlights or flak. The citation to the DFC he had been awarded in October 1943 had commended his prowess:

A most efficient air gunner, this officer has gained the complete confidence of his crew. He has shown the utmost skill and coolness in directing his captain in evading enemy night fighters, searchlights and anti-aircraft fire. On all occasions he has displayed a fine fighting spirit which, coupled with his great devotion to duty, has merited the highest praise.

A pity, Cranswick thought, that his tail-gunner had picked up a cold and been barred from flying on a night like this. However, abandoning memories of ops that had long since passed into history, Cranswick anchored his thoughts now upon the raid on which he was engaged. As the Pathfinder crews once more calculated their whereabouts, troop-laden trains were clattering over the points, for the Germans were pushing their reinforcing armies through the Paris rail centres from as far away as Poland.

Some few minutes' flying time short of the French capital, Cranswick learned from navigator Reg Kille that they would be early over the target – a cardinal sin in Path Finder Force where the whole essence of the plan was based upon exact time schedules. To avoid a premature arrival, Cranswick slackened speed and turned the bomber gently in a wide orbit while still clear of the Paris gun and fighter defences. All was well still and, on reaching Villeneuve-St.-Georges, *J-Johnnie* was exactly on the ordered timing.

The weather situation is not what they had expected. During the pre-raid briefing at Graveley the forecasters had been reckoning on a cloud base of 12,000 feet over the target area. Now, flying just above this height, Cranswick thrusts his control stick forward and anticipates pushing aside the cloud blanket quite quickly. At 8,000 feet, however, *J-Johnnie* has still not emerged. Down, down goes the bomber, for Cranswick will never shirk his job.

By now, *J-Johnnie* is clear of the clouds and considerably lower than the height scheduled for the attack. The young pilot knows this is the only way to accomplish the task – that exacting, dangerous task of finding, marking and bombing the marshalling yards of Villeneuve-St.-Georges. His hands steady, Cranswick manoeuvres the Lancaster into position while the bomb-aimer seeks out the objective. His gunners scan the skies for prowling night-fighters as he holds the plane rock firm for the bombing run. Now! Although the target indicators and the high explosives are gone, Cranswick must not waver for an instant until the camera he is carrying in the plane has photographed the actual bomb-bursts so that the Intelligence staff can establish the accuracy of the mission when he gets home. This is a time when bombers are most vulnerable to enemy opposition and the pilots are fighting an over-powering impulse to dive away to a safer spot in the sky. Somehow Cranswick, as always, musters the courage to resist that temptation. So on goes *J-Johnnie*, perfectly straight and perfectly level.

The ever-watchful Master Bomber is circling still, but now *J-Johnnie*'s part in the raid is completed and Alec Cranswick hears Navigator Kille call out the compass reading he must follow for a few miles to get them clear of the target. The two Air Bombers, Burt and Gibson Taylor, compare notes, while Gunners Wood and Davies maintain their constant watch for fighters; Engineer Jock Erickson keeps an eye on his engine temperature gauges and petrol supply dials; Wireless Operator Horner has just left his seat and is standing up in the narrow walkway which leads along the fuselage, about to move into the astrodome.

The battle-proud *J-Johnnie* has just a few moments of life left.

Enemy shells slam into the now empty bomb bay in the bomber's belly, unleashed with the sudden fury of a succession of vicious stomach punches. Tongues of fire eat hungrily into the fuselage aft of the bay. Soon a raging torrent of flame is sweeping the length of the plane, and Cranswick orders the seven men with him in the aircraft: 'Bale out! EMERGENCY! J-U-M-P!'

The end of Lancaster ND846 TL-J comes within seconds. The blazing fuselage shudders, sags and shrivels while the quivering wings snap free and the nose droops to begin an earthwards plunge.

A lone figure falls clear of the flame-ravaged bomber and a parachute opens out above the fields of France. Dangling in the harness beneath the parachute is the sole survivor from *J-Johnnie*.[2]

Chapter 2

# Groomed for Gallantry

There was no one quite like Alec Cranswick in the whole of RAF Bomber Command; the lanky, supple boy was one of the most extraordinary characters of the Second World War. Yet Cranswick was as far removed from the popular idea of an operational flyer as a multi-million-pound atom-bomber is from the flimsy little scout planes of the First World War.

Often Cranswick was alone in the shadows, ignored by his more exuberant fellows. He preferred listening to classical music on his radiogram to competing in a race to see who could sink the largest number of pints of beer.

The strangely unreal atmosphere of those fly-today, die-tomorrow days played havoc with a man's personality. Some who survived look back bewildered upon the fantastic changes in character that resulted. For, under this mounting pressure, men of a hitherto placid nature became roistering, brash individuals. Cranswick, always a man apart, never changed. The teetotal, non-smoking bomber pilot had had the benefit of a childhood upbringing in which the iron rod of discipline was tempered with a rewarding measure of parental understanding.

The doctor roared with laughter when Alec Cranswick was born on 7 September 1919, at No. 2, Ship Street, Oxford. Chuckling, he told the puzzled mother: 'He should be a fair baby but just you look at him!'

Sure enough there was nothing fair about young Alec. He had a mop of dark hair, almost black, and his mother thought he looked rather like a gipsy. She did not immediately realize what the doctor meant when he said that her son should have been a fair baby. He had come into this world at the same time as the St Giles's Fair had come to Oxford.

He was born a little earlier than had been anticipated, and the doctor had had to put off a day's shooting in order to dash along to attend to the birth of the new Cranswick. The doctor turned up at the house wearing a deer-stalker hat and carrying a gun slung over his shoulder. The shooting could wait, but not the baby. Near the Cranswicks' house the showmen were putting up their stalls ready for the St Giles's Fair, so the boy's arrival was heralded by the deafening crashes of hammering, clattering and assorted biffs and bangs that go along with such preparations. With the frightful noise and the sight of a gun in the house, there was something oddly prophetic about Alec Cranswick's entry into a world that had not long since seen the end of one great war and that would see the start of another before he reached manhood.

At that time Alec's father, Philip Cranswick, held the appointment of Staff Captain (Royal Engineers) to the Chief Engineer, Portsmouth, but he and his wife Maia had kept on their small house in Oxford for the sake of the children.

There were just the two youngsters – Sheila and Alec – the girl being eighteen months older than her brother. Mrs Cranswick considered that, with the two babies, she should stay on in Oxford until they were a little older and therefore better prepared to face the rigours of being members of a serviceman's family, which would certainly entail sudden postings from camp to camp.

She remained in Oxford until Alec was a year old and then moved down with the children to her husband in Portsmouth. The two children were devoted to each other. Alec called his sister Slave, but she only laughed at this; she adored him. Once, when Alec was only about eighteen months old, some clothes being aired by the nursery fire caught alight. Alec was sitting on the floor close to the fireguard. Sheila beat out a flame on his dressing gown, shouted a warning to their parents, and dragged Alec by the hand to safety. Then she gasped out:

'The nursery is burning, but it's all right, I've saved Alec.'

Mother and Father rushed into the nursery to cope with the blaze. Thanks to Shelia's prompt action the only damage was to some of the clothes.

Cranswick was a great music lover. This appreciation stemmed from his early childhood and once led to an amusing incident when he was a toddler. He had been taken to a military band concert in Portsmouth. During one of the items in the programme, Alec slipped away from his mother and calmly climbed the steps to the conductor's rostrum. There he reached in his pocket, pulled out a penny and solemnly presented the coin to the conductor, who took it with a grin. The audience was highly amused, though Alec's mother was extremely embarrassed.

When Alec was 3 years old, his father realized a long-desired wish and joined the Royal Air Force. He had wanted to transfer from the Army to the Royal Flying Corps in the First World War but there had been no chance to do so and he had remained in the Royal Engineers until the war ended. He was then offered a regular commission in the Army but turned this down, as he felt that a peacetime Army officer should be a person with private means – and he had none. He knew his post at Portsmouth was not permanent, so he applied to join the RAF – which the RFC had now become – and hoped for a regular commission on the expiration of the Short Service Commission with which he had enlisted.

He became a trainee pilot and spent some months at No. 2 Flying Training School, Digby, Lincolnshire, when the school was under the command of Wing Commander Arthur W. Tedder, later Baron Tedder of Glenguin, Marshal of the Royal Air Force and Chief of Air Staff. From early childhood, Alec Cranswick was brought up against a family background in which aviation played a prominent part.

The strong guiding qualities of gallantry and chivalry that stood out in the boy in later years had been handed down from his forebears.

**Alec Cranswick when a child, with his parents, Philip and Maia.** (Author's collection)

He had inherited in the blood of his ancestors both the fiery spirit of bravery and the gift of an artist's quick appreciation of beauty.

On his father's side of the family, Alec was descended from the first Lord Cranstoun, the former William Cranstoun who was appointed by King James VI of Scotland as Captain of the Horse Garrison, or King's Guard, under the Earl of Dunbar, Lieutenant of the Borders. In that office William Cranstoun so distinguished himself by his zeal and vigour in suppressing the lawlessness then prevailing throughout the Border region that he was raised to the Peerage on 19 November 1609, in the title of Lord Cranstoun. From his mother's conversations, Cranswick became familiar with the story of how the Cranstoun sons had quarrelled and separated, calling themselves thereafter Cranstoun, Cranston and Cranswick. He learned to draw the Cranstoun family crest of three cranes and he learned the family motto: 'Thou shalt want ere I'.

Courage came right down the line, and his father's gallantry as a Lieutenant in the Royal Engineers in action against the enemy on the Western Front during the First World War won him a Military Cross in the King's Birthday Honours List of 1918.

Alec's mother's family, Docwra-Panton, were descended from Sir Thomas Docwra, last but one of the Grand Priors of England in the Order of the Knights of St John of Jerusalem. He was engaged in a number of diplomatic missions on behalf of both King Henry VII and King Henry VIII. The Pantons were old Dorset yeomen stock from Corfe, Wareham and Swanage, with doctors, writers, farmers and brewery owners among their number. Alec's grandfather on his mother's side of the family was Harry Docwra, son of a brewery owner in Wareham, a man of independent means who had spent much of his life big-game hunting in Africa and collecting wild animals for a hobby.

True country folk at heart and by tradition, Alec and his sister loved the Wiltshire Downs where their father was stationed after he had completed his flying training and joined an RAF fighter squadron. All day long the two children roamed the hills and the woods together, living a wild, free life. Although Alec was the younger, he always arranged everything and made all the decisions for both of them. He was a happy, laughing child – often in mischief, but with a great sense of humour.

When the children were old enough to go to school, Mrs Cranswick returned with them to Oxford to live, and their father remained on his RAF camp in Wiltshire. By now Alec was slight, tall and handsome; he was very strong-willed and with dark brown eyes that used to fill with tears if he saw or read anything sad. He was strangely sensitive to recognize pain or unhappiness in other people.

The family lived in various furnished houses during term time and returned to Wiltshire for the school holidays to be with Alec's father. It was there that Alec wrote his first poem; he was then just 6 years old. One of the family's favourite spots was Savernake Forest, and often his mother would read poems to him while sitting in one of the leafy glades with the sun glinting down through the tall trees. It was in the quiet of these surroundings that his eagerness for poetry was fostered.

### *A Forrest*

*There is a haunted forrest; it stretches far and wide*
*And on the very edge of it there runs a river wide.*

*It ripples as it flows along, and jumps from side to side*
*And all along the banks there are*
*Such grate big stones that stretch so far.*

*And then there are such lots of birds*
*That wisell in the cooling air;*
*And lots of rabbits, foxes, heares*
*Go pitering, patering to their laires.*

*The rabbits squeel, the foxes bark;*
*The heares are lisening... Hark, hark, hark.*

*Horns are blowing, hounds do bark*
*So goodby all of you, and love from the lark.*

Later the Cranswicks moved into a flat in Oriel Street, Oxford, opposite the Church of St Mary the Virgin. The children's father sometimes had occasion to fly across to Oxford from Wiltshire, and when Alec heard a plane he would rush out on the balcony overlooking High Street. If the plane circled the church spire three times, and then dipped, he would yell: 'Come on up, Mummy, it's Daddy flying over.'

At the age of 7, Alec left his kindergarten school and moved to New College Preparatory School, Oxford, where one of his closest friends was Paul Blagrove, two years his senior. Cranswick quickly revealed himself to Blagrove as a perfectionist. Whatever he set his mind on doing he would do well, irrespective of the amount of effort required to achieve this peak. Blagrove noted repeated examples throughout their boyhood:

*He would go on and on and on until he had satisfied his ambitions. Take shooting, for instance. I would moan about the number of slugs Alec was using – we had to pay for them out of our own pockets, remember! – and he would fire on and on until he had hit the target. Another side of Alec's personality showed up in our shooting exploits. As a kid I would like to take a crack at shooting a bird. Not Alec! – he hated killing. He stuck to bottles and tin cans for his targets. I suppose shooting was one of his favourite sports. He was never much good at cricket, football or hockey but he always used to play them. He always gave them a try – he would have a go at anything.*

Paul Blagrove was one of the first people to notice Alec's growing passion for aeroplanes. The two boys used to play aeroplanes when they were knee-high to a real machine. The elder lad had a bicycle, but Alec did not possess one. Instead, Alec had a rough go-cart made from pram wheels and box-wood, which he rode behind Paul's bike. Most boys would have been content with a steering wheel for changing direction as he trailed along, attached by a piece of stout rope to his friend's bicycle. Alec was different. After days of careful thought, he made himself a joystick instead, so that he could pretend he was a pilot.

Cranswick always wanted to get up into the air, even if the highest he could reach was one of the sturdy trees in Blagrove's garden. He would make huts in the treetops and he would be for ever seeking a loftier elm so that his huts might extend higher and higher into the sky.

Although Cranswick was adventurous by nature he certainly knew the meaning of fear. He was terrified of the dark; he was terrified of spiders. Until he was quite old he used to wrap the sheet round his head at night – 'in case any spiders crawl on me'. He used to make his sister go upstairs with him because he was afraid of the dark. When alone in the house, he was always scared to walk along the dark corridors and endeavoured to sit tight wherever he was until someone returned to accompany him. He had a fear of dogs, too, when he was very small. Then, as he grew older, he hid this fear like all his others until finally he was able to conquer it. Alec came to acknowledge that the best way of overcoming any particular fear was to force himself to experience whatever was worrying him – like a child who is apprehensive of a dark wood slowly going further and further inside, instead of turning and bolting for dear life.

At school Cranswick's progress was not outstanding. He was a bit lazy and he was a dreamer – but he was capable of any effort when he wished. He was a good mixer and he made many friends. The Headmaster reported that the boy's progress was steady and satisfactory – 'except when he goes into a kind of a trance and we only know he is still with us then because he appears to be breathing and, strangely enough, thinking deeply'.

Alec loved the school, the playing fields and sports. In particular he enjoyed the visits to the swimming baths in Merton Street – the first cup he ever won was for swimming.

The trifling worries and fears of Alec as a small boy used to upset his mother. She told his father about this and he replied: 'Don't worry. You manage him well and he trusts you. One day he may surprise you with his bravery.'

Unhappily Alec's father did not live to see his son proclaimed a hero.

Alec's father was killed in a mid-air collision with a close friend over Salisbury Plain on 5 June 1928, while carrying out a mock air battle as a practice for the big annual RAF Display at Hendon.

Flying Officer Cranswick and Flying Officer Douglas McMillan had spent about three years at RAF Station, Upavon, Wiltshire, where they were both pilots in No. 3 (Fighter) Squadron, flying the Hawker Woodcock biplanes, which were then the RAF standard single-seater night-fighters.

Wing Commander W. R. Read had ordered them to be airborne, with two other pilots, half an hour before noon to practise formation attacks against two Horsley bombers. Cranswick and McMillan were paired off and went into the attack. The interception went according to plan, but then came tragedy. After levelling out from a dive, the wings of the two Woodcocks were seen to hit some 1,500 feet above the ground. Immediately the wooden machines collapsed. Both pilots were wearing regulation parachutes and at 500 feet McMillan jumped from his plane. By then, however, he was too low, and the parachute only just started to billow open as he hit the ground near his plane. The two aircraft crashed about 300 yards apart. Alec's father was unable to get clear and fell with his machine. He was dead when the first people reached the scene.

A verdict of Accidental Death was recorded at the inquest that same evening, and the two friends were buried at Upavon three days later with full military honours.

Not yet 9 years old, Alec was deeply distressed when his mother broke the news to him that his father was dead. As the months passed by she watched him with pride as he worked harder at school; he was no longer a dreamer. He assumed more responsibilities in the home and helped his mother in every way open to a lad who was still so young; he was determined to take his father's place in his mother's heart and home.

For Mrs Cranswick, the skies must have seemed to be filled with sadness and death. Her very first sight of an aeroplane had ended in tragedy with the death, at Bournemouth on 12 July 1910, of the Hon. Charles Stewart Rolls, the famous balloonist, motorist and aviator, while flying his Wright biplane – the same machine in which he had made the first double-crossing of the English Channel by air only a few weeks previously.

Then in the First World War, when aircraft were rather less of a novelty, her brother-in-law, George Alec Cranswick, a clever engineer, went missing without trace while a pilot in the Royal Flying Corps.[1]

As he had no father to guide him, Mrs Cranswick brought up Alec on all the old family stories and traditions. Her trust in him, firm discipline and a spirit of justice and freedom soon moulded his character. He grew up with a truthful nature, trustworthy and determined, yet always kind, gentle and humane.

There can be little doubt that his adventurous spirit stemmed from his mother. He loved the stories of her childhood and listened earnestly to the tales of how her father caught wild animals on safari and then sold them to various zoos. For her part, however, Maia Cranswick was afraid Alec would become a Mother's Boy. To avoid this possibility she pledged herself to give him a life of his own and encouraged him to reach decisions uninfluenced by her wisdom. He went on holidays without her except when he wished otherwise; thus he soon became completely independent and self-reliant.

Maia Cranswick had only a small pension, so, in order to provide a home and educate her two children, she took a house in Woodstock Road, Oxford, and started a school for foreigners, where she taught them English. Eventually she managed to send Alec to St Edward's, Oxford,[2] whose achievements and pleasant country setting particularly appealed to him. Going to this distinguished public school was truly a wish fulfilled.

Chapter 3

# School for Heroes

**Chapel at St Edward's School, Oxford, taken from The Lodge, c. 1935.** (Property of the St Edward's School Archives)

It was apt, indeed, that this air-minded boy should have gone to St Edward's. Now, in these later years, there is an RAF Memorial Window in the Old Library – a magnificent stained-glass window, designed by Hugh Easton, with the face of a young airman as its centrepiece. The inscription is simple: 'Given by The Air Council. To Mark the Fine Record of Boys from this School in the Royal Air Force.'

A fine record, indeed; during the Second World War over 250 boys from St Edward's served in the Royal Air Force, the Empire Air Forces and Allied Air Forces.

Forty-eight honours and eleven mentioned-in-despatches are known to have been awarded. The honours included one Victoria Cross, one George Cross, three double DSOs, one triple DFC, six double DFCs, eight DSOs and fourteen DFCs.

It is an impressive tally.

The window was presented and unveiled in the then Memorial Library on 19 November 1955, at a moving ceremony presided over by the Lord Bishop of Exeter, the Right Revd R. C. Mortimer, Chairman of the Governing Body. It was presented on behalf of the Air Council by Air Chief Marshal Sir Francis Fogarty, Air Member for Personnel, and accepted and unveiled by Air Chief Marshal Sir John Whitworth Jones, a member of the Governing Body.

To the hundreds filing slowly inside after the ceremony the airman in the memorial window symbolized the very spirit of those gallant sons of

St Edward's who flew and died in the service of their country. There is the merest trace of wind fluttering through his fair hair as he stands with his eyes on the skies. He wears a soft blue flying suit and gaudy orange Mae West life jacket in instant readiness for take-off. Round his neck there is the silk scarf that is all but an accepted item of a fighter pilot's uniform when on flying stand-by.

It is only possible to guess at the reasons why so many Old Boys of St Edward's chose to go into the RAF on leaving school. While some other public schools had distinct links with either the Army or the Royal Navy, St Edward's had no strong service attachment at all in the years between the two world wars.

Old Boys tended to branch out in many different directions to follow a particularly wide diversity of careers with few traditional pursuits to sway the undecided.

St Edward's was founded in 1863 in New Inn Hall Street, Oxford, by the Reverend T. Chamberlain, MA, Senior Student and Honorary Canon of Christ Church, Oxford, Vicar of St Thomas-ye-Martyr, Oxford. In starting the school, Chamberlain was realizing a personal ambition to provide education in Christian principles together with secular training.

As the years went by, the old, damp, miserable buildings in which the school began reached such a pitiful state of unhealthy uselessness that a move became not merely advisable but a sheer necessity.

In 1873 the Reverend A. B. Simeon, Warden at that time, provided the money out of his own pocket to arrange a transfer to the present site of St Edward's in Summertown, Oxford. Refusing to make the move himself, Founder Chamberlain formally handed over the school to Simeon by deed of gift.

The freer life and the new facilities for sport were readily appreciated by the forty-five or fifty boys then at the school. The future seemed more sound, and the school roll began to increase. In 1890 came Simeon's retirement, and St Edward's, which was still legally his own property, was presented to trustees. Not only had he saved the school from an unfortunate and an early end but he had laid the foundations of the school's greatness. Around the turn of the century, more buildings were added, the playing fields were extended and a tutorial system was introduced. In 1912 a Governing Body was formed, with St Edward's becoming technically an association limited by guarantee with the profits going into a development fund.

In the First World War nearly 120 Old Boys lost their lives, and many honours and awards were won. The Memorial Buildings – later called Tilly's House – were given by the Old Boys to commemorate their brothers who fell in that war.

The years between the two world wars saw a continued growth of the school in stature, prosperity and efficiency.

The Second World War drew a fresh generation of Old Boys to fight and to die for their country – at the same time winning equal distinction as those who served in the First World War.

From a mere handful of boys clustered enthusiastically around Founder Chamberlain in the inadequate premises in New Inn Hall Street, Oxford, had been built a vigorous living memorial to those idealistic days of the 1860s and early 1870s when the pattern was fashion-ed for the present-day St Edward's.


Those whose schooldays were spent at St Edward's between the First and Second World Wars all shared an intense admiration of two particular Old Boys, Louis Strange and Douglas Bader.

Although Bader's epic deeds were to come an appreciable time after Strange's colourful exploits in the pioneering days of aviation, both men probably influenced St Edward's boys subconsciously over the course of many years.

In fact, far from becoming a fading figure as the years drew on, Louis Strange jumped right back into the centre of operations as the bloody fingers of war began to entwine the world for the second time in his adult life.

At St Edward's, Louis Arbon Strange was an enthusiastic sportsman; he was keen on athletics and he played in the School Cricket XI. He left in 1907 to turn farmer, but his thoughts darted excitedly from the land to the sky when the earliest flying machines were rising uncertainly into the air.

He saw a fine future for flying – so much so, in fact, that during summer manœuvres with his volunteer cavalry unit in 1912 Strange had the audacity to declare that in another war aircraft were going to do away with the cavalry, and to add emphasis to his forthright views Strange began taking flying lessons.

Qualifying as a pilot a full year before the start of the First World War, Louis Strange recalls that in those early war days 'pilots were real maidsof-all-work – reconnaissance, bombing, dropping secret agents and so on'.

He was one of the first to take up a Lewis gun in an aeroplane. He had the gun lashed to the cockpit, and the experiments he carried out pioneered the use of machine guns in aerial combat. It was over a gun on 10 May 1915 that Louis Strange had one of the most amazing air escapes on record.

He was flying a Martinsyde biplane engaged in a running battle with an enemy plane over the Belgian battlefields. He reached up to change an empty ammunition drum on the Lewis gun mounted on the wing above his head, but the drum was jammed and refused to move. Suddenly the plane lurched out of control and turned upside down, flinging him out of the cockpit at 8,500 feet up, without a parachute.

Strange was still holding on to the stubborn drum with one hand and a strut with the other hand. He knew he could not hope to retain his perilous grasp, and the German pilot obviously did not think Strange had a chance, because he sped away to lodge a claim for one Martinsyde destroyed.

It was a pity the German left so soon, for he had discounted the determination of Louis Strange.

Strange kept kicking upwards for all he was worth at the cockpit and somehow hooked his legs around the control column. With his legs Strange now succeeded in righting the plane, and as he did so he shot back into the seat.

During the First World War Louis Strange's tremendous courage in action won for him the DSO, the MC and the DFC.

He was a go-ahead giant in the infant world of aerial warfare, helping develop one of the earliest bombsights, dropping some of the first fire bombs and pioneering leaflet raids. His deeds were symbolic of the daring spirit of those days; he tossed a hand grenade at a sentry who was taking pot shots at his plane with a rifle and then went on to bomb a troop train, killing or wounding seventy-five soldiers and blocking the line for three days.

He retired from the RAF in 1921 with the rank of Wing Commander and resumed farming. From 1928 until the Second World War he was a director of the Spartan Aircraft Company and Straight Corporation Ltd.

Within a short time of the start of the Second World War Strange was in the RAF once more. With the most humble of the commissioned ranks, Pilot Officer, he was soon flying again – probably the only one at that time who had been a pilot before the First World War. His job was ferrying some of the most senior RAF officers between London and France.

In June 1940, during the dying days of the British Expeditionary Force's fight in France, Strange was detailed to fly from Hendon to Merville in France to act as Ground Control Officer during the arrival and departure of aircraft carrying food supplies.

At the last minute, before the enemy advanced on Merville, Louis Strange climbed into the cockpit of the only plane left on the drome – a Hurricane fighter without any armament – and set course for Hendon.

The Germans were not going to let him slip away quite so easily. Messerschmitt fighters raced to head him off and shoot him into the Channel. Even so, by sheer experience in handling aircraft – an art he had learned probably before the German pilots were born – Strange manœuvred so cunningly that he must have bluffed his interceptors into thinking he had guns in his plane and that when the occasion was ripe he was going to use them with deadly accuracy.

He beat off attack after attack, and all the more remarkable is the fact that he had never before flown a Hurricane. For his action in bringing the Hurricane home there came the award of a Bar to the DFC he had won in the First World War.

The citation mentioned his work at Merville, France, and went on:

He displayed great skill and determination while under heavy bombing attack and machine gun fire at Merville where he was responsible for the repair and successful departure of two aircraft to England.

In the last remaining aircraft which was repaired under his supervision, he returned to Hendon in spite of being repeatedly attacked by Messerschmitts until well out to sea.

He had no guns in action and had never flown this type of aircraft previously but his brilliant piloting enabled him to return.

Before the Second World War was over, Louis Strange had risen to the rank of Group Captain and collected two further honours – the OBE and the American Bronze Star. He was mentioned in despatches for a fifth time.

Small wonder, then, that Louis Strange's name was never foreign to the boys of St Edward's. But what of that other hero of the years between the wars, the irrepressible Douglas Bader?

It is hardly surprising that Douglas Robert Stewart Bader has been described as unique among the Old Boys, for he was obviously destined for success, whatever the hurdles that were set up across his track through life.

Bader became a legend of indisputable courage in peace as in war – incredible all-round sportsman before the flying accident that robbed him of both his legs – and amazing ace fighter pilot in spite of the handicap.

One of his fellow pupils, K. J. Veitch, a post-war Assistant Master at St Edward's, says of Bader: 'He was absolutely unique. There was no one like him before he came to the School and I doubt if there will be anyone like him again.'

Douglas Bader joined as a sturdy, lively boy in the Christmas term of 1923, when he was just into his teens. He excelled particularly in sport and won places in the Rugger XV for three successive seasons and played in the Cricket XI for three summers, leading the side in his final year, 1928.

He left to go to the RAF College, Cranwell, winning a Prize Cadetship and going on to collect Cranwell Blues for Rugby, Cricket, Hockey and Boxing as well as representing the RAF at Rugby, Cricket, Boxing and Squash Rackets.

By 1931 he was a Pilot Officer with No. 23 (Fighter) Squadron at Kenley. He had thrilled the crowds at the big annual RAF Display at Hendon, for he was regarded as being one of the finest acrobatic pilots in the RAF.

But on 14 December 1931 Bader took up a single-seat Bristol Bulldog at Woodley Aerodrome, Reading, and began a demonstration slow roll. He was too low, and the machine smashed into the ground. Bader lost both his legs.

Within a few months he had not only learned to walk again but he had learned to fly again. He was quickly overcoming the problems of mastering his new man-made limbs.

With rugger now completely out of the question, Bader took up a new sport – golf – and he was soon displaying creditable proficiency. He danced, too, and drove a car, but what he wanted to do most of all was to go back into the RAF – and the RAF kept saying No.

It took a war to make them change their minds. Bader insisted he was perfectly fit for flying, and at last the RAF gave him a chance to prove his claim. He passed with flying colours and joined a fighter squadron.

He was awarded his first medal, the DSO, in September 1940; the
citation said of him:

> This officer has displayed gallantry and leadership of the highest
> order. During three recent engagements he has led his squadron with
> such skill and ability that 33 enemy aircraft have been destroyed. In
> the course of his engagements Squadron Leader Bader has added to
> his previous successes by destroying six enemy aircraft.

Three months later Bader received the DFC: 'He has continued to lead
his squadron with the utmost gallantry on all occasions. He has now
destroyed ten hostile aircraft and damaged several more.'

His personal toll of enemy planes mounted steadily, and two more
medals followed within a year of his first one. He was a Wing Commander now, and the citation to the Bar to his DSO in July 1944, said:

> This officer has led his wing on a series of consistently successful
> sorties over enemy territory during the past three months. His high
> qualities of leadership and courage have been an inspiration to all.
> Wing Commander Bader has destroyed fifteen hostile aircraft.

The Bar to his DFC was announced in September 1941, and the citation
accompanying the award stated:

> This fearless pilot has recently added a further four enemy aircraft to
> his previous successes; in addition he has probably destroyed another
> four and damaged five hostile aircraft. By his fine leadership and high
> courage Wing Commander Bader has inspired the wing on every
> occasion.

By now, however, Wing Commander Bader had had to parachute to
safety from his crashing fighter on a sweep over France, and an item in
the St Edward's *Chronicle* said tacitly that 'it did not envy the Germans
their task of keeping him within bounds'.

In fact the Germans twice failed completely in their task of keeping
the boisterous Bader within bounds. He escaped first from the hospital
to which he was taken after baling out and secondly from a prison camp,
but on each occasion he had the ill-luck to be recaptured as he valiantly

stumped along the hard road to freedom on his metal legs.

Bader used to reckon that he was one of the safest pilots in the world. He would give a sly chuckle and go on to explain: 'They can riddle my legs with bullets and it doesn't make the slightest difference.'

Fresh honours came his way as France awarded him the Legion d'Honneur and Croix de Guerre, and three times he was mentioned in despatches, too. Bader was everyone's idea of the fine, bold hero – a masterly sportsman and a daring knight of the skies.

The exploits of Louis Strange and later Douglas Bader must have sown in many pupils the earliest seeds of speculation on aviation as a career. There were immense and intriguing prospects ahead in aviation during those exuberant years between the two wars that sparkled with achievements in civil and military flying. The world was shrinking as pioneering aviators set the noses of their planes towards more and more distant points.

There were flights over the North Pole and stirring solo runs across the Atlantic. A plane called *Winnie Mae*, carrying two pilots, circled the globe in only a little over eight-and-a-half days – a historic feat that was excelled two years later by one man flying round the world alone in only seven-and-three-quarter days. Records toppled swiftly with every thrilling advance in the capabilities of the aeroplanes and the flyers handling them. Biplanes, monoplanes, balloons and airships, land planes and seaplanes, amphibians and autogyros all claimed their successes, while development followed development and excitement followed excitement.

Boys steeped in the spirit of adventure had their eyes on the skies. There were plenty of them at St Edward's.

As the 1930s flipped past, there came expansion in the RAF. The inauguration of the RAF Volunteer Reserve for part-time flying training and the chance of a Short Service Commission for those eager to sample the RAF as a career both enticed young men towards rather more than just a passing interest in the Service.

A succession of splendidly groomed Old Boys, smart in well-tailored Air Force blue, spoke avidly of life in the Service when making the annual pilgrimage to St Edward's for a renewal of former acquaintances.

Boys at St Edward's were taught the ideas of service – 'You learned loyalty to the community in which you lived; you learned the principles of service. You learned to be responsible; you learned how to hold authority,' explains one Old Boy. It is clear that these products of

St Edward's made good officers because of their solid grounding in loyalty, service and responsibility.

Guy Gibson, holder of the Victoria Cross, was also an Old Boy of St Edward's School. He went there in the Christmas term of 1932 and left in the summer of 1936 when he joined the RAF. He was remembered as a quiet, reliable type who was not likely to set the school on fire.

He flew bombers right from the start of the war. He was in the RAF's first raid of the war and he quickly gained a reputation as an outstanding pilot. It was practically impossible to stop Gibson from flying; he even attacked a German battleship on a night when he was supposed to be resting.

At the end of his first tour of ops, Gibson scorned the idea of an enforced rest and asked for another operational posting. Somehow he had his own way, and he was transferred to Fighter Command to become a night-fighter pilot.

In two months he destroyed three enemy aircraft and damaged a fourth. 'His skill was notably demonstrated when one night in July, 1941, he intercepted and destroyed a Heinkel 111', stated the citation to the Bar to the DFC already awarded to him in September 1941.

Returning to heavy bombing, Gibson raided targets as far away as Poland, and in one attack nearer home, Le Creusot, he bombed and machine-gunned a transformer station from as low as 500 feet – 'he is a most skilful and courageous leader whose keenness has set a most inspiring example', according to the citation accompanying the award of the first of his two DSOs.

At the conclusion of a third operational tour, Gibson pressed strongly to be allowed to remain on ops. He was selected to command a squadron then forming to carry out special tasks – No. 617 Squadron. He was to lead them on their most famous exploit of all in breaching the Moehne and Eder dams.

He carried out the first attack himself on the Moehne dam, bombing with great accuracy despite having to bear the full brunt of the ack-ack defences. He circled very low for half an hour to draw the enemy's fire so that the rest of the squadron might have a clear run over the target.

Gibson then turned the force's attention to the Eder dam and repeated the tactics. Again he invited the defences to blast him from the sky so that the remainder of his force could have a better chance to bring the raid to a successful end.

Gibson received the VC for his work in the epic flight of the

Dambusters:

> One of the most devastating attacks of the war and a task fraught with danger and difficulty. Both as an operational pilot and as leader of his squadron, he achieved outstandingly successful results and his personal courage knew no bounds.
>
> Wing Commander Gibson has completed over a hundred and seventy sorties,[1] involving more than 600 hours operational flying. Throughout his operational career, prolonged exceptionally at his own request, he has shown leadership, determination and valour of the highest order.

His service was marked in another way by an invitation to accompany Prime Minister Churchill across the Atlantic, where he lectured in both Canada and America. President Roosevelt made him a Commander of the Legion of Merit. Returning to Britain, Gibson begged permission to take charge of one more raid over Germany.

It was the night of 19 September 1944 and, as Master Bomber directing an attack on Rheydt, near Munchen-Gladbach, Gibson saw the mission through to a successful conclusion, flying throughout at a much lower level than the main bomber force. On the radio he congratulated all crews in his usual calm and unhurried voice before heading for home. Those were the last words anyone heard from Guy Gibson.

Some months later an issue of the St Edward's *Chronicle* recorded a brief note that Gibson and another pilot who were earlier reported missing were now known to have lost their lives. That other pilot had had a remarkable career in the RAF, too. His name was Wing Commander Adrian Warburton, and like Gibson his personal courage never seemed to accept any limitations.

Both the same age, Gibson and Warburton joined St Edward's in the same year, 1932, but they were in different houses. Warburton went there in the Easter term and became a valued member of Sinn's, while Gibson, going there in the Christmas term, went into Cowbell's. During their four years at St Edward's there came a milestone in the school's history with the Diamond Jubilee Commemoration in 1933.

As a particularly daring and highly successful long-range reconnaissance pilot, Adrian Warburton, son of a naval officer, gained one of the most impressive collections of gallantry awards earned by the Old Boys – DSO and Bar, DFC and two Bars and an American Distinguished Flying Cross.

The fine sense of devotion to duty he displayed at all times won for him his first DFC in February 1941. He was a skilled night-fighter pilot, too, and shot down two aircraft in the winter of 1940.

Only seven months later came a second DFC and he was paid the following tribute in the citation:

> This officer is a most determined and skilful pilot and has carried out 125 operational missions. Flying Officer Warburton has never failed to complete the missions he has undertaken and, in the actions fought, he has destroyed at least three hostile aircraft in combat and another three on the ground.

From ridiculously low levels Warburton skimmed over enemy installations and shipping to get the required vital information and photographs – apparently quite oblivious to the fierce opposition from flak and fighters. He flew at only 50 feet over an Italian battleship to penetrate Taranto Harbour, and, in spite of a useless engine and repeated attacks by enemy planes, completed the mission and made a safe return.

His valuable work, great skill and tenacity were rewarded by his first DSO in March 1942, while in the following November came the award of a third DFC, in which citation was revealed another fine illustration of Warburton's gallantry.

An Allied aircraft had been shot down, and the crew were safe in a dinghy awaiting rescue. The nearest ship in sight was an enemy destroyer. Warburton directed this vessel towards the dinghy. The destroyer's guns began opening up, and enemy aircraft engaged him in combat. Yet, despite these attacks on him, Warburton refused to fly away home until he had seen the enemy ship pick up the crew from their dinghy.

In August 1943 came a second DSO, and again there was an exceptional testimonial to his courage: 'His work throughout has been of the highest order and the information he has obtained has proved of incalculable value... Wing Commander Warburton's record of operational flying is outstanding.' It seemed there was no praise high enough for him.

When Adrian Warburton went missing in 1944, St Edward's *Chronicle* contained a tribute saying that his record in war came as no surprise to his friends because his achievements were based on modesty, devotion to duty and extraordinary application.

Like Gibson, Warburton had now flown his last mission, but there were others who were more lucky and survived the war. For some the end of hostilities was also the end of their flying days, although for many more the RAF was to remain their career.

For one of those who stayed on in the RAF, James Anthony Leathart, the foundations for success were quickly and firmly laid in the first few months of the war, when he was flying fighters over France.

The eldest of three brothers who all went to St Edward's, James Leathart joined the RAF in 1937. He was fully trained in time to lead a Spitfire squadron on offensive patrols over northern France when the German armies began swarming through Holland, Belgium and France ready to leapfrog across to Britain.

The odds in the air never seemed to matter in those days. The rougher the battle, the tougher the spirit of the fighter boys streaking into action, trailing their white vapour lines across the sky like a toddler scribbling with chalk on a blackboard.

Once James Leathart's few plucky Spitfires zoomed merrily into a formation of no less than sixty enemy aircraft.

In company with his squadron, Leathart shot down fifteen Messerschmitts and possibly a Heinkel He.111 and a Junkers Ju.88 as well in the course of a single month's furious fighting.

He showed his bravery, too, by flying an unarmed two-seater Miles Master trainer across the English Channel to snatch a squadron commander from right beneath the enemy's nose when he was forced down over France at a time when the Germans were set on defeating and capturing the British Expeditionary Force in May 1940.

Escorted by two Spitfires from his own squadron, Leathart landed on Calais Marck airfield and calmly picked up the stranded officer before the enemy had a chance to seize him; a truly adventurous piece of flying – but the situation did not look too happy.

A dozen Me.109s swept into the attack while the slow and defenceless little trainer was in the act of taking off.

With great coolness and by means of skilful evasive tactics, Leathart managed to shake off the enemy and landed again without damage. He took off a second time and flew the trainer back to England unmolested by any more Jerries.

The two fighters that had been escorting Leathart originally had in the meantime piled into the German planes. They shot down one apiece and shared in the destruction of a third, besides probably destroying a fourth and damaging two more of the enemy.

For this exploit, coupled with his fine operational record as a fighter pilot, Leathart was awarded the DSO. The citation noted that he had 'displayed great courage, determination and splendid leadership'.

James Leathart, St Edward's School, Oxford, 1928–1934, receiving the DSO from His Majesty the King. (Property of the St Edward's School Archives)

The escort pilots in the rescue, Pilot Officer A. C. Deere and Pilot Officer J. L. Allen, each received the DFC for their part in the rescue and for their courage in aerial interceptions, which were often made in the face of overwhelming odds. Both Deere and Allen served with Leathart in No. 54 Squadron at RAF Station, Hornchurch, Essex, before the war.

Leathart, twice mentioned in despatches, commanded Nos 54 and 89 Squadrons and No. 148 Wing during the war.

After that, he was an instructor at the RAF Staff College and commanded the Air Defence Operations Centre of the Royal Air Force Fighter Command. With his appointment as Officer Commanding RAF Station, North Coates, Lincolnshire, he became the first chief of an RAF guided-missile base.

In much the same way that a fighter pilot can reveal an intrepid spirit while flying a training plane – as did Leathart – so can a bomber pilot find himself forced suddenly into a situation calling for action while he is away from the controls of his aircraft.

In July 1941 an RAF bomber of No. 12 Squadron was taking part in a daylight attack on the French port of Brest. Once the raid was completed, the bomber headed back towards home. To the young officer in command, Pilot Officer Alexander James Heyworth, all seemed to be going extraordinarily well.

Heyworth was a St Edward's Old Boy too. The energetic six-footer, a vigorous member of the School Rugger XV in his final year, joined the RAF on his 18th birthday in 1940. After he had finished his training as a bomber pilot, he was posted to No. 12 Squadron.

It was during the Brest attack with his squadron that Pilot Officer Heyworth found himself faced with a state of affairs that demanded particularly clear-headed and decisive action if the bomber was to reach home. For racing towards them was an enemy fighter intent on a kill.

Heyworth, who had handed over the controls to his second pilot now that the actual bombing was over, spotted the plane from the bomber's astrodome – the Perspex observation bubble in the roof of the fuselage. From that astrodome, exposed to the fighter's guns, the captain had the widest field of vision of all in the big bomber. If he acted as the 'eyes' of the crew, the trapped plane might yet escape.

Disregarding his personal safety, Heyworth coolly directed the defensive fire of his gunners so successfully that not only was the bomber able to get home, but the fighter that pounced upon them was probably destroyed into the bargain.

Once Heyworth flew home a crippled bomber for five wearying hours with only one engine working after a night raid. His skill was recognized by the Air Officer Commanding-in-Chief of Bomber Command in an Administrative Order.

For these two instances of courage and devotion to duty in the execution of air operations, Heyworth was awarded the DFC.

Within a year he had completed his second tour of ops and he had been promoted to the rank of Squadron Leader. His bombing record was now marked by the award of a Bar to his DFC. Twice during his RAF Service he was mentioned in despatches.

In 1944 Squadron Leader Heyworth was posted to Special Duties – with a job as test pilot for Rolls-Royce Limited, with whom he was to make his career after the war.

In 1955 Heyworth was appointed their chief test pilot – a post his brother Harvey Heyworth had held from 1950 to 1954. This established him as one of Britain's most outstanding experimental flyers, and there was no one more proud of him than those associated with St Edward's, for yet another Old Boy had triumphed in peace as in war.[2]

In 1954 the Air Council expressed its appreciation of the school's association with the RAF by granting £1,000 from the RAF Prize Fund to endow a scholarship of £40 a year at St Edward's for the son of a serving RAF officer.

It was decided to name the scholarship after one of the school's bravest men, Guy Gibson.

At the same time the RAF Benevolent Fund declared its intention to commemorate the men who were educated at St Edward's and gave such valuable and distinguished service in the RAF during the last war by providing £1,800 for bursaries of £50 a year for twenty-five years for the sons of deceased RAF officers.

Those two grants were made in conjunction with the Air Council's gift of the RAF stained-glass commemorative window in the Memorial Library.

Since the end of the Second World War the school's links with the RAF have been maintained by a regular entry of boys to the RAF Colleges, where the highest awards have been won. For by such a splendid record of service in times of peace as well as in war there has been laid a great foundation of interest in aviation.

Yet perhaps there is nowhere in the whole school that reflects such an aeronautical interest in the more recent post-war years as the Combined Cadet Force's Air Section Headquarters – the Air Hut.[3]

Scale-model aircraft dangle from the ceiling; maps, posters, diagrams and pictures decorate the walls. Here the talk is always of aviation – the pioneering past, the palmy present and the fascinating future.

Side by side in a single picture frame hanging on one of the walls are photographs of some of the heroes of the wartime skies. The common factor is that they are all Old Boys of St Edward's.

One of them was Douglas Bader, who shrugged away mention of his own bravery – 'Fellows like Gibson were the brave ones by flying hour after hour in their bombers. I could not have done it. I didn't have the guts... I didn't mind doing short sharp bursts but not going for hour after hour in a bomber.'

Naturally another famous flyer in the frame was Gibson himself; ace reconnaissance pilot Adrian Warburton was also there; then there were A. J. Heyworth, bomber captain turned test pilot, and fighter ace James Leathart.

There was only one more picture in the heroes' frame. It was that of an outstanding young man whose gallant exploits have more than earned his place among the six courageous pilots from St Edward's, despite the fact that his name has remained totally unknown to the general public – Alec Cranswick.

When Cranswick went to St Edward's as a day boy at the age of 14, he soon realized that the day boys seemed less concerned with school

traditions than were the boarders. Alec considered that the day boys –
there were only a few – appeared to have no interest in the school after
lessons were over. 'They just want to get home,' Cranswick told his
mother with great regret.

He was intensely interested himself in the history and the spirit of the
school – it was his school and he wanted to belong to it and to have a
part in it. He wanted the day boys to be able to hold positions equal to
those of the boarders and to be allowed places of trust in the running of
the school. So, with the flair for leadership that had developed over the
past years, Cranswick set out to remedy what he considered were the
shortcomings of his fellow day scholars. Later his House Master
complimented Mrs Cranswick on her son's good manners and home
upbringing and said that he had improved the status of the day boys
beyond recognition.

In the holidays he often exercised the polo ponies on Port Meadow,
Oxford, becoming a fine horseman with extremely sensitive hands that
could manage any horse, however restive the creature might be beneath
him. Another favourite haunt was the boathouse at Godstow where the
boats of St Edward's were kept. At school he learned sculling and soon
approached the same proficiency that he had learned from his mother in
punting. He grew fond of rugger, but he was none too keen on cricket.
He was a member of the St Edward's Officers' Training Corps and
always enjoyed going to camp. It was another instance of his pleasure
in an open-air life, which he liked to feel was the main reason for keeping fit.

During the time Alec was at St Edward's he used to spend long hours
throughout the summer weekends on the River Cherwell with his
mother and the pupils whom she was teaching English. There was
hardly a language not represented at these river picnics. They often
decorated their punts with fairy lights and had late-night supper parties
and swimming – a cheerful, happy time for the youngsters at a period
when, with the rise of Hitler in Germany, the days of peace in the world
were beginning to run out.

When there was money available, Mrs Cranswick sent her son abroad
during the holidays to stay with the parents of some of her pupils. He
visited places such as Paris, Bremen and Hamburg. He watched with
alarm as columns of Stormtroopers marched stiffly through German
cities, their jackboots echoing along the narrow, cobbled streets. He
watched, too, while hordes of fresh-faced Hitler Youth members massed

in the open countryside for their rallies. He made many friends there but he came back saying: 'There's something peculiar going on in Germany, very, very peculiar...'

Cranswick had a deep affection for St Edward's, but after he had matriculated there he told his mother that he wanted to leave and find a job. He felt there was too much of a strain upon her to educate both himself and his sister, who was by now going to Reading University. His mother urged him to remain at school, but he insisted on leaving – he wanted, he said, to join the Royal Canadian Mounted Police.

Presumably his adventurous spirit and his eagerness for riding and a rigorous, open-air life prompted him to set about joining the Mounties. Whatever were his motives, the scheme came to nothing. Instead, he enlisted in the Metropolitan Police with the intention of going through Hendon Police College and making a career in the Force.

He had left St Edward's by the summer of 1937 with the following testimonial from his House Master, Mr G. H. Segar:

*Mr A. P. Cranswick has been a member of this school since September, 1933, and I have been his House Master since September, 1935. He has always had an excellent character. His work has not been below the average and he has done fairly well in sports. He has a quick intellect and pronounced social gifts and has always kept very healthy. He has left too young to enable him to take a leading position in the House, but I consider that he has the makings of a leader. I consider that he has chosen well to apply for police work and that he is very well fitted for this sort of work.*

Although Cranswick had not excelled particularly in his studies, he had made a lasting impression through the development of his character, intellect and charm. He was marked down as a credit to his school, to his mother and to himself.

In the Force he was sent to Limehouse Police Station in London's East End. He was quickly depressed by the district and overwhelmed by the prospects of what he imagined life was going to be like in the Metropolitan Police. Still, he refused to quit so easily. His heart was never really in the Force though and he never found true happiness.

As an observant teenage scholar on holiday in Germany, Alec had seen something of the growth of Nazism and the rise of the Hitler Youth Movement. The Cranswick family were left in little doubt about the grave danger of approaching war long before most people in Britain realized what was afoot.

Once Cranswick found a spy under his own roof. A new German pupil at his mother's school asked him for some information about railway junctions and aerodromes in Britain. The German was given a prompt answer – but not quite the reply for which he was hoping.

Angrily, Cranswick snapped: 'You can clear out, you swine. I'm not spying for you or your master.'

He was turned out of the Cranswick house in very quick time. For, although Cranswick was rarely heard condemning or speaking ill of anyone, he abhorred Nazism and viewed the system as a promoter of war.

In the early summer of 1939, Alec Cranswick went home on leave from the Metropolitan Police and told his mother: 'I want to join the RAF but I do not wish to cause you more worry. What shall I do?'

Mrs Cranswick realized that, with war obviously fast approaching, her son would sooner or later break the news that he wanted to fly. His decision must have caused her great worry, but she tried to hide her fears. Already she had lost her husband in the air; she had also lost her brother-in-law in the air. Must she now lose her only son the same way?

Both mother and son knew she was stifling back the truth when she answered: 'You have every right to arrange your life as you wish. Whatever you do, decide for yourself and I will not worry.'

So into the RAF Recruiting Office walked Alec Cranswick, happy to serve his country but never imagining for one moment the impact he would make in the war years ahead.

Chapter 4

# Enthusiast with Wings

Thunder was in the air the day Alec Cranswick joined the Royal Air Force. Grim black clouds reached like towering mountains into the darkening skies for all to see. But the threatening thunder rumblings that heralded the Second World War could easily be ignored if one was so minded.

For the sports-loving British there were much more pleasant events taking place on this sultry, storm-heavy summer day. It was 24 July 1939, and at Old Trafford the Second Test Match against the West Indies was being played – quite enough to claim one's attention if one wanted to dismiss from one's mind those disturbing thoughts of war. England was one up now in the series, and this second match looked like ending in a draw. That was the only battle worth worrying about this sticky, uneasy afternoon.

War? – plenty of time for such thoughts when the Tests were over for another year. Few people guessed that the Test series would come to an abrupt end on account of those very thunder clouds of war that everyone was trying so desperately to ignore. It was ridiculously easy to divert one's thoughts away from war when there was something as utterly peaceful to concentrate upon as a game of cricket.

Cranswick himself was not exactly mad on cricket, but if anyone had managed to talk him into visiting Old Trafford that day, even he must surely have cast war from his mind. Instead, Cranswick was spending his first day in the RAF as a pupil pilot at No. 7 Elementary and Reserve Flying Training School, Desford Aerodrome, Leicester. In those rather more sombre surroundings he had a distinct feeling of apprehension that war was now clearly drawing nearer.

There can be little doubt the Air Force felt much the same way, for it had him up in the air for his initial taste of flying almost before the ink had had a chance to dry on his RAF enlistment papers. He strode out eagerly to a waiting DH-82 Tiger Moth two-seater training biplane and climbed awkwardly into the passenger seat. With scarcely an explanation the pilot was in his own cockpit and the plane was scurrying bumpily along the coarse grass. The little trainer nosed gracefully into the sky during a merciful break in the storm that had been plaguing most of the country all that day.

The same routine was taking place at the other flying schools, for by now the RAF was really spreading its wings. In the previous week alone nearly 600 recruits had joined to bring the total number of pilots, observers, airmen and boys enlisted since 1 April to 14,252, a figure well over twice that recorded in the same period the previous year.

Cranswick sat intently in the open cockpit behind his pilot and watched with fascination as the control stick in front of him and the rudder bar at his feet kept moving in response to the handling of the pilot's own controls to which they were linked. Dare Cranswick touch the controls? Ever so gently so that the pilot would not know, he placed his hands on the control column and imagined that he was flying the plane on his own.

But that first flight lasted only twenty minutes – short enough to make Alec almost weep with disappointment that it was over, yet sufficiently long for him to know he had made the correct decision when he chose to train as a pilot. He felt wonderful, exhilarated. Tomorrow he would really fly the plane, just wait and see!

The tension of a pending war was mounting with each passing day. The nations were all displaying their might. German aircraft were exercising over the North Sea and some were reported over the English coast. The RAF was out a-roving, too.

The day that Cranswick settled down to his first lessons in the Tiger Moth – 25 July 1939 – 240 bombers set out from their bases in England for distant objectives in France. Seldom had so many been used at one time. They formed a vast procession, with the first bombers returning home from their circular tour before the last groups had started on the journey. The exercise was a gentle reminder that the RAF's bomber force was going to be something to be reckoned with seriously if war should come.

Cranswick's progress was steady. He went solo after just over thirteen hours' flying experience – by no means an unusually fast time, but all was going well. Again the instructor took him up, and the flying programme became more varied and intensive. There was no dawdling, because the threat of war was strengthening with every hour. The smooth days of peace were surely drawing to a close.

Up to now Cranswick's progress checks had been carried out by civilian instructors, but on 28 August 1939 came his first test by an RAF examiner. On the same day another test, of a different sort, was being conducted in many parts of Britain. It was a rehearsal of the school evacuation plans.

In London, Mr Herbert Morrison, MP, Leader of the London County Council, called upon everyone not already engaged to consider how far they might be able to assist local authorities or individuals in need during what might be difficult times immediately ahead:

> If unhappily war should come, London must expect to go through a period of great anxiety, as indeed must all other large cities of the countries involved. I would appeal to my fellow Londoners to be helpful, to co-operate with the local authorities, who will have to carry great responsibilities, and not to forget to extend a helping hand privately to each other as problems arise.

Cranswick's own hands were full just now – making his willing little Tiger Moth do everything that his RAF examiner ordered him to do while the examiner tried to assess his aptitude for flying. He had just twenty minutes to impress upon that RAF chappie in the other seat that he was well and truly up to standard. Why, after twenty-eight hours' flying time he felt a positive veteran!

As August drew to a close, the RAF was standing by at emergency stations. General mobilization was proclaimed, and all RAF reservists were being called up. On 1 September Adolf Hitler was promising in the Reichstag: 'I will not war against women and children. I have ordered my air force to restrict itself to attacks on military objectives.'

That heartening speech of Hitler's was to find a place in history as an example of yet another unfulfilled promise. For on that same day Germany invaded Poland with an unprecedented savagery directed equally against military objectives and civilians.

On the day Britain went to war, Cranswick was not flying. Many Bomber Command crews, however, were sent out that night to shower upon Germany more than six million copies of a statement by Premier

Chamberlain giving the reasons why Britain and France were now at war with Germany.

Alec was thinking: 'The Bomber Boys are busy already. They're going to be still busier soon. So that's the job for me.'

The following day RAF Blenheims and Wellingtons struck the first offensive blow of the war by bombing German warships in the Wilhelmshaven and Kiel areas – while Cranswick was peacefully putting in twenty far less hazardous minutes in the air himself, doing some more low-flying practice under instruction.

Cranswick was 20 years old on 7 September in that first year of the war. It was an important day. First he had to brush up on his aerobatic flying skill; then he had to face his final RAF flying proficiency test. He did well. The RAF gave him a birthday present – a progress report indicating that, unless he did anything downright stupid between now and the end of the month, when he could expect to move on to a more advanced training school, he was as good as accepted as an RAF pilot.

By 18 September, after twenty-five hours, forty-five minutes of solo flight and twenty-seven hours' dual flying, Cranswick had completed his initial training. He was assessed as being of average proficiency as a pilot; nothing startling, for, like everyone else on the course, he had been secretly hoping for an assessment of above average or perhaps even exceptional. Still, he was accepted. He was now Acting Pilot Officer Alec Panton Cranswick (Personal Number: 42696), holder of a Four-Year Short Service Commission in the General Duties Branch of the Royal Air Force.

The next stage would be a training course on bigger aircraft to pave the way for the bombers he hoped to fly. Cranswick's decision to apply for instruction as a bomber pilot came because he considered that this was the best way of carrying the war to the enemy.

He went on leave, and on 8 October 1939, when the Second World War was just five weeks old, Cranswick reported to No. 10 Flying Training School, Tern Hill, Market Drayton, Shropshire, where he would do his multi-engine training on the Avro Anson, a twin-engined plane that could race along about twice as fast as the tiny Tiger Moth on which he had carried out all his previous flying.

Two days after reaching Tern Hill, Cranswick first sampled the Anson. He was up for an hour and five minutes – familiarizing himself with the cockpit layout, taxiing, straight and level flight, climbing, gliding, stalling and making medium turns. Flying is like driving a car in one respect: simply because you can handle a bubble car with ease does not necessarily mean you can drive a huge limousine faultlessly at the first attempt. Anyway, nearly seven more hours elapsed at the controls before Cranswick was ready to take up the Anson on his own.

The first night flight came on 21 November – the very evening that German aircraft ventured over Britain for the first time in darkness and were met by ack-ack and interceptor fighters over the east coast. Cranswick was bringing down his Anson for the sixth landing of the evening's exercise at the time the Germans were nearing England.

Cranswick at the controls of a Wellington; he flew a 'Wimpey' when serving on bomber squadrons in Britain and the Middle East. (Author's Collection)

His flying log was filling up swiftly, and he clocked his first hundred hours in the air on 6 December while on a solo trip in an Anson to practise steep turns and precautionary landings. Then, as crisp winter turned to mellow spring, Cranswick was ready for the final stage of his training. Graded Pilot Officer on probation, Cranswick was posted on 7 April 1940 to No. 11 Operational Training Unit, RAF Station, Bassingbourn, Royston, Herts. He had satisfied the RAF that he knew how to fly; now he had to be taught how to bomb.

For the next eight weeks he flew Vickers Wellington twin-engined long-range bombers – the type that had carried out the first raid of the war on the Kiel naval bases in company with the smaller Bristol Blenheim. The Wimpey bombers were popular with the crews and packed a good punch. Cranswick would like them; he knew that from the start.

He often looked back on his training period and commented that not enough tribute was paid to the instructors who had such a difficult and responsible job teaching so many varied and unpredictable types to fly. These men showed, he realized, great patience and courage.

As Cranswick prepared to join his first bomber squadron, the war had reached a critical stage. The Germans were flooding through Holland, Belgium and France towards the coast facing Britain. The British Expeditionary Force was pulling out of Dunkirk, and the first German bombs were crashing down on English towns. He visualized a long and bitter fight ahead, with RAF Bomber Command having one of the toughest, most vital roles. On one point he was certain: he would be in at the beginning of the fight. Would he, he wondered, be there to see the final victory?

From the operational training unit, Pilot Officer Cranswick was posted to No. 214 Squadron at RAF Station, Stradishall, Suffolk. Only a few days afterwards he found himself in conversation with Squadron Leader W. P. J. Thomson, Flight Commander of 'A' Flight and the squadron's second-in-command. Although nervous, perhaps, in his choice of words in the presence of a senior officer, Cranswick left no doubt that he was dead keen to get in as much flying as possible in the shortest space of time in order to become sufficiently experienced to be given the captaincy of a bomber and a crew of his own.

The routine at that time on Wellingtons was that two pilots flew on each raid. One was the senior pilot and captain in charge of the plane; the other was second pilot, a junior to understudy the captain for probably a dozen or so operations before graduating to the point when he had his own plane. Cranswick made such an impression in his talk with Squadron Leader Thomson that Thomson said later: 'Cranswick's keenness and enthusiasm were so outstanding that there and then I decided to take him on as my own second pilot.'

No. 214 Squadron had just become an operational bombing force after some time as a unit where experienced aircrews received their conversion training to enable them to fly Wellingtons. This had come about through pressure by the Commanding Officer, Wing Commander F. E. Nuttall, and the pilots were now feeling a little strange at being allowed to go bombing after so long instructing others how to fly Wellingtons – so that their pupils could themselves go on bombing raids. Cranswick had been posted in among a batch of young officers straight from training who were needed to fly as second pilots now that the squadron was being reorganized from a training to an operational unit.

Naturally the boy was still very inexperienced in flying generally and in piloting a Wellington in particular. He had completed two hundred hours in the air only the week before joining the squadron and up to six weeks previously he had never so much as looked inside a Wellington. From now on, though, he never missed an opportunity to fly – not even the shortest, dullest routine test flight.

His determination was fortuitous, for, on 18 June 1940, a fortnight but for a day since Cranswick joined No. 214 Squadron, RAF Bomber

Command's activities entered a fresh phase. A new series of attacks was ordered upon aircraft factories, oil and aluminium-producing plant, communications connecting with the German industrial war effort and more especially railway marshalling yards and canals. It was the night Alec Cranswick made his first raid.

At 10.25 p.m. Cranswick flew with Squadron Leader Thomson to Leverkusen, 6 miles north of Cologne, where bustling factories were working round the clock to turn out chemicals and explosives. Flying high over Germany, a heavy load of bombs stacked in the fuselage, Cranswick thought of the happy times he had spent in that country before their Fuehrer had plunged Europe into war.

For an hour Cranswick handled the controls, gaining confidence as each minute ticked by. For the rest of the time he had to secure some insight into the duties of the remainder of the crew – navigator and bomb-aimer, wireless operator and gunners – so that in an emergency he would be ready to take over their work. But this was a comparatively peaceful debut as a bomber pilot and not until his fifth mission did Cranswick find himself in any real trouble.

The target was Monheim. Heavy cloud blanketed the Ruhr, starting at 8,000 feet and towering up to between 12,000 and 13,000 feet – considerably higher than had been forecast. Thomson tried to get to the target beneath the ragged base of the massive, angry clouds. Ahead one of the Wellingtons was trapped by searchlights and plastered by ack-ack fire. The best course for Thomson seemed to be to clear off into the cover of the clouds for safety for a while.

He pulled up the nose of the bomber and the cloud gave the climbing plane a clammy embrace. At around 10,000 feet the Wellington became so heavy with ice that Thomson could not get it to rise any higher. The port engine began surging – revving to maximum power and then falling off again. The ice-laden bomber, still with its load of high explosives aboard, was already difficult enough to handle, but now 'Tommy' Thomson was having to battle like mad to keep the plane on a reasonably steady course. By now Cranswick had left his own seat. He was standing beside his captain and saying quietly: 'Sir, I think we are going to spin...'

In his fierce struggle to keep the trundling Wellington on a steady flight, Thomson had failed to notice the airspeed dropping back dangerously. Just about this time the starboard engine, too, began surging as ice formed in the carburettors. The bomber was perilously close to going out of control. There was nothing to do but dive down low enough to escape the ice that was affecting the engines. The Wellington broke through the cloud layer at a little less than 8,000 feet – only to be picked up by the searchlights.

Flak was bursting all around the bomber. It was so intense that Thomson did not see how they could escape being hit at any moment. Into the intercom to all the crew he shouted: 'Prepare to abandon ship.'

In the tail-gunner's turret Flight Lieutenant Bill Fielding-Johnson yelled: 'Dive!'

As Cranswick checked his parachute straps and stood by to jump out of the plane, Squadron Leader Thomson pushed the Wellington into a dive that somehow succeeded in shaking off the searchlights and the flak. The crew could breathe again.

Back home again safely, Thomson said of Cranswick: 'During the most uncomfortable period he appeared to remain very calm – almost unconcerned, in fact. I have never flown with anyone who was so much on his toes and who could be relied upon to do the right thing at the right time.'

Three more raids and the pilot partnership of Squadron Leader Thomson and Pilot Officer Cranswick was split when the former was promoted to Wing Commander and left No. 214 Squadron to take command of a squadron of his own, No. 38 Squadron at RAF Marham, Norfolk. Cranswick, meanwhile, had qualified to take command of an aircraft after only eight ops as second pilot – more quickly than many others were doing at that time. But, in deciding to give Cranswick his own crew, Thomson considered him outstandingly fit for a captaincy.

He was still only 20 years old, and he had chalked up only 300 hours in the air, when he left 'Tommy' Thomson and the courageous tail-gunner Bill Fielding-Johnson to fly against Germany with a bomber crew of his own.

William Spurrett Fielding-Johnson had already served with distinction in the First World War and won the Military Cross in May 1915 for conspicuous gallantry with the Leicestershire Yeomanry near Ypres when his unit was under heavy attack and experiencing severe losses.

Soon Fielding-Johnson was seconded for service with the Royal Flying Corps and flew as an observer. Once he was in a plane crash in which the pilot was killed; Bill himself was badly injured and for about a year he lay on his back. When fit again, Fielding-Johnson returned to flying duties – training now as a pilot and gaining his wings in time to fly fighters in France with the renowned No. 56 Squadron, whose air aces won great honours. The squadron was credited with destroying 427 enemy aircraft – more than any other squadron – and among the flyers were two who won the VC, Captain Albert Ball and Captain James McCudden.

Promoted to the rank of Captain, Fielding-Johnson won a second Military Cross in May 1918 – again for conspicuous gallantry but this time in the fresh, open skies instead of on the muddy battlefield. He was flying a fighter escort to some bombers of another squadron when he and one other officer attacked ten enemy scout-planes. He destroyed two of them and forced another to land.

On leaving the Service after the war, with seven aircraft 'kills' marked to his credit, Bill joined his father's textile spinning business in Leicester but eventually moved down to London, retaining his links with Leicester-shire by running a small farm there for a hobby and hunting whenever he could get away from London. He went to live at Manor Farm, Compton Bassett, near Calne, Wiltshire, when he married, and by the time the Second World War was looming Bill Fielding-Johnson had become established as a leading farmer and one of the foremost breeders of Dairy-Shorthorn cattle in England.

He was commissioned in the RAF Volunteer Reserve in July 1939 in the Administrative and Special Duties Branch. However, he sought a chance to fly again, and in October 1939 transferred his commission to the General Duties Branch, training and qualifying as an air gunner despite the fact that he was in his late forties. His wife knew nothing of his switch to flying duties until one day she saw a newspaper photograph of him with the rest of the crew of a bomber. He had not told her because he did not want her to worry.

He flew on many raids over Germany and Occupied Europe and later commanded a camp of his own, RAF Station, Newmarket. In September 1942 he was awarded the DFC in recognition of his out-standing keenness and courage – his son Hugh was to win the same award two years later as a Mosquito pilot, but was killed flying over Germany within only a few weeks of gaining the award.

When the Allies invaded Normandy, Fielding-Johnson was back flying again. He was in a bomber over Caen when the plane was hit. One of the gunners was killed and Fielding-Johnson was wounded in the legs. He was in hospital for two months. In the autumn of 1944, when gunnery leader of an RAF Second Tactical Air Force squadron of Mitchell bombers, he was reputedly the oldest air gunner flying on operational service in the RAF.

One day in October 1944 he put himself as a substitute in a depleted crew detailed to make an attack on a target in Holland. The bomber was hit by anti-aircraft fire and the pilot, Jimmy Armstrong, an officer of the South African Air Force, ordered the crew to abandon the aircraft.

'Everything went beautifully,' Bill said later. 'This was a thing I had always wanted to do; as soon as I had pulled the cord I found the sensation a splendid one.'

The first his wife knew of his escape by parachute was when she was travelling in a train to go to a cattle show and some Americans were reading a paper. One of them pointed to a news item and said:

'Say, there's an old chap here jumped out of an aeroplane!'

Mrs Fielding-Johnson caught a glimpse of a photograph in the paper and asked if she might have a look – the picture was that of her husband.

At the cattle show a little while later her name was broadcast over the public-address system loudspeakers. She hurried across to the show-ground office to receive a message that her husband had just arrived in London on survivor's leave. Mrs Fielding-Johnson met her husband and the rest of the crew that evening. Jimmy Armstrong, the handsome and charming pilot, wore the khaki South African uniform and stood out among the rest, for they were all in RAF blue.

Armstrong was to gain notoriety the year after the end of the war. In his real name, Neville George Clevely Heath, he was accused of murdering two women and executed at Pentonville on 16 October 1946. Fielding-Johnson called him a schizophrenic – dull, dour and sullen in the daytime, but another man entirely when the bright lights were shining at night.

For Fielding-Johnson, his courage and devotion to duty a shining example to all who serve in the air, peace brought the heavy commitments of running his Wiltshire farm and at the same time retaining the chairmanship of the family business, Fielding and Johnson Limited, worsted spinners of Leicester.

Busy with the farm, Bill still made a practice of devoting a regular amount of time each month to the textile concern. In February 1953 he collapsed in his chair while conducting a board meeting. At 60, Wing Commander Fielding-Johnson, DFC, MC and Bar, gallant soldier and airman, successful farmer and businessman and staunch friend, was dead.

Britain's bombing efforts were still rather haphazard in the uneasy summer of 1940 when Pilot Officer Cranswick was made Captain of Aircraft for the first time with No. 214 Squadron at Stradishall. Yet what was lacking in precision was partially compensated for by the eagerness of the bomber crews. It was especially true of Cranswick and those who comprised his first crew early in August 1940.

Two of them, Sergeant N. P. Kerr, second pilot, and Sergeant Harry H. Brown, navigator and bomb-aimer, recall the mood of those early days.

'I soon discovered that Alec Cranswick was an enthusiast,' said Kerr. 'He was keen to go on operations and he was keen to hit the target properly – and in 1940 that wasn't so easy.'

'He was not a fanatic by any means,' Brown added, 'but he tackled everything with a boyish enthusiasm. Guess that is all we were at that time.'

In those days there were no Pathfinders to lead the way to the target, so Cranswick and Brown used to come to an agreement on the height to fly on each raid and the route to follow. The practice during that particular phase of bombing activities was to have RAF aircraft attacking many different targets in the course of each night. Perhaps only a handful of bombers would visit each place at a time – a mere pinprick compared with the deadly stabs to the heart of Germany's industry made by many hundreds of bombers on a single target in later years.

Cranswick summed up his attitude to bombing in comments such as this made to his mother when he was home on leave: 'I don't like what I have to do but I think of you and my country and know I must carry on and do all I can. I must do what my pals, who have not returned, would have done. I shall try to forget the horrors we are committing.'

Back in 1940 there was no radar to help find a target and allow accurate bombing through the clouds. If there happened to be a lot of cloud obscuring a target, the bombers had to move on to a secondary target decided upon before take-off. This occurred on 24 August 1940, when Cranswick's Wellington was in a batch detailed to attack the power station at Knapsack, near Cologne. Round and round they flew, but there was no improvement in visibility. The clouds gave them no chance. To try any more was simply to waste fuel. So Harry Brown, navigating, set course for Schipol Airport, Amsterdam, which had been chosen for their secondary target.

They reached Schipol without any trouble, and Cranswick roared along the length of the main runway to drop the bombs originally destined for the German power station. Second Pilot Kerr, stretched out on the floor in the nose of the Wellington, peering over Brown's shoulder in the bomb-aimer's position, saw the runway quite clearly as the bombs smacked down. The plane shuddered from the blast of the exploding bombs. And back at Stradishall the jubilant crew were able to report: 'We seemed to have caught Schipol completely unawares.'

Cranswick displayed relentless vigour in pressing home all his attacks, even when hampered by weather conditions as appalling as those on 8 September 1940. They were on a night raid against barges assembled at Boulogne while the Germans prepared to launch their invasion of Britain. The planes had to struggle through lashing rain, low cloud and an electrical storm. Icing conditions were treacherous enough for any aircraft, let alone those heavy with bombs like the Wellingtons as they battled along gamely towards the French coast. The bombers were tossed about the sky so violently that the pilots had the utmost difficulty in keeping either a steady speed or a constant height. They were flung around by violent up-draughts of air encountered in storm-cloud conditions. Surging currents such as these can snap aircraft wings with the ease of a child breaking a twig.

Over Boulogne, Cranswick started the bombing run at the normal 10,000 feet or so for a Channel port target. But the night was so black that no one could spot the barges. Cranswick pushed the bomber down to only 2,000 or 3,000 feet and made a succession of reconnaissance runs in the midst of a barrage of intense light flak. Still there was no sign of the barges. By now his second pilot, Norman Kerr, was becoming decidedly nervous.

'Skipper, we've tried long enough, surely,' he suggested.

The obstinate Cranswick turned a deaf ear.

*Cranswick just kept on going* [Kerr recounted later]. *Then, on account of the weather and the flak, we almost did pack up. Even at this point he changed his mind. He turned round again for yet another attempt. It was typical of him for he was so thorough. Down we went once more and this time we found the barges. We bombed them successfully and then went off home.*

The longer the trip, the greater were the hazards. The Channel ports missions were over in about three hours usually, but an operation as far as Berlin meant some seven or eight hours in the air, with most of this time being spent over enemy territory. Cranswick's turn to go to the *Big City* – the RAF term for Berlin – came on the night of 7–8 October 1940. This looked like being one of the much-of-a-muchness trips, and to the best of everyone's belief aboard the plane, *F-Freddie*, the attack was completed expeditiously and accurately. There was the minimum of interference from the German defences unless one counts a wayward lump of shrapnel slicing into one of the fuel tanks over the *Big City*. Still, that was what would come of spending three-quarters of an hour circling, circling, circling until the actual target was identified to Cranswick's satisfaction. So far, so good.

The trip back home after a raid was usually rather dull. There was little else to do but keep scanning the skies for any fighters that might be pottering about. No one seemed to want to say much. You drank your coffee and munched your sandwiches now that most of the tension was gone. However, *F-Freddie*'s crew did do a bit better for refreshments this time – thanks to the New Boy, Pilot Officer Wilfred Spooner, successor to Kerr as Cranswick's second pilot.

The son of a Newmarket farmer, Spooner was making only his third raid. The first had been against invasion barges in a French port; the second was against Hamm – the 'Hamm and Eggs run' it came to be known, because both the RAF and the Luftwaffe referred to bombs as eggs in those days.

On the Hamm raid Spooner had watched anxiously as the flak bursts crashed closer and closer, for within a few hours he was to be married. He was never so relieved as when the Wellington reached home safely. There was just enough time for a rest and to get spruced up before going into Newmarket for the wedding. As none of the crew could get to the wedding, Spooner cut a slab of the cake to put on one side for the next time he met them. And that turned out to be the Berlin trip.

With *F-Freddie* turning on to a home track, Spooner clambered through the bomber handing round the cake to each member of the crew. Away behind them the flak was still crunching and the bombs were still crunching. And in the freezing, draughty Wellington, 10,000 feet above Berlin, gloved fingers fumbled with crumbling wedding cake in staunch endeavour not to lose the merest morsel. Mouths that had parched with apprehension over the target now slowly munched the chunks of cake in place of the interminable spam sandwiches; shame, though, that there was no champagne with which to drink an accompanying toast to the bridegroom and the bride he had left behind in Newmarket. Sadly the bomber crew sipped lukewarm coffee as a poor substitute while the flak flashes over Berlin became fainter and fainter, and Stradishall nearer and nearer.

Fog blotted out everything below as *F-Freddie* crossed over the English coast. Cranswick brought the bomber down as low as he dared. Everyone peered into the murk, searching for some sign to indicate their whereabouts – some glimmer of light to show them the way home. Sky and ground had been obscured throughout the return flight. There was no radio contact with the ground to provide a position check, because the wireless set and the radio-telephone had gone dead.

However, one sure way of deciding where you were once across the English coast was to watch out for the identifying beacons on the ground, which flashed out a Morse signal. Each gave a different sequence of dots and dashes that was changed frequently so the enemy would not be able to deduce the code. Pilots could establish their position from these beacons without a great deal of trouble. So lower and lower went *F-Freddie*. But where were the beacons?

In a temporary clearing in the dense fog blanket came a speck of red light. Eyes straining, the crew stared at the light as it flashed out its Morse sequence. They wanted to satisfy themselves that they were reading the signal correctly before the light vanished in the creeping, swirling fog. This, at least, would indicate their position.

Suddenly another light flickered through the gloom. It was signalling the Morse letter 'K'. What the hell did that mean? The wireless operator suggested that in radio language 'K' meant Carry On. Cranswick's crew repeatedly flashed a Morse 'S-O-S' with their own lights to warn the people on the ground and were relieved to spot, some distance away, a flare-path glimmering weakly through the murk.

The fuel gauges had been showing 'Empty' for some time already, so Cranswick dared not waste a second. He had lost a substantial amount of petrol when the tank had been punctured over Berlin; he knew he must land at the first opportunity. He thrust the bomber's nose earthwards and the crew tensed themselves for the landing. In the gloom Cranswick could not make out where the plane was going but he followed the flare-path obediently. The friendly soil of home was but a few feet below the dipping bomber.

The next second the belly of the Wellington was bearing down on what were obviously the tops of some trees. Cranswick's first reaction was that he was landing short of the runway. With a horrifying cacophony of slithering, scraping, grinding noises the fuselage tore down the branches before the plane struck the ground with a jarring thud. It leapt into the air again, catapulted upwards by the sheer force of impact, and crashed down a second time. The wheels crumpled and the bomber lurched drunkenly along the uneven ground in a skidding, shuddering succession of bumps until it came to a violently abrupt stop.

In the darkness Sergeant Brown, the navigator, saw what he thought was one of the crew lying in the bomb-aiming position on the floor at the nose of the aircraft and assumed someone had been flung there in the crash. He scrambled forward to investigate and found it was only a pile of earth that had been pushed through the fuselage floor which had been ripped to pieces when the undercarriage collapsed. Brown made his exit by way of the pilot's hatch amid excited enquiries as to what had happened to him in the crash.

Fortunately no one was seriously hurt, but the Wellington was a write-off. The bomber had come down on a fake airfield some few miles inland in East Anglia. The flares had been lamps strung up on poles like fairy lanterns and the 'runway' turned out to be nothing more than a turnip field. There were wooden posts erected throughout the area and the bomber had skittled over several sets of these before one particular obstruction stopped the plane in its tracks. They had not been briefed on the existence of these dummy airfields and were unaware that one existed in that area.

Decoy dromes like this one drew more attacks from enemy aircraft at that stage of the war than the real aerodromes. They were so realistic that there were instances of lost pilots trying to land on them even in daylight. At night time, whenever enemy planes were approaching, boundary lights were turned on at these decoy dromes to invite an attack from Jerry. And to add to the illusion, dummy aircraft were often towed down the fake runways – the landing lights burning brightly on the mock planes.

Cranswick's unfortunate choice of a dummy drome for the emergency landing resulted in a great deal of anxiety for the next-of-kin of his crew members. Wilfred Spooner's bride of just over a week knew he was to have been flying that night and she expected him back about 4 a.m. to take her from her mother's home in Newmarket to their own flat. Mrs Spooner received no news at all about her husband – nothing to warn her that he was missing; nothing, either, to tell her he had come back from the night's bombing trip. It was not until after lunch that a telegram arrived from him to say he had been 'delayed' and would see her later in the afternoon.[1]

Those were dicey days. One of the biggest shocks that Cranswick experienced while flying with No. 214 Squadron happened when he was about to make the run-in over the target. Cranswick went to operate the dashboard control that opens the bomb doors, but his gloved hand brushed accidentally against another switch. He did not realize what he had done. There had been a fairish amount of anti-aircraft fire about at the time and the searchlights were wandering about the skies to pick up the raiders.

Suddenly there seemed to be a whole lot more flak and a whole lot more searchlights. And all of them appeared to be concentrating on Cranswick's Wellington as it droned along, straight and level, at the critical start of the bombing run. Cranswick hastily closed the bomb doors to make his plane more manoeuvrable and called off the bombing run in order to take evasive action and get clear of the bursting shells.

All of a sudden Cranswick leapt up in his seat – 'Jeepers,' he yelled. No wonder the Jerries were picking on them!

Cranswick's glove had caught the switch that turned on the Wellington's powerful landing lamps fitted beneath the port wing. These are used to illuminate the runway sufficiently for a safe landing if there is no proper flare-path. For a full ninety seconds those lamps had blazed down beneath Cranswick's aircraft, attracting every gunner and every searchlight crew for miles. Brown saw them first – two spectacular beams of light shining directly downwards – and he called out a warning to Cranswick.

As Alec plunged the flak-battered Wimpey into a dive, they were helped on their way by an ack-ack shell bursting beneath the tail. The blast punched the after end of the bomber and forced it into a still steeper dive. With the speed increasing alarmingly to what was a terrifying rate in a bomb-laden Wellington, Cranswick seemed powerless to pull out by his own efforts. His dashboard dials danced crazily as the bomber thundered earthwards.

Just about the only way to escape catastrophe was for the pilot and second pilot to join forces by pushing their feet hard against the instrument panel in front of them and lever with their legs while heaving back the control column with all their might. In any event, Cranswick and Spooner regained control of the plunging plane. Although their aircraft was extensively damaged by flak, they went on to bomb the target and returned safely to Stradishall.

Immediately Cranswick landed he made a full report to his superiors and this was acted upon right away. A safety device was fitted so that the lamps could not be turned on by mistake.

He might have been excused a little boasting about how he had managed to get away with his crew's lives even though the bomber had been lit up over the target as if it had been at a pre-war searchlight tattoo, but Cranswick disliked line-shooting. Once he had been in an attack on Magdeburg where large quantities of synthetic benzene and aviation spirit were being produced. One pilot came back claiming that his bombs had started a particularly devastating series of fires. This pilot was obviously highly delighted, for he went around telling everyone that he had put up a damn fine show. It did not seem quite such a good show, however, when the armourer took a look inside the bomb bay. The bombs were still there – every one of them. There had been an electrical failure that, unknown to the pilot, had prevented his bombs from being released.

After the landing lamp incident Cranswick's first tour of bombing operations was coming to a close. Still with Pilot Officer Spooner flying as his second pilot, Cranswick went on to bomb other targets in Germany, including Kiel, Berlin again and finally Bremerhaven, which brought his tally of ops to twenty-nine with No. 214 Squadron. Now he was due for a rest.

Maybe he would become an instructor. Maybe he would be given an administrative job of some sort. He hated the idea of either of these alternatives, but what could he do. There was one possibility.

In the winter of 1940 the Middle East war was promising to hot up quite a bit. Volunteers were wanted to man the bombers out there. Now was his chance. If he went to the Middle East, he could be sure of carrying on with his operational flying. That, then, was the answer; he would go to the Middle East.

Chapter 5

# Bombers over the Desert

Throughout the second half of 1940, Alec Cranswick's crew consistently demonstrated the truth of the saying that a happy aircrew makes a successful bombing team.

They were finding the targets and hitting them as hard as anybody could do in those early, exploratory days of the RAF's bombing offensive. Not once did Cranswick's crew go into an attack without the conviction that their bombs were going to fall exactly where they were meant to fall.

There had been many discussions among the crew about the possibility of going out to the Middle East. Cranswick seemed to be keener than the rest, somehow; he would snatch every chance to introduce the subject.

Eventually Alec was able to win them over to his way of thinking and, after completing only a few trips with No. 214 Squadron at Stradishall, the crew put in a request for a move to the Middle East. It was not until they had finished their bombing tour in November that the posting came through, however, by which time some of the earlier enthusiasm had worn off.

Alec was immensely eager to go, but navigator Harry Brown was not much in favour, and there were rather mixed feelings among the rest of the boys. Yet on one point everyone did agree – they did not want to split up as a crew. They were happy together, worked well as a team and had infinite trust in each other's capabilities in whatever awkward situation might develop in the air. For these reasons, then, Alec's boys let the decision stand.

The crew were sent on leave and ordered to report back to Stradishall at the end of it to fly their own Wellington out to the Middle East.

No one had any idea where they would be stationed and no one had any preference. They supposed that one stretch of desert would be much like any other, so what the heck! One fact was known: the route would be by way of Malta, where they would refuel and be told where in the Middle East theatre of operations they would be based. Certainly the Malta lap would not be a piece of cake – the crew had heard enough already about the losses en route not to have any false illusions on that score.

Only a few days earlier Air Marshal Owen Tudor Boyd had started out from England to fly the 1,400 miles to the island; his plane was forced down on Sicily. He became the first high-ranking British officer in the war to fall into Axis hands. Boyd was chief of RAF Balloon Command at the outbreak of war, and when he set off for Malta in a Wellington bomber he was on his way to Cairo to take up a new appointment as deputy to Air Chief Marshal Sir Arthur Longmore, who was then Air Officer Commanding-in-Chief, RAF, Middle East.

His long, cold night flight was coming to an end when the Wimpey ran into trouble. It happened near Sicily, almost within sight of Malta, where the enemy opposition was regarded as being just about the fiercest of the whole, hazardous journey. With the petrol tanks practically drained dry, Boyd's aircraft was spotted by enemy planes patrolling the Sicily area, and it was forced down in a field. When everyone had scrambled clear, Boyd drew his revolver and coolly fired into one of the petrol tanks in a defiant bid to destroy the Wellington before the Italian police arrived on the scene to take them all prisoner.

Many crews at that time were less fortunate; nothing more was seen or heard of them once they had left their base in Britain. The winter weather combined with the long, lone flight and the formidable enemy defences covering the greater part of the journey to make the England–Malta flight distinctly unhealthy. It was too far to allow fighters to provide a defensive cover and if the bombers set off in groups they would be easily spotted by the watchful enemy. So, in order to minimize the risks, planes used to fly singly to run the gauntlet of first the defences of the Germans and then those of the Italians. Crews had to keep a careful watch and hope for the best.

Cranswick's crew were reckoned to have roughly a fifty–fifty chance of reaching Malta. The journey would probably drag on for about nine hours, at least, and so far Cranswick had never taken his crew on a flight lasting any more than seven-and-a-half hours. Fatigue would be an enemy almost as dangerous as the German and Italian guns and fighters.

The trouble was that the crew needed to be particularly alert at a time when their endurance powers would be most severely taxed, on the last lap across the Mediterranean, and especially the final hour or two when within range of the Italian fighters.

The flying was to be shared by Cranswick and a Pilot Officer Cross from the Argentine who was with them for the first time. Twice the flight was cancelled because of bad weather. Finally, at twenty minutes past midnight on the night of 8–9 December, Wellington No. 1249 lumbered down the runway at Stradishall on the way to Malta. The throbbing engines shattered the quiet of the night in many a Suffolk homestead as the bomber struggled to gain height. It was so burdened with extra fuel for the unusually long journey that, once it was airborne, there could be no chance of landing again until the greater part of the colossal amount of fuel in the wings and fuselage had been used up.

Everyone was abruptly reminded of this particular point when the pilot's hatch blew off on take-off and an icy blast of wind roared through the plane. It was not an entirely unusual mishap, but the special circumstances on this occasion presented fresh problems. The hatch was the Perspex window above the pilot's head. It was in two separate, identical sections, which each hinged on the top edge of the cockpit and fastened down flat, side by side, forming the roof of the cockpit. In the event of a flaw in the locking device, or if the pilot should fail to ensure the hatch was properly secured before take-off, it would be tugged open by the steadily mounting wind force as the aircraft gathered speed along the runway. If this should happen, the easiest course was to turn back. However, Cranswick's bomber was so brim full of petrol that to turn round again and land would have been courting suicide. So Cranswick and his crew were forced into the uncomfortable alternative of going on to Malta, through a shivering winter night, with the hatch flapping open all the way. Flying at 10,000 feet on a December night, the conditions were not going to be exactly tropical.

The wind wrenching the hatch loose on take-off had twisted the mounting so badly that the strenuous efforts of successive members of the crew to close the hatch resulted only in frozen hands and lots of abuse. It was soon obvious that the hatch could not be fixed, and everyone bundled up as well as possible to keep reasonably warm. Navigator Harry Brown kept beating his hands on his chart table to keep the circulation flowing; he had never been able to work properly in the heavy aircrew gauntlets, so he wore only the silk linings.

He and Cranswick had decided to fly first to Marseilles and from there to Tunisia, which they hit just at daybreak. Brown thought how picturesque the sweeping Tunisian coastline was looking. In the subsequent brilliant sunshine the deep, glorious blue of the Mediterranean fully matched up to his anticipation. It was so splendid, so peaceful, dazzling and eye-catching. Yet now was the time of real danger. In the bright sunlight there might be lurking the Italian fighters from the island of Pantelleria. Cranswick ordered a vigorous all-round watch to be maintained so that the tiring crew would not be caught napping. Grimly, Brown remembered that the Italian fighter pilots from Pantelleria had been given most of the credit for the non-arrivals on the England–Malta gauntlet run.

It was just coming up to 9.30 a.m., British time, when Wellington No. 1249 circled the dot in the Mediterranean named Malta, untroubled by the fighters from Pantelleria after all. The island looked rather like a patchwork quilt, Brown thought, as he picked out the aerodrome at Luqa, where they were to land. Already there were a few Wellingtons at Luqa. These had been flown out from Britain the previous month. But the arrival of Cranswick's, and another on the same day piloted by a South African, drew interested batches of spectators from the Messes, Squadron buildings and the administrative blocks. It was a noteworthy event when any plane succeeded in getting through from England, but that day was a special one. It was 9 December 1940, and in the Middle East war history was being made.

As the first flickering of dawn light broke over the barren wilderness called the Western Desert, the Army of the Nile moved forward swiftly like a gigantic broom wielded from far-off Cairo to sweep the Italian invaders right out of Egypt. The Italians had been in Egypt just under three months. Marshal Graziani's forces had crossed the Libyan frontier into Egypt on 13 September, pressing forward about 80 miles to Sidi Barrani and halting there to prepare for the final advance upon Mersa Matruh, some 70 miles further on, which was the chief defensive position of General Sir Archibald Wavell, who was in supreme command of the Middle East Army. As the autumn turned to winter, one side or the other clearly must take the initiative – either Graziani must order his forces towards Mersa Matruh or Wavell must give the command for his troops to fling the Italians out of Egypt. Each was waiting for the supplies and support to carry out the blow.

Covered by a tremendous RAF strafing of the Italian airfields throughout Libya, and by the Royal Navy's thunderous bombardment of enemy land positions, Wavell's men moved first. This was the situation in the Middle East as Pilot Officer Cranswick flew into Malta and the crew climbed down wearily from their Wellington, leaving their kit inside in case of orders to move on.

Reporting their arrival, Cranswick and his crew were found sleeping accommodation on the camp and shown where to get their meals; they were also encouraged to have a look around Valletta, the island's capital, which was within walking distance if one had a mind to chance the heat of a sun that, to the new arrivals, seemed pretty fierce. The nine-hour journey from Stradishall to Luqa had lifted them from the cold and miserable dampness of winter to near summer-like conditions that were a pleasantly welcome if startling change.

The ripped pilot's hatch on the Wimpey was replaced and, on the second morning in Malta, Cranswick took the plane up on a forty-five minute flight to familiarize himself with landmarks on the island and the landing approaches of Luqa airfield. From high in the sky Malta looked no bigger than the foamy crest of a wave that glints unaccountably to catch the eye in the middle of a great, calm expanse of sea. It would not be an easy place to find.

On the third day Cranswick still had no news of when he and the crew were likely to move to a permanent base in the Middle East: 'Just how long I shall be here is hard to say as there is a tyrannical old pirate who has more or less shanghai-ed us,' he explained in a letter home that night.

He had sent a cable telling his mother about the safe arrival on Malta as soon as he landed and he gave an account of immediate impressions in his first letter home. Alec wrote:

*Malta is quite a nice island judging by my observations so far.*

*It is terribly barren, however, and full of weird and obnoxious smells.*

*Every building is built of stone and lots of them are marvellously carved, especially the shrines which are surrounded with minarets.*

*The commonest mode of transport is by a 'gharry' which is similar to the Irish pony carriage, but with a definite Spanish appearance.*

*The weather here is just like spring at home and as soon as I have time I am going swimming. We walked into Valletta this afternoon and felt as though we were being baked...*

*Most of the cars here are of the 1928 type and there is a marvellous old one that takes us in and brings us back from Valletta in the evenings. It holds six, but usually has at least eighteen on board and even then the driver never changes out of top gear.*

Cranswick knew several of the other aircrew personnel at Luqa. They were either with him on No. 214 Squadron at Stradishall or flew with squadrons from nearby bases. He even found one officer who had served with his father at Upavon.

Malta had special historical attachments for Alec, for the island's powerful fortifications and great treasures had been established by the work and wealth of the Knights of the Order of St John of Jerusalem, with whom his forebears had strong links as far back as the sixteenth century. The Knights governed the island fortress until its occupation by Napoleon in 1798, the Congress of Vienna eventually recognizing Malta as a British dependency in 1814.

The island, 17½ miles long, by 8½ miles wide, was only twenty minutes' flying time from the raiding enemy dromes in Sicily. It struck Alec Cranswick in much the same way as any other visitor – bare and stony, a mass of high stone walls instead of fences to protect gardens and fields from the fierce winds, and not a lake, a river or even a tree in sight, whether one strolled in the rugged valleys or on the terraced hillsides.

He made the most of the first day or two in Malta for sight-seeing expeditions while the stronghold was still reasonably intact. The enemy's air bombardment had yet to reach the peak of ferocity to demolish more than 15,000 buildings, among them seventy churches, eighteen convents and monasteries, twenty-two schools, eight hospitals and ten theatres.

The lazy, waiting days were over for Alec Cranswick's crew on 14 December, and there was no need to move on from Malta. They were posted to No. 148 Squadron, which was being re-formed that day as a sixteen-bomber unit to operate from Luqa. The squadron had been formed originally at Andover on 10 February 1918, and in the early days of the Second World War had trained crews to fly Wellingtons, until it ceased to exist on the formation of No. 15 Operational Training Unit.

Cranswick's crew joined a flight led by Flight Lieutenant Peter Forsyth, who had been flying Wellingtons with Special Flight, No. 115 Squadron, since reaching Malta more than a month earlier on a posting from England. He had flown on some of the raids that were ordered with the object of keeping the Italian Air Force grounded when General Wavell was preparing to launch his Western Desert offensive. With that attack now under way, a bad weather spell put a stop to air strikes from Luqa for five days. The bombers were brought to a state of readiness each morning, but by the afternoon the cancellation had come through and the crews were able to relax.

For those who fancied a trip to the cinema in Valletta, there was a Wallace Beery–Maureen O'Sullivan film, *Port of Seven Seas*. Failing that, there were bridge parties in the camp or social calls upon the Maltese, who used to delight in welcoming the RAF boys into their homes.

The period of inactivity ended with a raid on Naples on 14 December. The usual way to Italy was right beyond the western end of Sicily and up towards the Bay of Naples on a zigzag course to give the enemy the impression that the bombers were from England instead of Malta. The subterfuge was an effort to make the return journey less susceptible to fighter attack and avoid reprisal bombing attacks against Malta.

The Naples raid was not lacking in moments of drama.

One lump of shrapnel smacked into Cranswick's Wellington, but the enemy had the worst of the exchange, for his crew were credited with severely damaging an Italian cruiser in the harbour. It was Cranswick's first attack with his new squadron, so he had cause to feel pleased with himself. Bombs thudded down on the jetty to which two battleships were moored and fires blazed for a considerable time. One of the raiders dropped an entire bomb load close to a battleship; and five direct hits were scored on a concentration of cruisers and destroyers.

But Malta was under heavy attack, too, by now.

One night when No. 148 Squadron bombers were not engaged in operations, crews on Luqa watched with admiration as the Malta searchlights picked up one Italian raider, an SM79, and a Hurricane fighter was seen darting up from behind to blast the bomber out of the night sky with some rapid bursts from its guns.

The spirited Malta defences were in direct contrast to those functioning at Castel Benito aerodrome, just to the south of Tripoli. This was the target for Cranswick's next raid. The only defence appeared to be a single machine gun in the centre of the drome. And a burst or two of retaliatory fire from the nearest bomber was enough to quieten the machine gunner for a while.

The Wellingtons swept over the airfield in a clockwise direction at between 1,500 and 2,000 feet, dropping 250-pound high-explosive and incendiary bombs. The gravest risk was from colliding with another aircraft or, if you went in too low, of being hit by splinters from your own bombs. Aircraft and hangers were left wrecked and blazing, but the Wimpeys were not yet finished. Down they screamed in a dive attack to well below 800 feet to let the high-spirited gunners enjoy themselves with their machine guns. Cranswick skimmed down to a mere 150 feet – the lowest he had ever flown on any raid – and the machine guns spurted out a stream of bullets.

When the last of the Wellingtons climbed away from stricken Castel Benito, fires were burning over a large area of the drome. One of the bomb dumps was ablaze, and the fires were still visible 70 miles away. The raid was carried out without the loss of a single British plane, although several bore the scars of machine-gun fire from aircraft of their own squadron.

Three nights later No. 148 Squadron again attacked Castel Benito. Now everyone was forbidden to go below 3,000 feet to avoid the chance of getting hit by machine-gun fire or suffering damage from the blast from their own bombs. In the mounting Middle East offensive, bombers and crews were too precious to waste.

Alec's navigator bomb-aimer recalled: 'Everyone enjoyed Castel Benito... I think!'

It was almost more enjoyable than Christmas, for a day or two later Cranswick was writing home:

*Christmas was not a very cheerful affair. It rained all day. In the afternoon I went to tea with some Maltese people I have met and had quite a good time.*

*At present I am on leave but as there is nothing to do it does not mean much out here. If you want to get a letter to me in a hurry send it to my old station.*

This was a veiled hint, of course, for the England–Malta air gauntlet run was still going on and, as several of his old mates were flying out to Malta at odd intervals, any of them would act as a Flying Postman to carry his mail.

Shipping was a frequent target for No. 148 Squadron within its first month of activities from Malta. Through a gap in the clouds over Taranto, Alec's crew bombed units of the Italian fleet on 30 December and, on New Year's Day 1941, they sent high explosives raining down on ships in Tripoli harbour.

The cloud gap sealed before the Taranto results could be observed, but there was more luck over Tripoli. There were numerous ships in the harbour when the squadron's Wellingtons arrived, but one merchant vessel of about 10,000 tons stood out among them, and Alec made straight for it. Down spilled the bombs. Jackie Hoy, the rear gunner, yelled out that at least one direct hit had been scored as well as several near misses. The vessel was later confirmed hit and sunk and the credit went to Cranswick's crew.

It was not all such easy going. A week after the Tripoli raid, Alec Cranswick was giving his Wellington a routine seventy-five-minute air test before lunch with a full load of 250-pound bombs on board ready for operating that night.

The wind changed direction completely during the flight, with the result that Alec was landing down wind. This meant that the wind was coming up behind him to boost the speed of the aircraft instead of heading into the wind, which would naturally slow down the machine and so shorten the landing run.

The runways at Luqa were short enough at the best of times, but with the wind behind him Cranswick realized the plane was not going to stop under its own braking power. As it raced along, brakes screaming, he swung the Wellington to starboard and smashed into a heap of stone

blocks hewn out of the rock and used for construction work on the airfield.

The thought of the bombs still dangling in the belly of the plane sent everyone scampering out and fleeing for the protection of the stone walls, in case the plane blew up. Anxiously the flyers waited, tensed behind the sheltering walls, but the bombs remained intact. And no one suffered any more serious injury than minor scratches and the odd

Aftermath of a landing in Malta when Cranswick's Wellington hit a heap of stone blocks in January 1941. (Author's Collection)

bump on the head. The Wellington – No. 1249 – was the one Cranswick had flown out from Stradishall and had used constantly in the previous month on Malta. It was out of commission and then it was finished off completely by enemy bombing. Cranswick changed to a mongrel Wellington made from the serviceable parts of damaged aircraft, which, although it rattled a bit, chugged along a good twenty or thirty knots faster than any other Wimpey on the squadron.

Cranswick's crew considered the Malta ops were easy compared with those over the Continent from Stradishall, except that Malta was such a tiny island for the navigator and pilot to find on the return journey, with

the additional hazard that the surrounding areas were all hostile. They
were occasionally bothered by Italian planes prowling around over Malta
at some 20,000 feet, but no one seemed to encounter a night-fighter, and
enemy anti-aircraft fire was most erratic. This consisted almost entirely
of tracer bullets just pumped wastefully into the sky. In fact, the Italian
ack-ack used to guide the British bombers to the target, because the
gunners were in the habit of blazing away long before the bombers were
in range.

It was a different story when the Germans moved into Italy and to
Sicily, only 60 miles away. The Germans boasted that their dive bombers
would destroy Malta in a few hours. The first blow came when the
Luftwaffe trapped a British convoy in the Sicilian Channel on the
journey eastwards to Greece. In a spectacular and closely pressed attack,
the dive bombers singled out some of the powerful escort warships. In
particular, the aircraft carrier *Illustrious* had to face a frightful hammering.
Battered and crippled, *Illustrious* was detached to make for Malta, while
the rest of the convoy and escorts carried on towards Greece. Enemy
bombers scarcely left her alone as she limped along, with the crews of
her desperately overworked guns still beating off the frenzied attacks.
The defiant arrival of *Illustrious* in Grand Harbour, Valletta, further
infuriated the Luftwaffe, so they now began an intensive, continuous
series of raids against the island. Luqa was subjected to regular pastings.
Harry Brown noted:

*After giving the airfield a good pounding on one occasion the dive bombers diverted their
attention to the living quarters. About six of us jumped into the corridor of one of the
billets – it was too late to make the shelters – and we were all hiding under one steel
helmet and being buffeted backwards and forwards along the corridor by the blast. I've
often thought what a stupid sight this must have been.*

*Before any aircraft could take off, we were all called upon to fill in the craters in the
runways – some of them were a handy size, too. I remember Alec and I were driving
Army trucks around the place and taking turns filling holes with shovels and spades
and any tools that were to hand. In the middle of the procedure we would need to stop
while we were again pounded by the Germans. Whereas previously most had stood and
watched the raids it was now becoming quite a panic to get into the shelters. Up to that
time they had mainly been occupied by the Maltese. Everyone was becoming a little
jittery with the bombing – working to get the runways serviceable again and trying to
operate at the same time.*

In one day four hangars were hit and two damaged; one of the aircraft of No. 148 Squadron was destroyed, and all the rest were damaged by bomb splinters. Ground staff and aircrew joined in to fill up the craters left on the runway by an estimated twelve tons of German bombs.

Chances to hit back came with No. 148 Squadron's raids on Catania Aerodrome, Sicily, which were the first encounters with really accurate ack-ack fire since Cranswick had been raiding Germany. It shocked everyone back into reality. The airfield had a veritable carpet of German planes and the Wimpeys scored considerable successes with their bombs and machine-guns.

In one attack a petrol dump was set on fire. Bombs blasted the main runways and a railway line running along the west side of the drome. The fires and explosions were visible from Cape Passero on the south-east corner of Sicily, 45 miles away. A week later the Luftwaffe repaid the debt when fifty Ju.88s bombed Luqa from high level and some Ju.87s dive-bombed the drome, demolishing two hangars and two bombers completely, damaging all the remaining planes and shattering several camp buildings. Time again for Operation 'Clean Up' on Luqa.

Next day No. 148 Squadron returned to Catania. The enemy gunners were waiting for them. To date, this was the most intense, the most severe and the most accurate flak barrage thrown up against Cranswick in all his time as a bomber pilot. The stench wafting inside the aircraft from the explosives bursting outside was nauseating.

One of the crew remarked tersely: 'How we avoided damage I'll never know. The flak was bursting all around us.'

Remembering what the Luftwaffe had done to Malta, Cranswick purposely delayed making a quick return to Luqa. His bomb-aimer explained later:

*Whilst not instructed to do so, and strictly off our own bat, we saved one bomb for the living quarters in retaliation for the aircrew killed at Luqa a few days earlier. I retained one piece of shrapnel that passed between my head and my bed rail as I attempted to get out of bed. Had it not been for the blast of the previous explosion knocking me down it would no doubt have scored a hit on me.*

As the Wellingtons turned for home, aircraft were burning on the airfield and fires started near the administrative buildings were visible for more than 20 miles. There was no pride in creating a bloodbath in the midst of an enemy drome, but memories of so many friends lost in the blitz on

Luqa remained fresh in the thoughts of these RAF bomber crews.

One of the most outstanding acts of bravery on the Malta station in the winter of 1940–1 was that of a young NCO pilot of No. 148 Squadron, Sergeant Raymond Mayhew Lewin, whose Wellington crashed into a hillside shortly after taking off from Luqa.

As the bomber burst into flames, Sergeant Lewin scrambled out and saw three of his crew of four climbing out of the escape hatch. He ordered them to run clear.

Instead of racing for safety himself, Lewin deliberately ran round the blazing wing in which full petrol tanks were burning and crawled beneath the wing to rescue his injured second pilot.

Lewin was already injured himself with a cracked kneecap and severe bruises on face and legs, yet he half-dragged, half-carried his wounded comrade 40 yards from the plane to a hole in the ground, where he lay on top of him to shield him just as the bombs exploded.

Sergeant Lewin was awarded the George Cross and the citation ended with these words: 'This superbly gallant deed was performed in the dark under most difficult conditions and in the certain knowledge that the bombs and petrol tanks would explode.'

When Raymond Lewin recovered from his injuries he flew as second pilot with Alec Cranswick for a time before he was ready to have a crew of his own once more. It was an unfortunately shaky return to flying duties.

The main runway at Luqa was looked upon as too small for comfort, and at the end there was a deep gully, which claimed a number of aircraft that failed to get airborne in time. To facilitate the take-off, pilots used a few degrees of flap to give extra lift and even then virtually had to yank the plane off the ground by sheer brute force. That gully nearly claimed Cranswick's bomber the night Sergeant Lewin was second pilot for a raid on Tripoli on 31 January 1941, Alec's fortieth operational mission.

As soon as the Wellington had cleared the ground, Lewin attempted to lift the undercarriage but apparently pulled the wrong lever. By so doing he took up the flaps that had been lowered to provide extra lift at the critical time. Brown, the navigator bomb-aimer, standing in the astrodome, remembered the incident vividly:

*Down into the gully we went due to the loss of lift. We literally staggered up the opposite slope. No one ever understood how Alec avoided hitting the other wall of the gully. It was a particularly shaky start for Lewin's return to flying. I think that gully was the spot where his own plane had crashed, caught fire and blown up in the incident when he won his George Cross.*

Sergeant Lewin was commissioned as a Pilot Officer later in the year. He returned to Britain on leave and was killed only a few days afterwards.

Cranswick's last raid from Malta was on Castel Benito airfield again. The bombing force dropped several tons of high explosives and incendiaries that night, 2 February 1941, and at least seven enemy aircraft grounded on the drome were destroyed by fires. Planes left in the open in front of the hangars were machine-gunned, and several were damaged. Direct hits were registered on one big hangar and other buildings that were set ablaze. The hangar was demolished by bombs dropped from Cranswick's Wellington and one of the crew reported later: 'The whole hangar appeared to rise in one piece for some considerable height, dropping down again and disintegrating as though a child was lifting a house made of blocks and then letting them fall again.'

Two days later Alec had a lucky escape – only this time he wasn't flying. He was engaged in nothing more dangerous than making up a four at bridge with Flight Lieutenant Forsyth and two other officers named Waterfield and Astell in the Officers' Mess at Luqa. Hardly had the game started than an air raid alert sent them scurrying into the shelter beneath the Mess. Thirty Ju.88s chose this building for a special target, Forsyth commenting afterwards:

*There was not much left of the Mess when the bombers had finished. There were only about the four of us there at the time. All the others must have left camp – and it was just as well. Anyone who had stayed in their rooms must surely have been hurt and maybe killed. I lost seven pounds, a watch, my uniform and my raincoat. The clothing was all ruined by the bombing; the money and the watch were stolen from the wreckage.*

Cranswick's crew had some respite from the Malta bombing in a temporary posting to Heliopolis on the outskirts of Cairo. Alec himself lived at an Officers' Club in Cairo; the remainder, all NCOs, had to stay on the airfield. There was more sightseeing than duties to occupy them – trips to the Pyramids and the Sphinx and into the bazaars to watch the manufacture of beautifully engraved copper and silver plates. The RAF lads soon got the hang of the art of bargaining with the market vendors: 'They always ask three times as much as the article is worth and then you haggle like mad with them until eventually you get it at the price you want,' Alec wrote home.

Luqa, meanwhile, was receiving an average of three visits a day from enemy bombers, and the number of aircraft lost or damaged by these raids was beginning to affect No. 148 Squadron's efficiency. In one attack on 25 February, when Ju.88s and Ju.87s blasted Luqa for close on an hour, six of the Squadron's aircraft were burned out and four more damaged too severely to be repaired immediately. These losses slashed the effective strength of the squadron to only two aircraft.

It was then that orders came through for No. 148 Squadron to move to a less exposed base, RAF Station, Kabrit, Egypt. Even so, Axis planes gave them a fond farewell by attacking the ships waiting to take the squadron personnel and equipment from Malta to Egypt.

From Cairo on 1 March 1941, Cranswick flew his crew to El Adem, Tobruk's airport, which had been the Italian Air Force's main flying and repair base in Cyrenaica. By now El Adem was just a graveyard of Italian biplanes. Alec stayed on the drome, but his NCOs had to live in a transit camp in a wadi outside Tobruk. Apart from the obvious feeling of insecurity in a tent in the middle of an air raid, the crew had a reasonably enjoyable time. They had great fun organizing races on Italian motor cycles that had been abandoned in the desert with untold quantities of 45-gallon drums of gasoline and cognac – which were often hard to tell apart, for the motor bikes would run on either!

The reason for the delay at El Adem was that Cranswick's crew were waiting to fulfil their most unusual role so far in the Middle East war: escorting fighters, whose normal role was – escorting bombers!

At 9.40 a.m. on 8 March 1941, Wellington No. 2817, with Cranswick in command, climbed away from the desert air base to accompany three Hurricanes across the Mediterranean as far as Malta. To make the journey the fighters had to discard all their armament and fit overload petrol tanks. With the game little Hurricanes in such meagre supply in the Middle East, Cranswick's Wellington had to fly with the trio to show them the way and be ready to open up with its own protective .303 machine guns if any enemy planes should pounce on the defenceless fighters. The aerial convoy succeeded in reaching Malta unscathed and unhindered. So much concern had been expressed over the air defences of the island in the face of ever-increasing attacks from Axis bombers that the arrival of each new fighter trickling through to Malta was an occasion for jubilation.

Back at Kabrit now with the rest of No. 148 Squadron and after fifteen weeks away from England, Pilot Officer Cranswick wrote to his mother:

*Here I am, surrounded by swarms of flies, answering the letters I have never received. I have had only one letter since I left England and that was from you.*

*We wander about the whole time in khaki and have a marvellous time sunbathing. The Great Bitter Lake is just outside the Mess and the water is as warm as the hottest day in England... The other day I was stuck in the Desert in a sandstorm. It was so thick that we could not see across the Mess and all the food was covered in sand. When I went out to see if my plane was picketed down okay I had to put on my gas mask.*

*I was stuck on the roof of a building the other day when Jerry decided to dive bomb a place two hundred yards away and as I had my camera with me I obtained some marvellous photos. I got one of a dive bomber being attacked by three Hurricanes and having its tail shot off.*

Settled in well at Kabrit by now, No. 148 Squadron were able to commence a new series of operations aided by Wellingtons, which were arriving from England to replace the machines lost on Malta.

Malta, remembered by Cranswick as a proud and historic sun-swept land of whitened stone, figured in one of his poems. It was written just after he had returned to Egypt from escorting the first batch of Hurricanes, which were so sorely needed to fling into the defence of the besieged island.

He called the poem 'Malta Awakes':

*A peaceful sun-swept land of whitened stone,*
*Blissful with thoughts of your fraternity;*
*Gone were the wars to which you once lay prone,*
*Bright shone the Star of your Eternity.*

*Great was the prowess of your St John Knights,*
*Lengthy the siege against the Turkish foe.*
*Praised were the tales of your historic fights*
*Peace turned the wolf alas, into a doe.*

*Left was the joy which you attached to life,*
*Pleasure surpassed all fears within you born.*
*You were a carefree folk bereft of strife,*
*Working your scanty farm each rising morn.*

*Left were your towns where people flocked to pray,*
*Valletta, on the coast, Rabat, on high;*
*Amongst you all there was no one to say*
*Your greatest hour of trial was drawing nigh.*

*Deep was your fear when first the raider came,*
*Dumbly you watched your dwellings blown apart;*
*Could this be Malta, isle of worldly fame,*
*Surely a dream and yours the foremost part?*
*To God you prayed in terror to explain*
*Why should my neighbour seek to kill me thus?*
*You were a vital link of rusted chain,*
*Loud were your lamentations, great the fuss.*

*Razed was your ancient sacred Maltese Church,*
*Back came the ghosts of St John Knights of old;*
*Courage O People, nothing can besmirch Our Honour.*
*Courage, Maltese, and be bold.*
*Back came the Wolf for centuries at rest,*
*Fired were all souls with his defiant bay;*
*Back came morale, back came your former zest,*
*Malta for ever though great be the price we pay.*

*A peaceful sun-swept land of whitened stone,*
*Proud in the thought of your fraternity;*
*Faced with the war to which you now lie prone,*
*Bright shines the Star of your Eternity.*

*A. P. C. 12/3/41*

Although operating from Kabrit, No. 148 Squadron's Wellingtons continued to use Malta as an advanced base for refuelling and maintenance. A detachment of ground staff had been left on the island to carry out this work.

In the fortnight after the move to Kabrit, forty bombing sorties were made from Malta against Tripoli, all of them without loss. Some of the new aircrew from England were members of Cranswick's old unit, No. 214 Squadron at Stradishall, among them a crew led by Pilot Officer Maurice Hartford.

He and Cranswick had been in an attack on Kiel on 28 October 1940, which completed his own tour of ops with No. 214 Squadron, although Cranswick still had a couple more ahead of him.

Hartford and his crew then went to No. 40 Squadron at RAF Station, Wyton, to fly with them during the conversion period when switching from Blenheims to the more powerful Wellington bombers. With him were Sergeants E. C. Hargest, wireless operator; Potter, navigator; Evans, rear gunner; and Stevens, front gunner.

By February 1941, No. 40 Squadron was fully converted to Wellingtons, and Hartford's crew returned to Stradishall to pick up a Wellington to fly to Malta on 3 March with a Pilot Officer Tweedale as second pilot. The crew almost failed to reach the island – but this time the blame could not be placed either on the weather or on the enemy defences. The trouble was a jammed valve, which meant that the 160 gallons of fuel in one of the petrol tanks in the wings could not be pumped to the near-starving engines. When a check was made on arrival at Luqa, the other tanks were practically dry.

By the end of that month, March 1941, Cranswick had completed forty-six operational missions and those of his crew with the most ops to their credit were selected for return to Britain. Alec himself was due to play a new role a long way from the enemy's clutches but where disaster still lingered as close as some of the ack-ack shell bursts that had rocked his bomber many times in the previous ten months.

He was detached from bombing operations to go to the big RAF base at Takoradi, Gold Coast, West Africa, to fly urgently required aircraft across Africa on the Sudan Air Ferry to the Middle East operational dromes. The planes were reaching Takoradi either in crates on board ships or flown off carriers. To Cranswick, Takoradi was a new world – a world of excitement and beauty. Within a few days of arriving there he wrote a letter to his mother, telling her of his first experiences on the Gold Coast:

*Since my last letter I have been journeying across Africa through the Sudan, Belgian Congo and French Cameroons. At the edge of the Congo we saw herds of game and a few elephants. The person who said that the jungle steams was nearer the truth than he thought. It stretches for hundreds of miles and there is a continual mist rising out of it.*

*The contrast to Egypt is very noticeable as there it is a dry heat but here it is a wet one. You always feel clammy but soon get used to it. At nights I don't even pull the sheet over me and in daytime everyone wears a sun helmet. The beach is only four hundred yards away and we have a fine time surf-riding on the Atlantic rollers. It is really a marvellous sport.*

*At night there are thousands of little fireflies flitting about looking like sparks out of a fire. The only nasty customer here is the snake. There are several varieties, the worst being the black mamba, but when we go into the jungle we carry sticks to deal with him.*

*I went into the jungle in the Congo and came across several native villages. It is a marvellous sight to see the jungle on either side of the river. I have taken lots of photos and cine films of all these places.*

*We always sleep in mosquito netting, especially now as the rainy season is approaching, which means malaria will be much in evidence. Fruit is very cheap out here, in fact most of it, such as pineapple, bananas, oranges, dates, paw-paw and lemons can be picked in the jungle.*

Veteran now of forty-six flying operations over enemy territory from bases in Britain and the Middle East, Pilot Officer Cranswick had been taken off ops for a rest of between four and six months: 'Actually I shall apply to operate again in about three months,' he warned his mother.

Cranswick's return to operational flying was not going to be as soon as he expected. The malaria that he had mentioned as likely to be much in evidence struck him down within a day or two. He had to be stopped from flying for a month and go into hospital. He lost a stone in weight, and boredom was the enemy now. Sadly Alec wrote in a letter to his mother in utter desperation during his third week of the malaria attack:

*I now just sit around the Mess all day doing nothing and it gets very boring. There is no news much to tell you because nothing ever happens here. Every day is just the same as the last and all we do is listen to the radio and go bathing. There is not even a daily paper.*

*To fill in time I have written to everyone I know but I expect by the time the replies get here I shall be somewhere else!*

While tornadoes and heavy rainstorms swept steamy, tropical Takoradi, Alec's thoughts turned eagerly to home: 'What is the garden like now? I suppose all daffodils and tulips are in full swing,' he wrote.

After resting a month to get over the effects of malaria, Cranswick had to go before a medical board to see if he was fit for flying once more. He passed without any trouble and flew on 22 May for the first time in six weeks: 'It was a joy to do so again,' he said when he returned.

Another enjoyment was writing poems, and the slack hours provided him with ample opportunity to look back on both the pleasures of peace and the horrors of war and unite them in poetry.

His joy at being able to return to flying duties was short-lived. Within a fortnight Cranswick was back in hospital, laid low by another dose of malaria and off flying again for a further month. It was a miserable existence: 'At the present minute there is nothing at all to write about except that I have not been out anywhere for two months because there is nowhere to go,' he wrote despondently in one letter home. The only cheering note was in anticipating his return to operational flying the next month. And then these hopes were dashed – by another bout of malaria.

When Cranswick recovered from this attack, he went back to ferry-flying, back to those long, arduous journeyings across the continent of Africa, where the unfriendly jungle waited below in sinister silence to claim any erring flyer. It was on one of these ferry trips from Takoradi that he suffered the most frightening episode that had befallen him in two gruelling years as a pilot. In terms of fear, this experience at Wadi Halfa, on the Sudan–Egypt border, on 1 August 1941, was far worse than anything he had faced on bombing operations. Yet there seemed no reason why the flight should have been anything but quite straightforward when he set out for Cairo in a Bristol Blenheim.

He made his pre-flight check and satisfied himself that all appeared to be well with the aircraft. He taxied out, took off and began gaining height. Once airborne, however, Cranswick found the plane was playing tricks on him. It was sluggish and he found it a strain to get it to climb. He managed to get up to 500 feet but that was the limit. Uneasily, Cranswick struggled along, but when he was 10 miles from the airfield his starboard engine cut out. He knew now that he had no option but to turn back for Wadi Halfa. Could he make it? He glanced down at the hills. There was no chance of pulling off a successful forced landing unless he could get back to the airfield. It was a horrifying prospect; either coaxing the Blenheim back to Wadi Halfa on the one remaining engine or crashing to almost certain death if he failed. An escape by parachute was impossible, he was far too low.

The stricken plane dragged down – down towards the hills. There were no more than 5 feet between him and the hilltops as he scraped over and staggered on towards the haven of the drome. The full emergency drill was swinging into operation by now. An ambulance tore across to where the airfield personnel guessed the crippled plane would touch down, still some distance short of the airfield. It reached the point of touch-down seconds ahead of the Blenheim: 'Waiting to pick up the bits,' Cranswick thought wryly.

In his logbook Cranswick wrote: 'Worst experience so far.' That he survived to tell the tale is fair proof of his airmanship. Yet Cranswick's superb handling had achieved more than simply saving his own life. He had saved a plane, which, when repaired, would supply an urgent need in the Middle East theatre of war. And he had done this under great personal strain. Already he was sickening for what he thought to be a further bout of malaria. It turned out to be scarlet fever, however, and almost put an end to his flying career. Straight away the doctors rushed him from Wadi Halfa to Cairo and into the 63rd General Hospital, Helmeih.

He was placed in an isolation compound where he spent much of the time playing chess, reading and learning astronomy. He wrote home to say that this was very useful for night navigation, but he had gone wrong somewhere; by his calculations Cairo was just about 10,000 miles away from its true position!

Cranswick had little fun on his 22nd birthday on 7 September 1941 – just sitting in a chair in that Cairo hospital, staring straight ahead all the time because he was suffering from a stiff neck.

With huge, luscious grapes at only five pence a pound, Alec was leading as comfortable an existence as possible within the cramped confines of isolation. By worming his way into the good books of the nursing sisters, Alec charmed them into supplying him with quantities of fruit, biscuits and reading material. An old school friend and an airman from his previous squadron were both in hospital at the same time as Cranswick, but he was irked to find that both of them managed to get themselves discharged before him.

The scarlet fever left Cranswick with aches in his muscles and, after a further examination, the doctor ordered him to remain in bed for another week with what were diagnosed as scarlet fever complications and rheumatism, making a nine-week spell in all in hospital.

By the end of the first week in October 1941, Alec was out of hospital at last with what he described in one letter home as 'no worse an aftermath than slight rheumatics and a morbid feeling of illness in general'.

He was severely warned against attempting to do anything energetic for fear of weakening his heart, which almost certainly would have ended his flying career. Refusing to take the warning seriously enough,

Alec went swimming the second day out of hospital; he was left so weak he only just managed to reach his room.

The convalescent leave was spent in Cairo, where he joined a sporting club and filled in most of the time there. After only a few days of inactivity he was beginning to be bored and the heat was getting him down, too. Although the more brash of the Cairo population were complaining the weather was becoming colder, the temperature was still soaring well into the nineties. He could hardly wait to fly again.

His chance came on 14 October 1941, when he was posted back to his old bombing unit, No. 148 Squadron, which was still operating from Kabrit. The news made him begin to feel a new man. He sensed he was in real tip-top form again. The scarlet fever had not left him with a weak heart after all – he had had a double medical check to be quite sure all was well.

However, what he did have was an attack of nerves...

The Mail Run was in full swing as Alec Cranswick, now promoted Flying Officer, returned to No. 148 Squadron to fly Wellingtons again on bombing missions against the Axis forces secure in their Western Desert strongholds.

The squadron's main role in life at that time was bombing the port of Benghazi, capital of Cyrenaica, to halt the influx of supplies to Rommel's Desert Army. It quickly became known as the Mail Run on account of the monotonous regularity of the trip.

Benghazi, captured by General Sir Archibald Wavell's Army of the Nile on 6 February 1941, fell to the enemy again after only two months in the face of a determined advance by strong Italian–German forces.

There were four RAF squadrons engaged on the Benghazi Mail Run – No. 148 and No. 70, both based at Kabrit, and No. 37 and No. 38 at Shallufa, both airfields being on the Suez Canal.

No. 148 Squadron was then under the command of Wing Commander F. F. Rainsford, whose crews soon became familiar with the everyday pattern of events.

The modus operandi was to take off after lunch with lightly loaded fuel tanks and full bomb bays. They would fly to the advanced landing grounds around Fuka and El Daba; Benghazi was out of range from Kabrit without a stop for refuelling on the way.

After an evening meal and a further briefing, the crews would take off for Benghazi in the early evening and get back to the advanced landing ground around dawn. Following debriefing and an early breakfast, the bombers would fly back again over the Nile to the Canal Zone, generally returning to the Kabrit base around 11 a.m.

Wing Commander Rainsford remembered those timetable trips:

*At Kabrit it was our custom to adjourn then to the bar drinking beer and eating tinned asparagus and Japanese crab with which – for some extraordinary reason – we were very well supplied. The Station Commander used to wink a tolerant eye at the very scruffy officers in the bar when he came to the Mess for his morning drink.*

*After lunch we would go to bed and sleep very heavily indeed on the combination of fatigue, fresh air and the strange assortment of beer that used to come to the Canal Zone bases from India, Australia, Tasmania and even the United States. These were good days, both at the time and in retrospect. We worked hard, flew long sorties and had a great deal of fun. I don't think I have ever met a better bunch of people anywhere than we had in 148 at that time.*

*Our losses were moderate – through flak; through navigational errors; and due to the difficulties of maintaining fairly sophisticated aircraft in the desert, even at a semi-permanent base like Kabrit. In particular, we had trouble with glycol leaks causing fires in the Wellington 11s with which for some months 148 was equipped.*

The layout of Benghazi harbour with its long, finger-like moles and half-sunken ships that were used as jetties was firmly imprinted on the minds of the crews as the weeks and the months of bombing went on throughout the summer, autumn and winter of 1941.

The Cathedral at the end of the Cathedral Mole escaped almost unscathed in much the same way as the black and sombre twin-spired Cologne Cathedral was to be spared, although it stood close beside the city's main railway station, which was a common aiming mark.

Alec Cranswick's first three bombing sorties when he went back to No. 148 Squadron on 14 October 1941, were raids on Benghazi. A number of fires were touched off on the Cathedral Mole – one of them was marked down in the records as having been caused by a petrol store set alight.

A raid on Crete brought Alec up to his operational half-century, and just after he had returned from the mission he wrote a letter to his mother, in which he revealed briefly the drama of the illnesses he had been fighting before he was able to fly again.

*My dose of scarlet fever has not left me with a weak heart – I have had it checked up twice to make sure – but it has left me very weak and things take twice as long to get better out here. Also I have an attack of nerves, not flying nerves, but imagining I have got all sorts of diseases I have not got. It is a final fling of the scarlet fever and I have got the Doc to give me a tonic for it.*

The Kabrit–Benghazi Mail Run was not without drama, too.

In the first week of November 1941, No. 148 Squadron received the new 4,000-pound bombs, and Alec Cranswick was to drop the first of them on Benghazi. On the way back there was what he casually called a 'flare of excitement' when he was compelled to make a forced landing in the desert.

Faced with a toss-up between an emergency landing and baling out, Alec characteristically decided to try to save his bomber. It was just one o'clock in the morning as he brought down the Wimpey gently, skilfully and undamaged on a desert track about 20 miles inland – just missing some telegraph wires in doing so. Wires like these crossed the desert at the most unexpected places.

His crew were both hungry and thirsty after seven hours in the air. What the lads most wanted was some hot grub, so they lit a fire from camel grass and unpacked their emergency rations. No one liked the taste of the water – it was particularly nasty. Alec said he would play Mum and make them all some tea, so like six old tramps the crew sat patiently around their fire boiling water in two fruit cans.

As there was no milk Alec suggested cheerfully: 'I know, we'll use our malted milk tablets in place of milk.'

Alas, Alec was to be teased mercilessly afterwards for he had to confess when he had dropped in the tablets that 'something went wrong and we were only too pleased to drink the water after all'.

The crew achieved a more spectacular job with two cans of roast bully beef, however, and dipped in vigorously with their fingers instead of using the more orthodox knives and forks that had unfortunately been omitted from the emergency kit on that particular flight.

The six weary flyers were about to bed down uncomfortably for the night in the shadow of their bomber beneath the desert skies when someone spotted a light away in the distance. Eagerly they fired Very cartridges into the sky with all the brilliance of a small-scale fireworks display in the hope of attracting the attention of whoever was moving around out there with the distantly gleaming lamp.

Eventually a rescue truck rolled up, and the crew were taken back to camp. A rumour had gone around, meanwhile, that Cranswick's

Wellington had been shot down by a Jerry night-fighter and the Jerry had been destroyed in turn by Cranswick's gunners. What had really happened was not quite so spectacular. Before the forced landing became necessary, Cranswick's rear gunner had decided to relieve his boredom by firing a few bursts on his machine guns. The crackle of gunfire was mistaken for a mid-air duel and when the bomber failed to return on time the rumour was born.

Some hours later Cranswick returned to his plane. When the trouble that had made the forced landing necessary had been rectified, he took off and within ten minutes was safely down again on No. 10 Advanced Landing Ground. And that night there was a big party in the crew NCOs' tent to celebrate their safe arrival.

They went back in the same plane to Kabrit – just in time to resume the Mail Run to Benghazi.

Alec's boys were luckier with their bomber than others in No. 148 Squadron. One pilot found an engine had failed when he was making his bombing run over Benghazi, but he managed to bring the plane home over 350 miles through rain and sleet until it plunged out of the sky at Sidi Barrani and disintegrated. The crew fortunately all escaped unhurt.

Around this time No. 148 Squadron was establishing a record service-ability rate among Middle East heavy bomber units in having eighteen aircraft available for ops although complete crews could be found for only seventeen.

Every plane was needed, for now was the time for a British push in the desert. Operation Crusader was all but ready to sweep the enemy out of Cyrenaica to make way for the advance into Tripolitania. In an eve-of-battle report to the Chief of Air Staff, Air Marshal Tedder was saying proudly of his Middle East Air Force: 'Squadrons are at full strength, aircraft and crews, with reserve aircraft, and the whole force is on its toes.'

At dawn the following day, 18 November 1941, Operation Crusader was launched. It was elaborately planned yet rapidly thwarted. But in the opening stages the progress was encouraging and Cranswick was writing home: 'The news is pretty good about our advance; let's hope it goes on as well as it has been doing. It will be very interesting later on to visit towns we have bombed and admire our handiwork.'

Cranswick joined in a series of bombing and machine-gunning onslaughts upon enemy airfields, transport and supplies to harass Rommel's retreating columns. On 19 December 1941, five days before

Benghazi fell to the British advance, Cranswick's Wellington came in for plenty of attention from the ground defences when trapped by the searchlights during an attack in which the last 4,000-pound bomb was dropped on the port. A month later the wily Rommel's triumphant troops were back in Benghazi. The Afrika Korps was surging forward to Cairo.

After about a year in the desert, and 200 hours of operational flying, No. 148 Squadron's crews started to split. A few went south to Kenya, Rhodesia or South Africa; a handful remained in the Middle East. But most of the squadron's aircrew were going home to Britain in a slow sea convoy. And Cranswick was among them.

Chapter 6

# Posted to Path Finder Force

While Alec Cranswick was on his homeward-bound troopship from the Middle East, Britain's bombing offensive was treated to a king-sized pep pill with the appointment, on 22 February 1942, of Air Marshal Arthur T. Harris as Air Officer Commanding-in-Chief, RAF Bomber Command.

He came on the scene with the impact of a bomb – an explosive force sending shock waves rolling far and wide. Under his vigorous leadership the mounting bomber force began dealing fresh blows upon the enemy's war production. On taking over Bomber Command, Harris had less than fifty heavy bombers on average for a raid. He demanded more planes; and still more. Previously, RAF bomber attacks against Germany had often been pitifully small compared with the kind he wanted to see. Harris intended changing all that by concentrating his strength on one place at a time. A staunch advocate of the policy of slamming hard at Germany's industrial towns, Harris would pick a single choice target and gather together as many aircraft as he could muster. If there were not sufficient front-line bombers, Harris would bring in men and machines from the operational training units.

In his first year in command, Harris saw the average number of heavy bombers available for ops increase more than sixfold, although this was still well below his aim. Bombsights were improved and bigger bombs were delivered to his squadrons – bombs that weighed as much as 8,000 pounds, twice the size of the largest in use in 1941. A new aircrew category, bomb-aimer, was introduced to relieve the already hard-pressed navigator on the bigger aircraft. A new bomber came into squadron service. It was the Avro Lancaster, which had a higher ceiling, carried a greater bomb load and was more manœuvrable than either the

Stirling or the Halifax, Britain's only other four-engined bombers. The first radio navigational and bombing aids were ready, and these also progressively cut down the disturbing toll among homecoming bombers. Frequently in 1940 and 1941 more aircraft and crews were lost through crashing in England on the return flight than were lost over Germany. These tragic accidents often occurred through errors in navigation when crews were tired and the fuel was running low.

The first of the radio navigation aids, GEE, was almost ready when Harris became Bomber Command's chief. Radio signals from a trio of wireless stations in Britain were picked up by the GEE-equipped bombers so that the crews could fix their position accurately and quickly, day or night, irrespective of the visibility. It could be used in an arc extending as far as the Elbe, Hanover, Kassel and Mannheim; well in range was the Ruhr, Germany's great industrial empire, where the location of targets had so far proved difficult. However, Britain's boffins anticipated that their opposite numbers in Germany would work out a means of rendering GEE useless to the bombers in about six months. So, with the Ruhr cities high on the priority list of targets, Harris flung all his might against them in order to gain the greatest advantage from GEE. The thousand-bomber raids on Cologne, Essen and Bremen came during this heyday of GEE.

Bombing became a highly specialized art. Routes were devised to avoid strongly defended areas and to keep the enemy guessing about the target and homeward route; at the same time they were required to be as direct as possible so as to reduce the strain on aircrews. These flying timetables had to ensure that the bombing force arrived over the target at the right moment without a risk of collisions. Speeds, courses and heights had to be worked out with infinite care so that aircraft flying in the upper streams could not release their bombs on planes flying beneath them.

The Germans discovered and jammed the GEE radio navigational aid in less than the estimated six months. By the second week in August 1942, enemy jamming considerably reduced the effective range of GEE, so that targets in Germany now dropped out of range. Nevertheless, GEE had brought about increased accuracy in locating the bombing target areas. Now improved equipment was required for the bombers, equipment capable of use over a much extended range and embodying the means to pick out the target aiming points, too. For, once the target had been identified and fires started, bombing crews would find their task simplified.

Gradually there grew up the practice of employing the most experienced crews to lead the way. And so Path Finder Force was born. In *Royal Air Force, 1939–1945, volume 11, The Fight Avails*, by Denis Richards and Hilary St George Saunders,[1] the authors record:

> The Pathfinders came into being only after protracted disagreement between Air Marshal Harris and the Air Staff. That the main force would have to be led by specially selected crews was not at issue, for this was already our practice. But the Air Staff's proposal to take these crews from their squadrons and concentrate them in a single corps d'elite seemed to Harris – and to his Group Commanders – destructive of squadron morale. Throughout the spring and summer of 1942 the Bomber chief had accordingly fought the project with all his accustomed vigour; but his opposition, if spirited, soon developed into a rearguard action.

On 15 August 1942, Path Finder Force was formed under the then Acting Group Captain D. C. T. Bennett. In his book *Pathfinder*,[2] Bennett declares that Harris had been given a direct order from the Prime Minister, through the Chief of Air Staff, and, since it 'was forced upon him, he insisted that I should command it, in spite of my relatively junior rank. ... He told me that whilst he was opposed to the Path Finder Force and would waste no effort on it, he would support me personally in every way.'

Harris, writing in his book *Bomber Offensive*,[3] comments that Bennett, whom he had known since 1931, was 'the obvious man at that time available for the job of head of the Path Finder Force. He was in his early thirties, very young indeed to become a Group Commander, but his technical knowledge and his personal operational ability were altogether exceptional.'

The RAF Station, Wyton, Huntingdon, one of the best-situated bases for flying weather conditions in Britain, became Bennett's Path Finder Force Headquarters. Oakington, another permanent station, was turned over to PFF, and so were two satellites, Graveley and Warboys. Four squadrons made up PFF in the early days – No. 7 with Stirlings at Oakington, No. 35 with Halifaxes at Graveley, No. 83 with Lancasters at Wyton and No. 156 with Wellingtons at Warboys.

Path Finder Force's role was to seek out the target and drop some sort of unmistakable object for the bomb-aimers of the main raiding force to use as an aiming point. It was decided that parachute flares would be the best means available at that time to provide this 'unmistakable object', and these were used in the very first Pathfinder operation against the German submarine base at Flensburg. The attack was ordered before the Pathfinders had had a chance to put in any practising of their techniques. It was carried out in such unexpectedly poor visibility that some of the aircraft brought back their bombs because they could not find the target. It was a bitterly disappointing debut for the Pathfinders. However, Bennett's crews quickly gained proficiency as the attacks continued and were soon providing an effective spearhead for raid after raid. During this proving time many crews fell by the wayside. They had failed to reach the standards demanded and were weeded out of the squadrons. But as the weeks progressed Path Finder Force's specialist crews became more and more expert in navigation; they became more and more efficient in target-marking; and there were new radio aids on the way to strengthen these acquired skills.

The overall pattern of action against the enemy was dictated by the War Cabinet; the Air Staff related their handling of the air war to the confines of this policy. When a bombing target had been decided upon, Harris's staff at Bomber Command's underground headquarters in Buckinghamshire passed on the name, size of the bombing force and time of attack in code messages sent on the teleprinters to the units selected to carry out the mission, and in more detailed instructions over the scrambler-telephone to the senior officers responsible for the various phases of the raid.

On a typical day, Path Finder Force's leader learns during the morning the target selected for the night's operations. With his planning staff he works out the tactics his crews will use. These will depend on the size of the bombing force, the nature of the target and the anticipated weather conditions.

The strength of the Pathfinders varies, too. Sometimes the proportion of Pathfinders to Main Force planes is as low as one in fifteen; some-times, when an attack is divided into several phases, Pathfinders' contribution may be as high as three in ten.

When the general plan of attack has been decided, Bennett's squad-rons receive their orders. At PFF dromes, all planes are checked on the ground and in the air so that they will be ready for the night's activities.

The crews, eyeing the weather at frequent intervals, know that, unless there is any deterioration in existing conditions, they will be aviating tonight. In the squadron offices a list of stand-by captains goes up; the nominated captains move around the various sections notifying their crews – the navigators, the gunners, the wireless operators and the flight engineers – saying that they have been put down for flying tonight.

For those who are taking part in the forthcoming raid there is the briefing session to be attended during the early evening when the crews gather to hear the target chosen for them and learn about the arrangements for take-off, the route to be followed and the weather conditions forecast along the journey and over the target. They are told the method of attack and assessments of the enemy defences, too; meanwhile the aircraft are being loaded with the fuel, ammunition, markers and bombs. As darkness begins to fall, the crews sit down to supper before collecting their flying kit, parachute, flasks of coffee, cans of fruit juice and chocolate and have a fitness check from the doctor before scrambling into the trucks that take them out to the waiting bombers.

It is the turn of one of the Ruhr towns to receive a Pathfinder-led blasting tonight. There are a dozen Halifaxes forming the trailblazers, flying high above the Dutch coast, while the Main Force squadrons are still streaming over East Anglia and the North Sea. The Pathfinder planes are manned by operational veterans, experts in the triple arts of navigating, bomb-aiming and flying. Installed inside each aircraft are the scientists' latest contributions to the bombing campaign. The finest crews, the finest equipment; Bomber Command cannot afford mistakes in identifying and marking a target.

Searchlights are weaving patterns in the night sky, and the curtain of flak is drawn across the path of the Halifaxes. Each shell explodes with a sudden flash, heralding the thump that seems to come from just outside the aircraft. This is Happy Valley, Germany's most heavily defended area, but the Pathfinders have been here before many times and know what to expect in the way of a greeting from Jerry.

A pilot needs fantastic guts to keep his bomber flying straight through a barrage as intense as Happy Valley. Jagged red-hot splinters from the bursting shells bombard the plane; blast sends it shuddering and skidding across the sky. But the pilot must ignore these distractions when he is trying to pinpoint a target with the precision of the Pathfinders. The Finders go in first, flying parallel a couple of miles apart, each releasing a stick of flares across the target area. These are special flares, hooded to stop their glare from blinding the next Pathfinder crews, who are known as the Illuminators; their task is to explore the 10 miles of territory already lit up and then drop a close pattern of coloured flares round the point to be bombed.

All the time the enemy guns are pumping up enormous quantities of shells, but the Pathfinders cannot waste time waiting for the barrage to ease because the flares will go out and the Main Force planes will arrive and not know where to drop their bombs. So in go the last of the Pathfinders. These are the Markers, and their role is to put down a carpet of incendiaries so that, when the flares indicating the actual target have burned themselves out, there will be fires already raging on which the bombers can aim.

Tonight the target is free of cloud, but the Pathfinders are able to pave the way for the bombers even if the clouds completely mask the whole area. They locate the target with their instruments and drop a special type of parachute flare to mark a spot in the sky, above the clouds, which the bombers can use as a substitute aiming point. These sky-markers burn for four or five minutes – long enough for a stream of bombers to send down a sizeable weight of high explosives on top of the unseen objective. Replenishing markers can be dropped by successive Pathfinders.

A device known as H2S is one of the instruments that has been developed as a magic eye for the Pathfinders. A rotating scanner in a blister beneath the fuselage throws out a beam which bounces back and forms, on a cathode ray tube inside the aircraft, a picture of the ground below. Practised crews are thus able to seek out the target by reading the television-type tube face as they would a map. Land, water and built-up areas each produce a different sort of echo on the screen, so the result is a shadowy map rather like an X-ray plate.

*Oboe*, which is an alternative radar system, uses signals from wireless stations in Britain to keep certain designated Pathfinders on a set course. These are picked up by each pilot and navigator in his earphones. If the plane should deviate, the signal changes from a continuous note to a series of dots or dashes, depending on which side of the flight path the plane has strayed. It is then up to the pilot to alter course accordingly and resume the correct track, indicated by the continuous note. The last ten minutes of flying time to the target are punctuated by Morse signals at specified intervals; the closing seconds are counted by a succession of pips at set timings. The bombs are to be released on the final pip.[4]

When the Pathfinders have blazed their trail, Main Force bombers stream across the target spilling out their high explosives upon the flares and fires. On this Ruhr mission, the Pathfinders are involved only in an initial flare-laying duty, but where many hundreds of bombers are engaged the Force will be required to have further waves of target-marker crews coming on the scene to drop a new batch of flares when the aiming point is blotted out by the great clouds of smoke that form in these mammoth pulverizing raids.

The homeward stretch is a dangerous drag. The element of surprise, which provided some security on the outward trip, has gone, because the enemy knows roughly the route which the bombers must take to get back to their bases. On a clear night the German fighters fly up and down these home-bound aerial roads in anticipation of making an easy kill. By now the bomber crews are tiring; for some the only indication that a Jerry fighter is within striking distance comes when he opens up with his guns. For the vigilant, and for the lucky, there may still be another day to live – and another night to fight and perhaps to die.

Such was the basic form of a Pathfinder-led bombing assault. Each attack suggested new lessons to be learned, so consequently fresh techniques were always being tested. And, of course, the inclusion of a Master Bomber later on provided flexibility of the procedure even while a raid was in progress.

Within a few days of returning to Britain, Cranswick had cause for a double celebration. It was on 7 April 1942, two years to the day since he had been graded Pilot Officer and started his operational training as a Wellington bomber pilot at Bassingbourn. That day saw him both promoted to the rank of Flight Lieutenant and awarded the Distinguished Flying Cross for gallantry and devotion to duty in the execution of air operations. Alec's citation said of him:

> This officer has carried out sixty-one sorties over Germany and enemy occupied territory, against Italian targets and in the Mediterranean. Throughout, he has proved himself a most capable captain whose determination to complete his task, often under difficult conditions, has been exceptional. He has excelled in the training of new crews in whom he has instilled the greatest confidence.

From Air Commodore L. L. MacLean, Air Officer Commanding, No. 205

Group, Middle East Air Force, under whom he had served with No. 148 Squadron, Alec received the following personal letter: 'I was delighted to learn that your very fine operational record has been recognised by the award of the DFC. My congratulations on a well-earned decoration.' At last the courage of the tenacious Flight Lieutenant Alec Cranswick had received official acknowledgement.

He had come a long way since first climbing into the cockpit of a Tiger Moth at Desford to begin his flying training, gradually and carefully developing a pilot's skill until he was successfully through his elementary and operational training programmes and joined No. 214 Squadron at Stradishall to start flying bombers over war-torn Europe.

He had shown tremendous guts in every attack he was ordered to carry out, and his immense spirit and vigour became the talk of the squadrons with whom he flew in both Britain and the Middle East. He was no daredevil pilot, reckless and wild. He knew bombing for what it was – an art that had to be studied with infinite and painstaking care.

He trusted his crew members. He encouraged them to accept responsibility for their own particular task without interference yet still showing a strong interest. Alec – invariably 'Skip' to his crew – must have been aware of their unfailing trust in him and that may be why he could become such a capable captain. Each relied on all the rest to take exactly the right action throughout every flight and realized full well that that would be done.

He was a capable captain because he had a capable crew.

When Cranswick was once more based in England he was expecting to be sent back to bombing duties after only a short rest. In fact he was not going to be so lucky.

As the size of the RAF's attacks swelled throughout the spring and summer of 1942, Alec was compelled to wage a battle on his own account against recurring bouts of ill-health that threatened to end his flying career. This personal setback came at a time when every trained pilot was needed in Bomber Command. Mass raids were in progress, which had necessitated even calling upon crews not yet fully qualified in order to make up the numbers.

Instead of adding the weight of his experience to the growing might of the bomber offensive, Cranswick was forced to alternate between trying to fight off a nervous breakdown and undergoing first training and later instructor duties on the American four-engined Liberator bombers that were being used by the RAF.

He had pushed himself too hard in taking his bomber over enemy territory again and again. He was in a nervous, highly strung state in which he needed rest. There were times when the sweat poured from his body as he relived the agonizing strain of a raid.

Like so many eager young warriors of the air at that time, Alec was an unwilling casualty of excessive stress and operational fatigue.

He saw doctors; he saw psychiatrists. He was given medical treatment; he was given rest. He laboured readily in the open air on a farm. Happily, recovery was only a question of waiting long enough. His mind often dwelled on the past, for he had so much time idling on his hands. Alec revealed some of these thoughts in a poem he wrote one summer's day. Under the title, 'Memoirs of a Pilot', he wrote:

*Oft as upon my bed I lie*
*And live the thrilling past anew,*
*My brain regains its distant tie*
*With lands o'er which I flew.*

*Then rising up before my sight*
*Come fleeting views of foreign lands;*
*The star-filled Eastern sky at night,*
*The sun-swept Desert sands,*
*The noisy, crowded wooden Mess,*
*Brings to my vision friends of old*
*Whose bones now fill the wilderness,*
*My comrades gay yet bold.*

*The placid blue Great Bitter Lake,*
*The curling breakers' foaming wake,*
*The convoy route across Sudan*
*Up from the fertile Western shore;*
*And how the herds of wild beast ran*
*When we went flying o'er,*
*The lengthy, freezing trips to Greece,*
*The humid air of tropic climes,*
*The khaki drill or silky fleece*
*We wore at different times.*

*Out of my sight these pictures fade,*
*I lose the tortuous jungle track;*
*In future sorties to be made*
*My thoughts switch swiftly back.*
          *A. P. C. 15-8-1942.*

One wonders what he was thinking as he wrote the closing lines: '*In future sorties to be made | My thoughts switch swiftly back.*'

It was still to be some weeks, however, before he was to fly those future bombing sorties.

A bombing sortie carried out by the Luftwaffe on a Sunday morning in the autumn of that year, 1942, spurred him into a renewed burst of endeavour to get back into an operational bomber squadron. It happened while he was convalescing at the Palace Hotel, Torquay, which was then an RAF Officers' Hospital. The doctors allowed him home one weekend and during the time he was away four German fighter-bombers carried out a rooftop-height terror raid on Torquay. One bomb struck the hotel, killing more than a dozen patients and staff, and the planes then turned their attention upon the nearby areas of Babbacombe, Plainmoor, St Marychurch and Hele, killing and injuring many civilians with indiscriminate machine-gunning of houses, streets and a church. This savage attack upset Cranswick greatly, because when he arrived back in Torquay he had to help dig out the victims at the Officers' Hospital – and he found many of them were his own friends. His impelling desire to fly again was not so much the result of any itching for revenge but more the determination that he must follow through to the end of the war the job for which he had been trained.

He tried desperately to be allowed to go bombing, but each time he was told he must wait. He had to be absolutely fit or he could not do his job properly. But this he knew full well.

Meanwhile, Cranswick was seconded to the Ministry of Aircraft Production to give a series of pep talks at factories that had built the aircraft he had flown in raids against the enemy. Chosen for his personality and operational bombing experience, Cranswick had the job of telling the people who were making the aircraft something of the people who were flying them and the uses to which the planes were put once they came off the factory assembly lines.

It was only natural that so much talk on his part about what happened on bombing raids must inevitably inspire him into a further series of 'sorties' of his own to try to induce his RAF superiors into letting him return to a bomber squadron.

Soon, Cranswick discovered that RAF Bomber Command had a pilot's seat all ready and waiting for him. In the first week of December 1942, his factory liaison lecture post was terminated and he was able to resume flying duties. He was ordered to go to No. 1659 Conversion Unit at RAF Station, Leeming, Yorkshire, to learn how to fly the Halifax – a far bigger, heavier, more powerful and more complex bomber than the old Wimpey that had served him so faithfully since he went to Bassingbourn for his operational training course more than two and a half years earlier.

On reaching Leeming, Cranswick found that Bomber Command Headquarters had taken the unusual step of selecting in advance the crew he was to lead when he had mastered the art of handling the new bomber. There was an obvious advantage in this. The whole crew, starting together from scratch on Halifaxes, would train as a team and so form themselves into a single bombing unit capable of working swiftly and faultlessly under the most pressing conditions. At Leeming, Cranswick first met tail-gunner Ivor Howard and navigator/bomb-aimer William McRobbie, both of them highly experienced and opera-tionally seasoned NCOs. Warrant Officer McRobbie had already won the DFM for gallantry and devotion to duty in the execution of air operations in the first year of the war; Flight Sergeant Howard had had his fill of action, too, while flying as an observer on Lysander spotter planes at Dunkirk and during the Battle of Britain, and then as a gunner on Wellington bombers.

For three weeks Alec's crew worked together to accustom themselves to their new duties in the Halifax. They flew whenever the chance presented itself – which was not often that wild and bitter December. With more and more hours in the air, however, they increased their proficiency until they were considered to have reached a sufficiently high standard to join an operational bombing squadron. Then the posting came through – to No. 419 Squadron, Royal Canadian Air Force, more familiarly known as the Moose Squadron, which was stationed at Middleton St George, near Darlington.

The arrival of Cranswick's crew at No. 419 Squadron coincided with the establishment, on 1 January 1943, of eight Canadian squadrons as No. 6 (Royal Canadian Air Force) Group of Bomber Command under Air Vice-Marshal G. E. Brooks – the first Canadian bomber group to be formed in Britain. It was a popular decision, for at that time nearly 40 per cent of Bomber Command's pilots were from the Dominions or the Colonies and somewhere around 60 per cent of that number were Canadians. The eight squadrons now grouped together were Nos 408, 419, 420, 424, 425, 426, 427 and 428, all of which had come into being in Britain between June 1941 and November 1942.

When Cranswick returned to an operational bombing unit after his illness, he had changed.

His health breakdown had left him in a challenging mood. By now, of course, the RAF doctors were satisfied that he was perfectly fit both physically and mentally. Yet Alec still had to prove to himself that he retained the courage to fly a bomber into the teeth of the enemy opposition. That opposition had been fierce enough when he was last on ops in the Middle East, but now it was a far tougher proposition.

He was as sure as he could be that all was going to be well. To be honest, though, how could any person really predict how he would shape in an action of war? Cranswick had never been boisterous or brash, but now he accepted that he was even quieter and more reserved than he had been in his earlier days on a bomber squadron. Alec found that many of the lads in the bomber crews seemed ever anxious to build up their stock of courage at the bars of the nearest hostelry, but he could not entirely bring himself to share their beer-stained companionship. Instead, Cranswick kept himself apart and sought comradeship in a collection of classical records and a little fluffy, blue Alsatian named Kluva of Kentwood.[5]

He bought Kluva as a puppy from the Kentwood Kennels, Cumnor Hill, Oxford. At once, dog and master became firm friends. Alec was tough in his handling of Kluva, yet the dog quickly warmed to the fresh-faced young man who, he knew, was as much his friend as he was his master. Kluva was completely a one-man dog. He would do anything for Alec; he would go anywhere with him. Alec took him flying scores of times; he gave him the rank of Temporary Sergeant and found him a place in the crew as Assistant Engineer. Cranswick did not dare imagine what Bomber Command would have said if ever they learned of the four-legged crew member whose name had never appeared in Air Ministry's records.

Cranswick even had an official RAF aircrew flying logbook for Sergeant Kluva in which he recorded every trip the dog made. He kept that log as meticulously and as neatly as he kept his own; he included dates, take-off times, pilot's name, Kluva's role on each flight, general remarks about the purpose of each flight and the actual time spent in the air. In the front of the logbook Cranswick wrote: 'Is liable to desert from his post of Assistant Engineer and assume the role of Assistant Wireless Operator' – which rather indicated that no one quite knew where in the plane Kluva would turn up next!

Kluva enjoyed complete freedom in the bomber. Quickly and carefully he soon found his way around the aircraft, scrambling warily from crew station to crew station, from nose to tail. The wireless operator's position was one place in particular where Kluva enjoyed taking up temporary residence. He was allowed to settle down into a comfortable position with the earpiece headphone of a spare flying helmet pressed against his head so that he might listen to music picked up on the bomber's radio during training flights.

He was house-trained and plane-trained. He normally showed neither apprehension nor fear while flying by day or by night, nor while the aircraft's guns were firing or bombs were being dropped. There were exceptions when he would appear to become a trifle worried and agitated, with the result that, if the navigator chanced to leave any maps on the floor, he might well discover that Kluva, in the unusual stress of the moment, had been responsible for a number of new rivers flowing across them in the most surprising places.

Bad weather imposed a considerable delay to Cranswick's return to bombing. Day after day there were briefings for night raids. Night after night the projected raid was cancelled because of the weather conditions. Then, on one of the worst of all, Cranswick was ready to set off for Lorient, the big U-boat base on the Bay of Biscay. The night was not fit for a dog to be out.

Not fit for a dog? There would be no holding back Cranswick's Alsatian. Already Sergeant Kluva had recorded 19 hours 25 minutes daytime and 6 hours 55 minutes night-flying experience up to that late afternoon of 29 January 1943, when his master's crew were detailed for the Lorient attack. And Kluva was not going to miss that trip for all the bones in the biggest butcher's shop in the whole world!

It was coming up towards dusk when the crew settled themselves into Halifax No. 623. Kluva, smuggled aboard beneath his master's flying jacket, scampered around inside the bomber he knew so well. The weather grew steadily worse as the Moose Squadron flew south. The huge bombers wallowed in a sea of lashing rain. Ice began dragging down the aircraft as they struggled to get clear of the storm. There was no path to freedom – and ahead there was worse to come. Over the crackling wireless – barely working at all in such atrocious weather – there came the recall signal for some of the bombers while the force was droning on gamely through the storm clouds towards the English Channel. The wireless operator passed the message to Cranswick. There was a moment while he digested the implications and then he retorted: 'Not us. We've come this far, we're going the rest of the way.'

It would be easy for Cranswick to talk his way out of any blame that might be awaiting him back at Middleton St George. He knew that all he had to say was that the storm had made his radio fade intermittently so that he must have missed the recall message. The resolute Cranswick had no intention of missing his first operational mission for a year when he was already a good part of the way towards the target. So on went Halifax No. 623, onwards to Lorient.

That was one hell of a trip. The engines iced up and spluttered pathetically amid the angry black clouds. An electrical storm battered them. Then, to cap the lot, came Jerry ack-ack over Guernsey and over the target with such fury that Cranswick fought the controls to heave his great plane upwards, downwards and sideways to dodge the worst of the heavy, accurate barrage. He reflected for a moment that he had been sticking his neck out when he ignored the radio recall. Once his Halifax was nicely on the bombing run, Cranswick was a different man. He knew then that he had won the challenge he had set himself. He had proved to his own satisfaction that his courage had not been sapped dry by his previous ill-health.

Ripped and scarred by Lorient's defences, Cranswick's Halifax reached home seven hours and twenty minutes after starting out from Middleton St George. The plane had just rolled to a stop at the end of the runway when the undercarriage gave way. The bomber collapsed on the rain-drenched concrete like a wounded bird. As Cranswick slithered out of the escape hatch, clutching hold of Kluva, he vowed that he would not take the dog on a bombing raid ever again for fear of prejudicing the lives of his crew in an emergency. In any case, RAF regulations expressly forbade the carriage of dogs in aircraft because of the safety factor. There was also the humanitarian point of view in that animals that were not at their fitness peak were liable to suffer lasting injury through rapid changes of altitude – and these could hardly be avoided in desperate manoœuvres to escape the guns of the enemy. A medical check confirmed that none of the crew had been hurt in the landing, and that went for Kluva, too, but Cranswick was adamant. Kluva would not fly on ops again.

For a while Cranswick had been keeping something from the members of his crew. He had told them a little earlier that he had volunteered the whole lot of them for Path Finder Force. What he had not told them,

| | | | | | | Time carried forward :— | 17·45 | 3·15 |
|---|---|---|---|---|---|---|---|---|
| Date | Hour | Aircraft Type and No. | Pilot | Duty | | Remarks (including results of bombing, gunnery, exercises, etc.) | Flying Times |  |
| | | | | | | | Day | Night |
| 2/1/43 | 10·30 | HALIFAX | F/LT CRANSWICK | ASST ENGINEER | | AIR FIRING IN FILEY BAY | 1·40 | |
| 26/1/43 | 11·00 | HALIFAX | F/LT CRANSWICK | ASST ENGINEER | | X COUNTRY. RATHER A FAILURE | | 3·40 |
| 29/1/43 | 16·50 | HALIFAX | F/LT CRANSWICK | —"— | | To LORIENT ON OPS WITH INCENDIARIES HEAVY ACCURATE FLAK OVER GUERNSEY AND TARGET. U/C COLLAPSED AFTER LANDING | 1·20 | 6·00 |
| | | | SUMMARY FOR | JANUARY 1943 | | | 3·00 | 9·40 |
| | | | 419 Sqd. | | | | | |
| | | | | | | .... al. b.luch. Sp/Ldr 'B' FLIGHT | | |
| | | | | | | .......... OC 419 Sqd. | | |
| | | | | | | Total Time .... | 20·45 | 12·55 |

Page in the flying logbook of Cranswick's Alsatian, Kluva, detailing flights that included a bombing raid with No. 419 Squadron, RCAF – The Moose Squadron. (Author's Collection).

however, and this he now had to do, was that they had been accepted. They were to drive down to the new squadron once they had had a few hours' sleep after the Lorient trip. It said much for Cranswick's strength of personality that no one voiced a protest. The new base: Graveley, Huntingdonshire. The squadron: No. 35 (Madras Presidency) Squadron, one of the four founder squadrons of Path Finder Force.

It was an appropriate time to join the Pathfinders. The Force was now in its sixth month of operations and pressing on from strength to strength. The crews that had not shown sufficient promise had been winkled out and replaced by others of the calibre of Cranswick's flyers. By now Cranswick himself had completed two tours as a bomber pilot,

**Alec Cranswick, during his early days in Path Finder Force.** (Author's Collection)

Cranswick was flying a Lancaster bomber with the lettering TL-J, 'TL' for No. 35 Squadron; uniquely, this one has different squadron letters on each side of the fuselage ('HW-R' visible and 'BQ-B' starboard), effectively commemorating the crews of both squadrons, Nos. 100 and 550. Painstakingly restored post-war – and wearing the markings of EE139, which had 30 ops to its credit with No. 100 Squadron and a further 91 with No. 550 Squadron – this RAF Battle of Britain Memorial Flight aircraft and one owned by the Canadian Warplane Heritage Museum became the only remaining Lancasters (out of the 7,377 built in Britain and Canada) with airworthy certification. (Damien Burke/HandmadeByMachine.com)

Reg Kille, left, one of the seven crew members who lost their lives when Cranswick's Lancaster was shot down over France on 5 July 1944; and Wilfred Horner, the sole survivor, who became a POW. (Author's Collection)

Ivor Howard, pictured with his dog Simba, missed Cranswick's 107th op on doctor's orders; and Alf Wood, who lost his life on that final operation, target-marking at Villeneuve-St.-Georges. (Author's Collection)

The glare of a Pathfinder's target-indicator is reflected in the River Seine as smoke from the fires drifts across the target – the railway yards at Juvisy-sur-Orge, attacked on the night of 18 April 1944, by 200 Lancasters of No. 5 Group led by three PFF Mosquitos using *Oboe* radar. (Imperial War Museum)

**Aerial view of St Edward's School, Oxford, during Cranswick's first year – he was there in the years 1933–7.** (Property of the St Edward's School Archives)

**Arthur Banks, a pupil from 1937 to 1942 and later a pilot with No. 112 Squadron in the Desert Air Force, would be awarded a posthumous George Cross for his courage and endurance when held captive in Italy – a unique instance among its Old Boys in the RAF in being honoured for conspicuous actions on the ground as distinct from in the air.** (Property of the St Edward's School Archives)

**Douglas Bader, St Edward's School, Oxford, 1923–8.** (Property of the St Edward's School Archives)

**Guy Gibson, St Edward's School, Oxford, 1932–6.** (Property of the St Edward's School Archives)

Cranswick with members of his first crew, in No. 214 Squadron, standing on the right, with – alongside, from left – Sergeants Husbands, Robinson and Hoy; and, foreground, Sergeants Brown and Kerr. (Author's Collection)

*K-Katie*, a Wellington belonging to No. 214 Squadron, entering a hangar at Stradishall for repairs after carrying out a bombing raid. (Imperial War Museum)

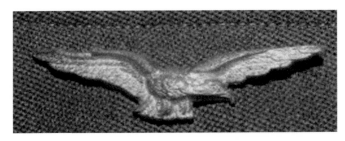

The Path Finder Force Badge, the coveted gilt emblem Cranswick would wear below the pilot's wings on his uniform when a member of PFF.

No. 35 Squadron has a proud history that spanned two world wars. The illustration shows its badge as approved in October 1936 by Edward VIII, with the specific designation 'Bomber Squadron' above the winged horse's head representing the Squadron's cooperation with the Cavalry during the Great War, though 'Bomber' does not appear in some representations of the badge in later years. (Air Historical Branch)

Post-war, Kluva made his home with Cranswick's mother for the rest of his life. (Author's Collection)

Cranswick with members of one of his first PFF crews – from left to right, standing, Sergeants Johnson, Mackenzie and Williams; and, front, Sergeant Arnott, Flight Sergeant Howard and Warrant Officer McRobbie. (Author's Collection)

Cathode ray tube and controls of the H2S airborne radar system for navigation and target-identification purposes. No. 35 Squadron took part in the first bombing raid to use this device, which scanned the terrain for several miles around the aircraft and presented on the screen what was virtually a map of the ground showing towns, rivers, lakes and coastlines. (Imperial War Museum)

**Her Majesty The Queen touring PFF bases with Air Commodore Donald Bennett.** (Imperial War Museum)

**Halifax HR926, *L-Leather*, flown by Alec Cranswick on raids against targets in Peenemünde and Berlin – the family crest beneath the cockpit.** (Author's collection)

**The burned-out wreckage of the Halifax landed by Julian Sale to save a crew member with a useless parachute.** (Author's Collection)

**A Halifax bomber silhouetted against target indicators descending over a V1 storage dump. Cranswick's op against the V1 site at Oisemont was his only one in daylight; it was his 106th and his role was Master Bomber.** (Imperial War Museum)

**Leading Aircraftwoman Valerie Parr, teleprinter operator at PFF Headquarters – the future Mrs Alec Cranswick.** (Author's Collection)

A Blue Plaque beside the entrance confirms No. 2, Polstead Road, Oxford, as the home of
T. E. Lawrence ('Lawrence of Arabia') from 1896 to 1921, a period that included the First World
War; much later, during a period that included the Second World War, this house was the
Cranswicks' home – the place where, on Christmas Eve 1943, Alec took Val home to be introduced
to his mother and to become engaged. (Author's Collection)

Alec Cranswick and Valerie Parr were married at Holy Trinity Church, Brompton, London, on 14 April 1944. (*Sport and General*)

Kluva beside the grave of Alec Cranswick's father at Upavon; on the left is a commemoration stone for Pathfinder Cranswick himself, added by his mother as a tribute to the 'gallant son' killed in action 'on his 107th air operation at the age of 24'. (Author's Collection)

**In the New Communal Cemetery in Clichy, France, the final resting place for Squadron Leader A. P. Cranswick, DSO, DFC.** (Author's Collection)

Mrs Ly Bennett, widow of Air Vice-Marshal Donald Bennett, unveiling the commemorative plaque when a newly-refurbished building at RAF Station, Wyton, was named Cranswick House. (Author's Collection)

Marker stone at RAF Station, Graveley, where No. 35 Squadron was based. (Fighting High)

although statistics showed that only one man in three could expect to live through a single tour. His flying skill and operational efficiency had impressed his superiors. And he had proved his enthusiasm over and over again. It was the right time to get into the Pathfinders, and Cranswick was the right man for them.

In Path Finder Force, Cranswick and his crew were destined for an astonishing run of success. The inspiration for these achievements came from a fine bunch of flyers – the pilots and crews of No. 35 Squadron; lads who were constantly living up to their motto: 'We act with one accord.'

Chapter 7

# Trail-blazing to Glory

The proud history of No. 35 Squadron has spanned two world wars. Royal Flying Corps crews from the squadron were the eyes of the big guns entrenched on the Western Front in the First World War, while their Royal Air Force successors in the Second World War repeatedly formed the vanguard of the giant bombing fleets ranging far across enemy-held Europe.

The squadron was raised at Thetford, Norfolk, in February 1916, and went to the Western Front in the following year with Armstrong Whitworth biplanes – 'Ack-Ws' – on reconnaissance, artillery observation and bombing duties. Battle honours came swiftly at Ypres and Cambrai in 1917 and on the Somme in 1918. The squadron worked in close cooperation with the Cavalry Corps and, to commemorate the long and happy association, No. 35 Squadron chose to incorporate a winged horse's head in the unit badge. With the end of the war there came the disbanding of the squadron, but it did not go out of existence for long.

Re-formed as a bomber unit after ten years, its next operational venture came with the Abyssinian crisis and their Fairey Gordons moved out to the Sudan for a year.

The early months of the Second World War were spent on training duties, and soon the squadron was growing impatient for an opportunity to win fresh battle honours. The time for action could not be long delayed. It came towards the end of November 1940, when No. 35 Squadron became the first squadron to be equipped with Handley Page Halifax bombers.

The Halifax followed the Short Stirling to become the second four-engined bomber to go into service with the RAF. Money for the aircraft came from the people of Madras Presidency, one of the earliest British settlements in India, and, in appreciation of the gift, No. 35 Squadron has since been known officially as No. 35 (Madras Presidency) Squadron. The first crews had their familiarization training on the new Halifaxes at RAF Station, Leeming, Yorkshire, and then in the following month, December 1940, the squadron moved to its operational base at Linton-on-Ouse. Once more the squadron was poised for attack.

On the night of 10–11 March 1941, the Halifaxes carried out their very first operational sortie with a raid on Le Havre, and in subsequent months the squadron struck at a great variety of targets. They made their first attack on Berlin in July 1941, and in the following September opened a series of 1,700-mile round trips to Turin. In February 1942, No. 35 Squadron was one of the units that attempted to stop the German battlecruisers *Scharnhorst* and *Gneisenau* on their Channel escape dash. April 1942 saw the squadron joining in the raids on the battleship *Tirpitz* in Trondheim Fjord, and at the end of May 1942 eighteen Halifaxes from the squadron flew in the historic 1,000-bomber raid on Cologne. The chance for still greater achievements and renewed honours came during that same summer.

On 16 August 1942, No. 35 Squadron moved to Graveley airfield, which was a satellite of Wyton, and launched into secret operations with twenty picked volunteer crews for a most important task. It was the birth of Path Finder Force. On the night of 18–19 August, No. 35 Squadron flew in the first Pathfinder operation and from then until the end of the war supplied target-marking aircraft for 425 attacks, including 5 on Berlin – the crews winning over 500 DSO, DFC and DFM awards in their service with Path Finder Force.

If Alec Cranswick needed any further encouragement towards gallant action, No. 35 Squadron aircrew certainly could produce the springboard with examples of bravery such as these...

High above northern Italy a Halifax was speeding homewards after disgorging a bellyful of marker flares and bombs onto some of Turin's war plant. It was a crisp, winter night in November 1942, and in the moonlight the streets and bridges of the target town stood out distinctly as the RAF raiding force set about its task of levelling the great Fiat works. The particular Halifax that was now hurrying home to Graveley had successfully accomplished its mission as one of the Pathfinder leaders that night and now there was an easier and more relaxed air inside the big bomber.

The towering Alps were looming nearer when suddenly the bomb bay filled with flames while choking smoke began pouring into the cockpit. The situation was dangerous.

'Bale out!' commanded the Skipper. It seemed he had no choice.

One by one the crew of the doomed Halifax slipped out into the silence of the night to become prisoners of war. Out billowed the parachutes, one by one, but in the plane there still remained one man – Wing Commander Basil Vernon Robinson, DSO, DFC, Commanding Officer of No. 35 Squadron and Skipper of the burning bomber.

Robinson, born at Gateshead in 1912, became an Acting Pilot Officer in the RAF on 1 September 1933. He was on a bomber squadron when war came, and within eighteen months of the start of the war he was a Wing Commander. He won the DFC in July 1941 for gallantry with No. 78 Squadron, shortly before moving to No. 35 Squadron. He was a noted Rugby footballer and played wing-three-quarter for North Durham, Durham County and the RAF.

He was a colourful personality, powerfully built and with a distinctive big bushy ginger moustache. He was a popular figure in the Mess, where he had his own method of carrying his beer tankard – thrust down securely between his uniform belt and tunic front. When he was in command at Graveley he organized a mass riverside picnic one day when the planes were on stand-down from operations. Motor transport was commandeered, cooking utensils were gathered in great quantities and the personnel from Graveley were all whisked away under Robinson's personal directions to have a tremendous day of high jinks beside the river near Cambridge. He was held in unusually high regard throughout the length of his time at Graveley.

Flying with No. 35 Squadron many months before the advent of Path Finder Force, Robinson was in the forefront of a daylight attack on the German battlecruisers *Scharnhorst* and *Gneisenau* at Brest in December 1941, which was regarded as an especially remarkable instance of accurate bombing under the heaviest fire.

The warships were lying side by side in two dry docks when the bombers, flying under fighter escort, reached Brest. The enemy flung a swarm of their own fighters into the sky, and the raiders also had to cope with a curtain of accurate, blistering anti-aircraft fire over the target.

The citation announcing awards to some of the men who took part in the raid stated that the attack was pressed home to the utmost, scoring hits on their objectives and shooting down several enemy aircraft. It went on to say: 'The success of the operation, which demanded the highest degree of skill and courage, reflects the greatest credit on the efforts of the following officers and airmen who participated in various capacities as leaders and members of aircraft crews.'

Singled out for awards were Wing Commander Robinson, who received the DSO, and nine other officers and NCOs from Nos 7, 10, 15, and 76 Squadrons who shared seven DFCs and two DFMs.

Wing Commander Robinson was appointed Commanding Officer, No. 35 Squadron, in September 1942, in the earliest days of Path Finder Force. The fire drama over northern Italy came when he was returning after leading the squadron against Turin on the night of 18–19 November 1942.

Robinson's own part in the assault had been carried out successfully except that, through no fault of the crew, one of their own marker flares, powerful enough to have lit up a huge slice of Turin, had jammed inside the aircraft. It was this that had started the blaze in the bomb bay when the Halifax was still some miles short of the Alps on the homeward flight to Graveley.

Robinson ordered the bomb doors to be opened to see if the blazing flare would dislodge. It was no use. The flames spread to the port wing and the great bomber began filling with smoke and fumes. Robinson gave the command for the crew to bale out. One by one the crew obeyed him and drifted down by parachute towards the safety of the Italian countryside and the security of the waiting prison camps. For them there was to be no more bombing, but for Wing Commander Robinson, however, still at the controls of the burning bomber, hope was far from gone.

He was about to bale out himself when miraculously the flames vanished as rapidly as they had begun. Robinson hardly dared believe his eyes. He made a quick check, which proved that somehow the blaze was truly extinguished. It also confirmed that he was quite alone in the plane – utterly alone in an aircraft that normally carried a crew of seven, each with a full-time job to do, and he was still some 700 miles from home.

Robinson decided he must accept the immense challenge to get his plane back single-handed to Britain. He faced a flight of some four hours or so in absolutely ridiculous circumstances. He had no second pilot to relieve him at the controls; no navigator to plot the course and check that the aircraft was sticking to it; no flight engineer to nurse the four engines; no radio operator to take and send messages and no gunners to scare

away any fighters that might choose to investigate the lone bomber
plodding the weary journey home.

His action after telling the crew to abandon the aircraft was a classic
example of determination and heroism for which he received a Bar to
his DFC. The citation explained:

> Undeterred by the difficulty of the flight which involved crossing the
> Alps and flying many hundreds of miles over enemy occupied
> territory, Wing Commander Robinson continued alone, completed
> the return journey, and landed his large four-engined aircraft
> successfully in this country despite very adverse weather, accomplish-
> ing a most praiseworthy and skilful feat of airmanship.

It is hardly surprising Wing Commander Robinson missed his own
airfield at Graveley. Instead he landed on an RAF fighter drome in the
south of England – all his lights ablaze, for he had no other means of
telling the airfield personnel who he was and what he was going to do.
There were astonished glances from the ground staff when they ran over
to the bomber, for everyone expected to see an entire crew filing out
instead of finding just the pilot aboard the plane. He climbed down
sheepishly and confessed:

'I've had to leave the other lads behind in Italy... '

The Italians were baffled by Robinson's deed of valour. They found the
baled-out crew and assumed the bomber must have crashed. However,
Air Ministry announcements insisted that all the aircraft had returned
home from the Turin raid. The Italians were quite prepared to accuse
the Air Ministry of a deliberate lie until the story of Robinson's astonishing solo flight was eventually revealed.

In May 1943 Wing Commander Robinson left No. 35 Squadron, but
he remained at Graveley. He was appointed Graveley's Station
Commander and promoted to Group Captain. His operational flying
activities were restricted when he accepted the new office, but he still
demanded permission to fly in a number of major attacks against
Germany.

The last raid he made was on the night of 23 August 1943.

The target that night was Berlin – the seventy-fourth RAF assault on
the German capital and the heaviest up to that time. Group Captain
Robinson briefed the Graveley crews himself, and a groan went up when
the target was announced, for no one relished the prospects. The

Germans knew that an attack on Berlin must come soon, for the nights had drawn long enough for the RAF bombers to get to Berlin and back under the cover of darkness. The Jerry defences were ready – and the bomber crews at the RAF bases knew that, too.

When the bombers were nearing Berlin, the sky became alarmingly clear. It was then that the trap was set. Enemy night-fighters soared away from their airfields to wait in ambush high over the expectant city. As the Pathfinders reached Berlin, the fighters pounced. One bomber pilot saw fourteen fighters in the space of three minutes. The raid was one of the most concentrated up to that stage of the war, with more than 1,700 tons of high explosives and incendiaries tumbling down within fifty minutes – double the weight of the previous heaviest assault. Yet the success of the raid was marred by the toll taken by the enemy defences, for fifty-six bombers failed to return. It was Bomber Command's most costly raid up to that time.

For Path Finder Force there came a particularly grievous blow with the loss of Group Captain Robinson in that attack as well as several of the most experienced aircrew personnel in the Force. They were casualties that the Pathfinders could ill afford.

A pale-faced figure wobbled uneasily as he pedalled a bicycle nervously through the streets of Turin one morning in November 1943. His legs were weakened by a long spell in hospital, but he was prepared to suffer a certain amount of discomfort, for only a few minutes before mounting the bicycle he had discharged himself from hospital without permission. It was his only way out – for he was an RAF aircrew officer. If he had delayed the bid for freedom, he would soon have found himself penned inside a prisoner-of-war camp deep in Germany.

The man on the bicycle was Flight Lieutenant R. Denis Ferguson, a navigator from No. 35 Squadron at Graveley, who was one of the two survivors from a Pathfinder Halifax shot down while about to light the way for a concentrated raid on Turin on the night of 16–17 August 1943. Only three days previously Ferguson and the captain of his bomber, Squadron Leader Patrick Haggarty, had each been awarded the DFC for gallantry and devotion to duty on air operations.

An enemy fighter had darted in to attack the Turin-bound bomber while it was flying just east of Mont Blanc in the French–Italian region of Haute Savoie, but the skill of Paddy Haggarty at the controls, coupled with that of his alert gunners, had enabled them to shake off the fighter temporarily. The thwarted fighter intercepted the Halifax again north of Turin, and there was no chance of getting away for a second time. Flight Lieutenant Ferguson and the wireless operator, Warrant Officer Ronald Hooper, DFM, just managed to make a parachute jump before the bomber blew up over Front, Canevese, 17 miles north of Turin.

For many hours Denis Ferguson lay injured and unconscious in a field where his parachute had deposited him. He had a fractured pelvis, severe concussion and bruising of the base of the spine. After spending a night in a military hospital in Turin, he was transferred to Novara Military Hospital. It appeared that he had played his last hand in the war.

Within three weeks of Ferguson parachuting out of the doomed bomber, Italy surrendered unconditionally to the Allies, and for some days confusion reigned in northern Italy. German forces poured in to occupy all the important towns – Milan, Turin, Verona, Pavia, Padua and Vicenza. At many centres Italian troops fought hard to stave off German efforts to take control, but their resistance was finally crushed. In Novara, German units took command of the hospital where Ferguson and the other survivor, Ronald Hooper, were still under treatment. Soon the patients were moved to a gaol in Turin, where over the course of a week they were examined and divided into two categories – the 'cureds', who were to go to a prison camp in Germany, and the 'non-cureds', who were to be returned to hospital. Warrant Officer Hooper was sent to Germany, but Ferguson was classed as requiring further medical care, and he was transferred to Turin Military Hospital.

The Italian surrender was the signal for an undercurrent of Italian hostility against its former Axis partner as soon as General Eisenhower, Commander-in-Chief, Allied Forces, Mediterranean, announced the Armistice and promised the assistance and support of the United Nations for all Italians acting to overthrow the German aggressor. A resistance organization known as the Italian Committee of National Liberation was soon flourishing in northern Italy and, even as Ferguson's wounds were beginning to heal, a doctor tending him in hospital was already in touch with the Committee urging them to effect an escape plot.

It was decided that Ferguson would be helped out of the hospital as soon as he was sufficiently recovered to be able to move about on his own. While the doctor was carrying out his scheduled examinations of the injured navigator, he was able to pass on verbal messages for him from the resistance workers, with the result that a rendezvous was soon arranged for him outside the hospital.

The Germans had been able to devote particular attention towards keeping Flight Lieutenant Ferguson in custody. He was in a single room in the officers' block – the only prisoner of war in the building. His window was barred, and the door was kept locked. Outside there was an armed guard, by day and by night. As a further deterrent against escape, there was an armed guard patrolling the grounds of the hospital.

On the night chosen for the escape, 7–8 November, Denis Ferguson waited until the guards had changed over at midnight and he asked to go to the lavatory. The guard unlocked the door and escorted him along two passages to the toilet, where Ferguson locked the cubicle door on the inside and remained for four or five minutes until telling the guard he was ready to return to his room. Already Ferguson was setting the scene for his dash to freedom. He feigned diarrhoea and repeated the journey under escort to the toilet several times throughout the seemingly interminable night. With only a few minutes still to go before the lifting of the night's curfew at seven, he paid another visit to the lavatory. Again he locked the cubicle door behind him and the guard waited outside. Now for it!

Ferguson pulled the chain and climbed through a window which had been left open by a friendly Italian orderly. Wearing a hospital nightshirt and battledress blouse, Flight Lieutenant Ferguson dropped a distance of about 9 feet to the ground and ran round the side of the hospital to the main road, where he found a wall pitted by bomb fragments. Using for his footholds a 'ladder' of these holes that had been punched out of the stonework so conveniently, Denis Ferguson clambered over the 12-foot-high wall and down the other side in the same way to reach the street. A minute or two later the Italian doctor's contact was at Ferguson's side with a pair of shoes, trousers and a hat and with a cycle on which to make the journey of almost half an hour through the city to a house near Cavoretta where the airman was promised shelter.

The wearying cycle ride was completed without incident and, once the refuge was reached, Ferguson was given an enthusiastic welcome from the family who were to be his hosts. He spent three weeks recuperating there away from enemy eyes. He grew stronger with each passing day. Each day, too, Ferguson became more restive for some means of re-paying the debt of gratitude he owed the Italian Committee of National Liberation for arranging the escape and ensuring his safe-keeping from the Germans out of whose grasp he had slithered with such cool cunning.

Flight Lieutenant Ferguson's host, a keen underground worker, had been arranging to look after some of the Allied ex-prisoners of war who had been roaming northern Italy since the Italian Armistice in a haphazard search for a path that might lead them home.

Now the Englishman himself became an emissary for the Liberation Committee.

His role was meeting these Allied wanderers and liaising between them and the doctor who had helped him in his own escape from the Turin hospital. With the doctor, Ferguson travelled into the mountains to link up with those former prisoners of war and convince them that the Italians were anxious to help them. So often phoney Italians had caught them out in the past that now the escapees had become reticent to work with those who professed to be friendly. The Liberation Committee's plan was to arrange for the ex-prisoners to get across to neutral Switzerland, or to lie low in the mountains with adequate supplies, or to join the partisans in underground work against the Germans.

Time and time again in the bitter, midwinter of 1943–4, Denis Ferguson made his way through the bleak and dangerous mountains to unite Allied Servicemen with the underground movement that was pledged to steer them safely out of the enemy's reach so that they might renew the fight against Nazism. He was pursuing a role that could not be maintained indefinitely.

By mid-February the underground group with whom Ferguson was working was warned that they must now be regarded as marked men and therefore more of a danger to the organization than useful. Ferguson, the doctor and the contact who had been the navigator's host at Cavoretta were all put on the escape chain into Switzerland.

Two partisans guided them across the mountains linking Italy and Switzerland, but on reaching Swiss territory they found that a vertical precipice of ice was blocking their way. By now the guides had gone back to Italy, and the three men had no option but to retrace their footsteps in the snow, too.

They rested in some shepherds' huts on the Italian side of the frontier and made a second attempt lower down the Alps three days later, and this time the trio was successful in reaching the welcome haven of neutral Switzerland. Suffering from acute frostbite of the feet and toes, Ferguson was put into hospital. He was able to contact the British Legation, and eight months later he was repatriated home to Britain.

He had been away from No. 35 Squadron for fourteen months –

fourteen months in which a remarkable pair from the Royal Canadian Air Force named Gordon Carter and Julian Sale had become not only a staunch, fearless team in a Halifax aircrew but a squadron legend, too.

Flying Officer Gordon Carter's face flickered into a wry grin as he floated down by parachute in the moonlit sky over Brittany, for he had to admit that his ill-luck in getting shot down was not entirely unexpected. Although he was not a slave to superstition, Carter had not completely overlooked the rather disturbing fact that the fateful number thirteen had cropped up with nagging monotony. The date was 13 February 1943, he was on his thirteenth bombing raid and an issue of maps and sundry items useful in avoiding capture if forced down on the Continent bore the number thirteen. That all seemed to add up to a sizeable slice of foreboding.

Gordon Carter had joined No. 35 Squadron as a newly commissioned navigator four months earlier. On this thirteenth raid, which was against the U-boat base at Lorient, the four-engined bomber in which he was flying had become hemmed in by heavy flak at 10,000 feet over the town, and the port inner engine was set on fire. Efforts were made for some minutes to check the blaze, but the task was hopeless, and the seven men had to take to their parachutes. Carter dropped into a ploughed field in the hamlet of Kerlescouat, where a young man flung his arms round him and kissed him with as much warmth as if he had been greeting a long-lost brother.

Almost immediately Carter was reunited with one of the crew, Napoleon Barry, a French-Canadian air gunner, and the two airmen spent the night in a farmhouse, where gifts were offered them – wine, cider and even clothing that had been obtained with precious ration coupons. At dawn Carter and Barry set out on foot towards the south-east, and on the second day reached Pontivy, where the two men were told that the rest of the crew were on their way to Spain. The truth came out later that one had been killed, one captured, one successfully reached a neutral country and the remaining two arrived in England some months later.

The travels of Carter and Barry led them to an extraordinary French Resistance agent who carried around with him in a cage a ferret named Hitler, while at his heels trotted a dog he impudently called Raf.

The agent planned that Carter and Barry – who had helped him with gun-running and participated in transmitting radio messages for the underground movement – should be smuggled back to Britain by submarine. The escape bid collapsed when the dinghy that was to ferry them out to the waiting submarine apparently mistook the rendezvous cove and went to a similar spot a mile away. With sad hearts, Carter and Barry turned their backs on the sea and went with their guide to a Trappist monastery, where they were received without any questions being asked of them. Now the two men could only wait to be contacted by a fresh link in the escape organization chain.

The link turned out to be a young Frenchman named Geo Jouanjean, an escapee himself who had fled from a prisoner-of-war camp in Pomerania. He took them to Paris, where the flyers arrived to find that the Gestapo had already arrested the contacts who were to have led them along the next leg of the journey down the escape route. Carter and Barry lunched at a swank restaurant on the Champs Elysées amid an assortment of German officers and their ladies. The airmen wanted more than food – they needed some sort of morale boost, for now the escape chain had snapped and back they must go to Brittany to try all over again.

Here Carter separated from Napoleon Barry, who began his own trek through enemy-held Europe, eventually reaching Britain by way of Spain.

Carter, meanwhile, cycled away with Jouanjean and his fair-haired sister Janine to stay with their sister in the small town of Gourin, through which Carter and Barry had passed within a couple of hours of starting out on foot on their first morning in France. Thus began a deep friendship between Gordon Carter and the pretty Janine. From then on-wards they were to be always in each other's thoughts.

One evening Carter was asked to consider an invitation to join a particularly daring escape plan in which a number of Frenchmen posing as technicians were to be crowded on board a new German motor torpedo boat to undergo trials in the Bay of Douarnenez. After a night-long battle with his conscience, Carter decided next morning that he would join the scheme, despite his apprehension that a host of so-called technicians like himself had slim hopes of overpowering the German Navy crew.

At Douarnenez, a fishing port on the nose of Brittany, south of Brest, Carter found that the anticipated German motor torpedo boat was nothing more than an unserviceable fishing vessel lying on its keel in the nearby Treboul harbour. A band of Frenchmen, eager to get across the 150-mile stretch of sea to Britain to join the Free French Forces, had managed to purchase and transform the boat into some reasonable state of seaworthiness. When darkness fell, Carter and sixteen Frenchmen crept across the harbour's carpet of mud and secreted themselves inside the hull, scarcely daring to breathe for fear of attracting the attention of a German sentry patrolling a jetty just above the boat's mooring.

By 9 a.m. the tide was flooding into the harbour, and the vessel was now afloat. Five of the Frenchmen remained on deck, while the other twelve flattened themselves below deck, and the boat nosed towards the Douarnenez sentry station, where all vessels were compelled to submit to a rigorous inspection. Comrades of the escapees on shore began to stage a methodically planned diversionary scheme to draw the Germans' eyes from the boat while those on board held their breath. The confused sentries impatiently waved away the boat without the usual check – probably for the first and the last time – and the escape party slipped out right beneath their noses. Now, ahead, lay the open sea and England.

A storm almost drowned the seventeen men on their first night out of harbour. The engine failed and practically everyone on board was fearfully sick. There was no food and there was no water to drink. With the arrival of daylight and calmer seas the boat was kept on a due west heading to clear the Continent as far as possible, but during that night, having veered north-east, they apparently drifted right through the Scilly Isles in a thick fog. Early next morning land was seen ahead. It might have been France or even the Channel Islands – in each case enemy-occupied territory – or, equally, the land might prove to be either England or Ireland. There was just no way of telling. Only when a fishing boat came bobbing towards them was the answer revealed. The boat was a crabber from Cadgwith, Cornwall, and the skipper guided them to the Lizard lifeboat station.

Soon afterwards the BBC relayed a message on their French Service: 'Sainte Anne a bien fait les choses.' Its literal translation meant nothing to the Germans who monitored the broadcast: 'St Anne made a good job of it.' To the waiting families in Brittany, however, the message was more easily understood. It was the agreed signal that the slip-away boat from Douarnenez had arrived safely in England. St Anne, patron saint of Douarnenez, had watched over her flock with the loving protection of a mother for her children in time of danger.

After interrogation about his activities in France during the previous two months, Flying Officer Carter returned to No. 35 Squadron and resumed bombing operations within a month. In October he was crewed up with a fellow member of the Royal Canadian Air Force, Julian Sale, who had successfully evaded capture on the Continent himself when he was shot down over Germany. It was the foundation of an unusually close comradeship, and the two became inseparable. In the words of Gordon Carter: 'Julian was one of those exceptionally fine persons every one of us occasionally meets in life.'

Sale, a pilot whose home was in Toronto, had just won a DSO when Carter joined his crew. The citation said of him: 'This officer has displayed skill and has achieved many successes against the enemy's most heavily defended objectives. His unconquerable spirit of determination, great gallantry and fortitude have set an example beyond praise.'

Some of that tremendous spirit had been shown over the course of a considerable period earlier in the year when he had been shot down inside Germany yet managed to make his way through Holland, Belgium and France, down into Spain and from there home to Britain. He had some remarkable close shaves, for he spoke no French, and, although he was often helped by various people on his travels, he was never aware of being in the hands of any underground organization. He was once challenged by a German sentry on a railway bridge and dived into a river to escape.

One classic example of Julian Sale's heroism occurred on the evening of 20 December 1943, when a layer of haze masked Frankfurt, and he made five runs over the target area at successively lower levels and down eventually to only 5,000 feet before releasing the bombs. In the role of primary visual marker, Sale's bomber was also carrying target indicators to release as markers for the main bombing force flying a short distance behind. The orders were to use them only if there was no shadow of doubt at all that they would fall exactly in the right position on the target. Sale's crew could not guarantee such extreme accuracy on account of the haze and had to return home with the indicators. The flight back to Graveley was safely accomplished, but when the Halifax was overhead at only 1,500 feet, and about to land, the target indicators blew up in the bomb bay.

Flames burst out near the rear turret and the underside of one of the wings. The aircraft quickly filled with smoke and fumes, and the blaze spread swiftly. Sale knew that at any moment the petrol tanks in the plane were certain to explode. He made an instant decision. He turned away from the airfield, struggled for extra height and ordered his crew to abandon the aircraft. First out should have been Squadron Leader Alan

Dowling, a navigator, who was in the nose of the bomber unloading a machine gun. He was on his forty-fourth Pathfinder raid and had only one more to do before leaving No. 35 Squadron for a prolonged rest. When he saw that the Halifax was fast becoming a blazing torch with the flare-path of his own airfield visible directly underneath, Alan Dowling was thinking to himself: 'What a damned silly time and place to get killed.'

He turned to face the rear of the aircraft and seized the escape hatch cover from the fuselage floor at his feet. The drill was to lift the hatch from the opening, turn round and drop the hatch on the floor in the nose of the plane. If an attempt was made to discard the hatch through the hole there was a strong chance of the slipstream sucking it and jamming the exit so that no one could get out that way. Dowling was having some difficulty in shifting the hatch and, while he was still grasping it in his hands to deposit it properly in the nose, Gordon Carter and the wireless operator dropped rapidly through the hole. The way was now clear for Dowling, and he wasted no time in plunging out after them.

Still at the controls, Julian Sale assumed everyone had left the aircraft and he opened the hatch above his head to lift himself out of his seat and make his own escape. The smoke was so dense by now in the cockpit that he could hardly see the instruments. But Sale was not quite alone.

He sensed a movement and then saw standing at his side a shadowy figure amid the belching, choking smoke. It was the mid-upper gunner, Flight Lieutenant Bob Lamb, and in his hands he was holding up his parachute – burned and useless when caught by the flames shooting out of the bomb bay. Again Sale was forced into a decision where he must scorn any thoughts for his personal safety. To save Lamb, Julian Sale decided he would try to land the blazing bomber. In a cloud of bakelite and smoke the courageous pilot opened his port window, stuck out his head and made a complete normal circuit approach. He landed and roared off the runway with the floor of the fuselage, equipment and stores ablaze. The two men bolted and, when they were only a bare 200 yards away, the great bomber exploded. Neither of them was hurt.

The crew members who had baled out had already landed. The first pair dropped heavily and sustained some injuries, but as the others had left the aircraft at slightly increased altitudes after Sale had gained height none of them became a casualty. Alan Dowling was just thinking that once the parachute had opened there was supposed to be a pleasant, exhilarating sensation when he plopped without warning into a soft, ploughed field near the Graveley aerodrome perimeter track. The plane was still so low when he had jumped that he reached the ground within a matter of seconds and in the darkness he did not realize how rapidly he was going to hit. He tumbled on his face and the earth jammed the parachute harness quick-release mechanism. A sharp slap with the palm of the hand was normally enough to free the catch and abandon the parachute, but that night there was a fairly high wind blowing and Dowling found himself in the strangely comical situation of being jerked across the field as the parachute billowed open with each gust of wind, while he was still fighting with the wedged release catch. Finally, Dowling had to stalk up on the parachute in the intervals between being pulled headlong over the ground by a fresh gust. He managed to flatten the huge silk shroud so that the wind no longer blew inside and eventually he freed himself from it. He clambered through the barbed wire boundary of the airfield and made his way over to the Ops Room. Only then did Dowling learn that Sale had stayed behind with Lamb and that he had succeeded in achieving something of a miracle in landing the fire-swept bomber.

Julian Sale's comrades expected he would be awarded a George Cross for his gallant action. Instead he received a Bar to his DSO. The citation to the award, which was announced six weeks later, ended with these words: 'In circumstances of great danger, Squadron Leader Sale displayed great courage and determination, setting an example of the highest order.'

Julian Sale and Gordon Carter flew twelve operations together against Kassel, Cannes, Ludwigshafen, Mannheim, Frankfurt – twice – Stuttgart, Berlin – twice – Stettin, Braunschweig and Leipzig. They flew low and often marked perfectly – many times making an approach from as low as between 4,000 and 10,000 feet. 'A rather special get-through-at-any-cost crew was gathered around Sale in October, 1943,' Carter recalled. 'Nobody asked us to adopt such a motto. We were very young and Julian was such an inspiring, able pilot that it came naturally that we should want to do the near-to-perfect job.'

The partnership ended tragically 4 1/2 miles up in the night sky at 2.43 a.m. on 20 February 1944, when for the second time in a week Bomber Command sent out close on a thousand aircraft. They singled out Leipzig as the principal object, but the German fighters were waiting for them as soon as the bombers crossed the North Sea.

A Ju.88 night-fighter from Wunstorf managed to approach unseen and climbed steeply beneath Sale's Halifax to open up with its guns as the bomber passed overhead. The fighter zoomed away in a dive directly after scoring a hit on the bomber's port overload fuel tank. Sale gave the command for the crew to bale out immediately, and Gordon Carter, dangling on the end of his parachute, lost sight of the plane as it plunged down through a cloud bank – one of seventy-eight aircraft lost that particular night when packs of roving enemy fighters reaped the largest harvest of RAF bombers since the raid on Berlin six months previously, when the Graveley Commanding Officer's bomber was one of fifty-six that failed to return home.

Later Carter did spot the distant glow of his blazing bomber through a forest near Celle. He was not to know then that Julian Sale, his closest friend during their previous five months together on No. 35 Squadron, had crashed with the plane to die in enemy hands. Sale's accumulation of past bravery yielded one more medal – a DFC that he never lived to see.

Carter, meanwhile, had dropped safely from about 22,000 feet as the plane began to spin. He slipped on a suit of civilian clothes that he and Sale always carried in special packs underneath their parachute harness. He trudged 100 kilometres west, but some children spotted him, with the result that he was challenged by a German sailor who happened to be there on leave. The airman failed to persuade him he was a forced worker from France, and the police were summoned. While awaiting them, Gordon Carter was offered schnapps by a German housewife – and invited back to see her family after the war was ended. The police arrived and roughed him up a bit, although to the obvious disgust of the local civilians, and he was finally flung into a prison camp.

By now Carter had flown fifty-one operations – thirty-seven over Germany, eight over France and six over Italy. He had become Squadron Leader and won two DFCs for great devotion to duty in bombing operations, outstanding enthusiasm and exceptional accuracy in carrying out his work as a navigator and bomb-aimer.

His fourteen months in prison camp were sustained by the love he had tendered towards a girl he had not seen since escaping from Occupied France in April 1943 – Janine Jouanjean, sister of the fearless Geo Jouanjean who, after Carter had been shot down the first time, had escorted him from Brittany to Paris and back again and then shielded him.

Carter's prison camp was liberated in the closing hours of the European War. His thoughts were always with Janine, and he begged immediate compassionate leave so that he might return to France to see her. Within a fortnight he and Janine were married.

High, indeed, were the examples set by the aircrews of No. 35 Squadron, and, only a few days before Alec Cranswick joined them at Graveley, the award of a DSO to one of their most distinguished pilots, Wing Commander P. H. Cribb, DFC, was announced. The citation explained:

> This officer has an outstanding record as a captain of aircraft and has displayed exceptional qualities of leadership in many sorties against the enemy. He has attacked his targets with unfailing regularity and accuracy. Wing Commander Cribb has a thorough knowledge of air warfare, and his high qualities combined with his consistent keenness have set a high example to all.

In December 1942, No. 35 Squadron was engaged in an attack on Duisburg when a bomber flown by one of the NCOs, Sergeant R. E. Wilkes, was heavily raked by flak at the start of a bombing run over the target. The plane was badly hit, but, although two of the four engines were put out of action, the pilot ignored the heavy damage and carried on to release the bombs. On the return flight, Sergeant Wilkes's bomber was attacked three times by a Junkers Ju.88 night-fighter, but he manoeuvred the crippled plane so successfully that he was able to escape the fighter's guns every time and reached Graveley safely. The sergeant-pilot won a DFM for displaying quiet confidence, fine leadership and an outstanding example of devotion to duty in the face of heavy odds.

He was not alone in triumphing over engine failure during a mission against the enemy.

One night in February 1943, Pilot Officer E. T. Ware was flying a Halifax to raid Lorient when one of his starboard engines failed over the French coast. Despite the handicap, Pilot Officer Ware continued with his assignment. Then, as he approached the target area, he had to face fresh trouble when one of the port engines showed signs of overheating. He kept on, bombed the target, enticed the overheated engine into behaving properly and flew back to Graveley on three engines. His great skill and determination in completing his task successfully under difficult circumstances was recognized by the award of a DFC.

Another pilot flying with No. 35 Squadron also ran into engine trouble over the French coast in the same month. Squadron Leader D. F. E. C. Dean was on the way to Saint-Nazaire, but he, too, carried on with his mission and pressed home a vigorous attack while held by enemy searchlights and battered by heavy ack-ack fire. No sooner had he headed for home, however, than a second engine failed. Even so, Squadron Leader Dean coaxed the bomber back to Britain on the two remaining engines and pulled off a masterly landing in arduous conditions to win a Bar to the DFC he had been awarded in June 1942. Later, Squadron Leader Dean was appointed to command No. 35 Squadron, and during this period he won a DSO – 'He has at all times displayed the highest courage and keenness whilst his enthusiasm and ability have been reflected in the excellent operational work performed by the whole squadron.'

Undismayed by the most severe handicaps, No. 35 Squadron crews constantly refused to be deterred from pursuing their attacks.

High over Berlin one night in March 1943, one of the Halifaxes was damaged by heavy anti-aircraft gunfire that put an engine out of action and severed the rudder controls. The captain, Flight Lieutenant Harry Malkin, DFC, a Canadian, mustered all his skill to control the bomber and carried out a successful attack. The damaged engine was restarted soon after leaving the target area, but, before the plane could fly clear of the Continent, further trouble was encountered. The bomber was again caught by ack-ack fire, which made another engine unserviceable. The mid-upper gunner was wounded, and all the lights failed in the pilot's cockpit. By superb airmanship, Flight Lieutenant Malkin brought the bomber back to Britain, and he was awarded a second DFC for accomplishing these feats of endurance.

A large number of the No. 35 Squadron flying personnel were members of the Royal Canadian Air Force, and there were many instances of their exceptional valour.

In April 1943, a Halifax with a Canadian crew was engaged in an attack on Stettin when a load of incendiaries from another aircraft showered down upon them while they were flying over the target. One of the fire bombs lodged behind the seat of the pilot, Pilot Officer W. S. Sherk, DFC, jamming the aileron and rudder controls. Flames and smoke rapidly filled the cockpit, and the pilot's clothing caught alight. He struggled with the steeply diving plane while the wireless operator, Flying Officer G. G. McGladrey, fought the blaze and the flight engineer, Sergeant D. G. Bebensee, battled to free the locked controls. Just as the situation seemed hopeless, Pilot Officer Sherk regained control of the bomber and Flying Officer McGladrey succeeded in putting out the fire.

By now, however, much of the navigational equipment had been lost in the blaze, but the navigator, Flying Officer K. G. Morrison, plotted accurate courses with great skill. After forty-five minutes of untiring effort, Sergeant Bebensee managed to free the controls, and the badly damaged bomber was flown home. Honours were shared among the four Canadians – Pilot Officer Sherk was awarded a Bar to his DFC, Flying Officers McGladrey and Morrison each received a DFC and Sergeant Bebensee was given the DFM. The citation to the awards said that the four men had displayed great courage, skill and determination in circumstances fraught with great danger.

Individual acts of bravery and total disregard for personal safety were revealed with every operation.

One of No. 35 Squadron's fearless 'Tail-end Charlie' air gunners, Flight Sergeant Norman Francis Williams, DFM and Bar, became Australia's most-decorated airman with the award of the Conspicuous Gallantry Medal for contributing in a large measure to the safe return of his bomber after a raid on Düsseldorf in June 1943. He won the two DFMs with No. 10 Squadron for gallantry and devotion to duty, exceptional skill and resource, as well as setting an example that inspired his colleagues. During the Düsseldorf operation two night-fighters intercepted the Halifax in which he was flying as rear gunner. In the first attack his turret was riddled by enemy gunfire and he was hit repeatedly by bullets in the legs and body. When the second fighter raced in, Flight Sergeant Williams skilfully gave his captain directions for evasive tactics and then he delivered an accurate burst of fire that caused the enemy plane to explode in the air. There was still one fighter quite near and biding time to swoop. The Australian was now in considerable pain, with both legs partially paralysed, but, when the remaining fighter resumed the attack, he gave a well-placed machine-gun burst from close range and shot him down, too. The plucky gunner made light of his injuries, but the shattered turret had to be cut away before he could be freed and taken to hospital for two months. There was no holding him, and the first night back on the squadron saw him in the air for yet another raid.

There were repeated instances of aircrew personnel refusing to quit even when suffering the most intense pain.

One of them was Sergeant H. D. S. White. He was the navigator of a bomber detailed for an assault on Gelsenkirchen. On the outward journey the plane was hit by anti-aircraft fire while still many miles from the target. White sustained three wounds in the leg, but in spite of considerable pain he continued to navigate the bomber to the target, where a successful attack was completed. The injured navigator remained at his post throughout the return flight, plotting the courses back to Graveley and finally collapsing through loss of blood. He received a DFM for displaying outstanding fortitude and courage and for setting an example worthy of high praise.

It was a truly cosmopolitan squadron in those fast and furious days with Path Finder Force – England, Ireland, Scotland, Wales, Canada, Australia, South Africa, New Zealand and Norway, all were nobly represented.

The wartime skies, filled with perils such as the world had never known, did not intimidate these flyers. Seven – or eight-man crews, crammed inside a metal-ribbed skeleton framework wrapped in a thin metal skin, faced nightly journeys that often dragged on for six or eight hours, with most of the time spent in sight or sound of enemy fighters and anti-aircraft gunfire. Frequently the bombers endured unbelievable poundings, to stagger home in shreds, saving grateful and astonished crews. Unrelenting storms and ice repeatedly sought to rival the night-fighters' bullets and the anti-aircraft shells in bids to pluck the aircraft from the sky. Ever onward rode the crews, protected by scarcely more than a sturdy airframe, alert and keen-eyed gunners and the skill of a watchful pilot. Death winged along, too, for almost every minute of the journey – death that might come with the merciful suddenness of a chance direct hit in a hail of machine-gun fire or the explosion of a single flak shell; death, perhaps, in a hundred other ways, each beyond the bounds of human control and so agonizing in its slow certainty.

Such was the recognized lot of the aircrew members throughout RAF Bomber Command, each one a volunteer. In particular, No. 35 Squadron was never lacking for men with the right measure of boldness to carry through every mission, but, in the arrival of Alec Cranswick at the end of January 1943, there came one of the most extraordinary pilots to fly with Path Finder Force.

Chapter 8

# Captain Courageous

Although twelve operational missions were the normal minimum required for acceptance into the Path Finder Force and he had already flown sixty-six, Alec Cranswick certainly did not anticipate that his wealth of experience as a bomber pilot would give him an open sesame when he drove up the hill from Offord village and swung through the gates of the RAF Station, Graveley, at the end of January 1943.

The first to be equipped with Halifaxes, No. 35 Squadron was one of the four founder units of Path Finder Force, and within a matter of hours of Cranswick joining them at Graveley he saw the squadron notch up another important milestone by taking part in the first bombing raid to use the H2S radar device. It was this system, which presented on a cathode ray screen an impression of the ground beneath the aircraft, that eventually gave RAF Bomber Command the ability to attack in great strength and with uncanny accuracy, even if the target was hidden by heavy cloud or blanketed by fog. But, when Cranswick entered the Pathfinders, H2S was fitted in only a tiny percentage of aircraft, and a full month passed before his crew were able to commence training with this prized equipment.

They first received classroom instruction in the Pathfinder methods and in the function of H2S and the other special navigational and bomb-aiming apparatus. Within a fortnight the crew was ready for operations and joined an attack on Cologne, playing a modest role. Two nights later they followed this up with a raid on Lorient in which their participation assumed greater importance. In this attack Cranswick was selected to pilot one of the illuminator aircraft, releasing his batch of eight flares from 14,500 feet to bathe the port in artificial moonlight, followed by a coloured marker to pinpoint the target for the benefit of the main bombing force.

After marking further targets at Wilhelmshaven and Bremen, Cranswick's crew began their airborne H2S training programme. Standards were high in the Pathfinders, but, although they failed in their first attempt, they passed the exacting test schedule after a further spell of rigorous practising. By now Cranswick was settling down well to the tasks in hand. He had succeeded in surviving six ops with the Pathfinders, which was more than a good many chaps had done. Yet this knowledge was liable to instil a feeling that, having gone so far, one was pretty sure of going on almost for ever. This was a feeling to be watched; it was a breeding ground for carelessness. And very often the first mistake was likely to be the only one.

A few hours after passing the H2S test on 16 April, Cranswick and his crew were on ops for the third time in six nights and trundling along in a moonlight marathon high over enemy-occupied Europe to blaze the trail, Pathfinder fashion, to the great Skoda armament works at Pilsen in Czechoslovakia. It was a formidable journey. The round trip was some 1,800 miles, and two-thirds of the way was over fiercely defended enemy territory. Bomber Command had been waiting for favourable weather before venturing quite so far into the heart of Occupied Europe. As the crews began assembling at their stations in Britain, everyone knew full well that the enemy night-fighters would be stalking the skies in their dozens as the main line of defence. And one of those Jerry fighters was going to give Cranswick his biggest shaking so far.

His Halifax was flying in the forefront of the attack – 'Belting along minding our own business with no opposition at all,' explained tail-gunner Ivor Howard. What happened next has never been completely made clear, but beyond dispute is the fact that no one in that bomber ever realized there was another aircraft chugging along quite unconcerned in their little patch of sky. Maybe there was cloud, maybe a freak haze, but not even the pilot of the other plane could possibly have known what was going to happen. The plane that no one had spotted until almost too late was a Messerschmitt Me.110 – a German night-fighter.

Howard noted down the next few perilous seconds in his logbook as 'A shaky do!' – something of an understatement.

*Imagine yourself standing in a rattly old tin hut when a plane roars across the top at what might be fairly accurately described as zero feet.*

*The hut dances wildly and seems ready to topple like a pack of cards unbalanced by a breath of wind.*

*The sound of the aircraft is magnified many times by the shuddering metal all around you, and the hut reverberates madly as the plane sweeps past.*

That is how the episode struck Cranswick's crew.

Cranswick and the Messerschmitt pilot must have seen each other at about the same time as the two aircraft raced together and closed at a frightening speed at 200 yards a second until little short of a miracle could prevent the collision.

Only the two pilots had the remotest control over the situation. The surprising point is that both acted without any hesitation and miraculously both took exactly the right action.

Cranswick plunged his bomb-heavy plane into as steep a dive as he dared in a desperate bid to escape the black shape of the Messerschmitt flashing towards him; Jerry, meanwhile, wrenched his smaller, lighter aircraft into a crazy climb.

The Me.110 zoomed over the top of the shaking, vibrating Halifax – its slipstream buffeting the bomber and the sound of the racing engines shrieking at full power in a torrent of noise fit to drown even the row from their own four throbbing engines.

From the rear turret Ivor Howard had a momentary glimpse of the fighter soaring away overhead. Not surprisingly the Messerschmitt never came back. All the way to the target area the Halifax crew were wondering who had had the biggest shock when the two planes nearly rammed each other. It is a pretty safe bet the Messerschmitt crew were wondering, too.

The episode had well and truly put the wind up them all, particularly Alec, for his father had died in an aerial collision.

Cautiously, Cranswick recovered his proper height and course for Pilsen, and no bomber crew kept more careful watch so as to be sure no aircraft came within a dozen miles of them.

The Pathfinders were over Pilsen about an hour-and-a-half after midnight. Down below the flares and the moonlight combined to present a perfect panorama of the 320-acre target area, which was reckoned at that time to be employing somewhere between 30,000 and 40,000 people.

Down went the incendiaries, down went the big high-explosive bombs. Pilsen was being pasted.

As far as Cranswick was concerned, all seemed to be going now without any particular snags. The routine was becoming a familiar one. The target had been marked, and their work was now done.

It was as uneventful as the trip out to Pilsen had been memorable. Perhaps, on reflection, this was just as well. One shock like that was quite enough for any man.

All that remained was to toddle off back home to Graveley – he was at least making up for the rather dismal effort of two nights previously when trouble developed in the port inner engine on the way to Stuttgart and he had reluctantly turned back after little more than an hour in the air.

The Halifaxes and Lancasters were laying it on thickly on Pilsen as Alec set course for home. The bombs were screaming down at an incredible rate – 'Four just missed us,' one pilot reported in all seriousness when he returned to base.

The ack-ack fire was only moderate, and the number of searchlights could be counted easily. Maybe all was going just that little bit too well. The men who flew by night were sensitive to such thoughts. Concentrate, concentrate, concentrate... 'We're not safe until we've landed on terra firma.'

In a flash Cranswick's Halifax was trapped by one of the lone, inquisitive searchlights sweeping the skies from the outer ring of the Skoda defences. Another searchlight swung round eagerly to pick up the bomber. Now another. And another.

He was caught in a cone of them to become a brilliantly illuminated and perfect sitting target for the ground gunners.

For five agonizing minutes – five minutes that seemed to drag for just as long as the entire journey to Pilsen – he pulled every trick in the book to dodge out of the searchlights.

Those blazing lights flooded the whole interior of the bomber. The figures of the crew members at their positions stood out in stark, black relief against the brilliance of the searchlights' glare.

The gunfire barked, boomed, crashed and crunched like thunderclaps as the pilot flung the machine about the sky like a fighter and everyone wondered whether they would ever be free of the dazzling beams that had the bomber in their grip.

The dodge that eventually rid them of the beams was one that Ivor Howard had often seen put to good use when he was bombing in 1941 and he shouted the instructions over the intercom to Cranswick.

The idea was to drop a wing and slide a few hundred feet down the searchlight beam. The crew operating the light would see the bomber moving away and try to swing the light round to what they imagined was the bomber's new position. It was really too simple.

Instead of the aircraft having to dodge away from the searchlight, the searchlight crew were smartly tricked into moving away from the aircraft.

Another way of outwitting the searchlights was to dive steeply and carry out a marked and sudden change of direction in a steep turn on dragging the plane out of the high-speed dive. If that was unsuccessful, the manœuvre was repeated at the cost of a further few thousand feet of precious height – which took you into increased danger by dropping into the range of medium and light ack-ack gun batteries. There were a number of cases where aircraft sacrificed too much height in trying to shake off the cone and fell quick victims to the ground gunners.

To be coned was one of the most alarming things that could happen to a bomber. Close liaison was maintained by radio between ground control stations, night-fighters and heavy ack-ack posts. If there was a night-fighter in the area, he would close in for an easy kill – the bomber's gunners would be almost blinded by the fierce glare of the cone – and, if there were no fighters, the ack-ack would concentrate on the unlucky plane.

Once one was free of the powerful beams, the scheme was to get as far as your engines would carry you in the least possible time – which is precisely what Cranswick did on this occasion. His ruse had taken the bomber clear of the searchlights, and everyone was able to relax again. Relax? Well, relax as far as anyone could when he knew full well that there were more flak, more enemy fighters and more searchlights to hound them all the way back to the coast on the final lap back to base.

Home was still far away, but the even throb of the bomber's engines was joyous music to the crew in the realization that every revolution of the propellers biting into the cold night air was taking them nearer and nearer base.

Soon there appeared below the tell-tale landmarks that the bomber boys of Graveley knew so well. Another night, another raid, was over.

Small wonder, then, that someone murmured as he clambered wearily down from the now silent bomber: 'Boy, what a night! What a night!'

After the Pilsen searchlights drama, Cranswick came to rely on Ivor Howard more and more to help him escape night-fighters, anti-aircraft fire and searchlights. It was the start of a warm team comradeship that dominated their activities both in the air and on the ground.

It was one night just forty-eight hours after the raid on Pilsen, when they were crossing the Alps, that rear gunner Flight Sergeant Ivor Howard came to realize that Alec Cranswick was a real sticker of a guy where flying heavy bombers was concerned. Their Halifax was on the way to Spezia, a key Italian naval base on the Gulf of Genoa, which was due to be raided in excellent weather by a bomber force thundering away from their bases in Britain at dusk.

Cranswick's plane was carrying a single 1,000-pound bomb and two 500-pound bombs as well as the target indicators and flares to light the way for the main force. The flight was going to be a long one and maybe the target none too easy to crack, but no one expected any particular difficulty. The route was well planned, and the possible opposition had been intelligently anticipated. The snag, unexpectedly, turned out to be the massive, towering Alps, which lay between him and his target.

The snowy caps were gleaming ahead in the moonlight – a wonderful, impressive sight – but they began to take on a grim, menacing appearance when Cranswick started to realize that his engines were not providing enough power this night to climb above them. He knew that he must beat this hurdle to do his job in leading the attack on Spezia.

Rather like an unskilful high jumper having a crack at beating his own record, Cranswick desperately pushed his hulking Halifax at the great mountains in a series of runs as he tried to eke out sufficient power from his engines to clear them.

But, unlike the high jumper, he knew he had no alternative but to cry off the attempt the moment he was positive the plane was still not going to be able to scramble over the top.

He had to lighten the aircraft somehow and so give it a better chance of clearing the Alps. As a Pathfinder he clearly must keep his flares and target indicators to blaze a trail for the main force following some distance behind. So he ordered the 1,000-pound bomb to be dropped – set safe before release in order to avoid an explosion on the ground that might damage civilian property or cause casualties. He did not want the innocent to suffer.

With the heaviest of his bombs now released to ease the burden on the weary engines of the Halifax, Alec tried another bid at the mountain barrier. Again he failed. He turned back and decided to drop one of the only two remaining bombs. The same safety precaution was observed once more. Again Cranswick was coaxing and straining to entice the maximum power from his failing engines so that the bomber could stagger over the Alps.

He began another run and the snow cap rushed nearer. The engines raced. Then – success! As the big, black Halifax slipped triumphantly over the mountain range the crew had an uneasy feeling that the fuselage had actually scraped a layer of crisp snow off the peak – it was as close as that.

Bright moonlight guided them easily to the Italian base, and the buildings were picked out without difficulty in the dock area, the target being marked by powerful coloured flares. There was little opposition, although crews who had been there before considered that the Italians had obviously made a special effort to improve both their ground and air defences.

It was nine hours after take-off that the Pathfinder Halifax was sweeping along the Graveley runway at the end of the mission – but at least Alec had had the satisfaction of dropping one 500-pound bomb on the target.

To him the Spezia attack was just another mission, yet he could easily have cried off the raid when he found he was unable to clear that Alpine barrier on the way out to Italy.

He was a sticker, though, Cranswick.

The fact that he did not choose to dodge out of the raid by pleading engine trouble was an instance of the indubitable courage that made him stand out among the select Path Finder Force flyers.

Alec Cranswick felt on top of the world up there in the skies he loved during those days and nights of April 1943, when the bombing programme was heavy and all was going so well in raid after raid.

There comes a time, unhappily, when your spell of good luck runs out. Whether you know it or not, there is trouble ahead. It came to Flight Lieutenant Cranswick on the night of 20 April – the night of his seventy-fifth operational mission since he had started flying from Stradishall in June 1940.

It was remembered afterwards as the Fiasco of Stettin.

The cardinal sin of a Pathfinder was to fail to reach the target exactly on time – to be too early or too late was equally wrong – and by a mix-up on someone's part Cranswick's Halifax arrived over the Baltic port rather early. A ferocious barrage of ack-ack fire greeted them, for they were all alone in the moonlit sky simply waiting to be picked off by the first gun battery skilful or lucky enough to find the correct range. That point alone gave everyone on board a most uncomfortable feeling.

The route out from Graveley had been planned as a 'dog-leg' course north of Denmark and then turning south-east to sweep in straight towards Stettin. The turning point was to be marked by a flare dropped from Cranswick's aircraft. This part of the programme was duly carried out, and the flare blazed in solitary splendour in slow descent on the end of a parachute – a beacon of brilliant light suspended in the night sky to attract the following planes so that they would know precisely where to change course towards the target. At this point the crew in Cranswick's plane knew something had gone wrong, because the plan laid down that within a moment or two another Pathfinder should be along to drop a fresh flare at the turning point when their own flare was almost burned out.

There was no sign of either the second bomber or the second flare.

Cranswick pressed on according to instructions, however, but reached Stettin ahead of time. The net result was that he had to sweat and strain manoeuvring his Halifax in a stomach-wrenching succession of evasive tactics in the face of a murderous flak barrage, unable to drop the target-marking flares because they would not last long enough for the main bombing force. And the bombers, manned by less-experienced crews, had to rely on those indicators as a signpost to the target.

Cranswick had to waste time, awkwardly, by stooging around the Baltic and going back again at the time they were supposed to be there. In due course the target was properly pinpointed on schedule, and Alec swung his aircraft on to the track indicated to take them home. So far, so good. Then – panic stations! They were lost, hopelessly lost.

When you have been flying over Germany regularly, there are places that are quickly recognized. But the landmarks below them now were unfamiliar. And to make matters worse the flak was bursting all around the plane with great thumping crashes that were much too near to be safe.

Shrapnel peppered the wings and fuselage. One lump, jagged and blistering hot, whined like a rifle shot midway along the fuselage, ricocheting from side to side against the metal spars and finishing up by knocking off the heel of the flight engineer's flying boot.

Cranswick slammed his control stick forward and the plane screamed earthwards. The altimeter spun crazily. Down, down, down – down from 17,000 feet to a mere 5,000 feet in a defiant and calculated act to escape the ravages of a merciless battering of flak. Flight Sergeant 'Johnny' Johnson, the Canadian engineer, now minus the heel of one flying boot, had tight hold of the control stick along with Cranswick to exert all their combined strength to haul the great bomber out of its frenzied dive before it plummeted into a vertical plunge that would be impossible to check.

'We all decided we must have been somewhere over Flensburg,' Ivor Howard said later, 'when we were hit – probably by the anti-aircraft barrage defending Kiel. Eventually I saw an island ahead, with the unmistakable shape of Sylt, so I called out to Alec to keep going straight and we wouldn't be far from home. We thought we had had it that trip. It just shows what can happen when you get yourselves lost.'

It seemed that everything had gone wrong on that Stettin trip.[1]

First they had arrived early at the turning point; then they had reached the target too soon. On top of all that they had lost themselves. They had almost lost their lives, too, for how they had managed to escape a really severe beating from the guns was a proper mystery – not that anyone felt like trying to solve it.

The one redeeming feature was that on this occasion the first error had not been their last. Maybe the arrival of a new navigator named Leslie Hulme might see a return of their good luck spell. It was obviously needed.

Where navigators were concerned, Cranswick was a bit of a devil. Veteran now of seventy-five operational missions from heavy bomber bases in Britain and the Middle East, Alec was among the most experienced flyers in Bomber Command. And there was no doubt whatsoever about his navigational capabilities being pretty high. Perhaps it was not surprising, therefore, that he made stern demands upon the navigators who flew in his crew.

Pathfinder planes were flying with two navigators now. The First Navigator's job was to feed courses to the pilot to maintain the specified track and to ensure correct timing on target. The Second Navigator's job was to operate the special radar devices and supply information from this equipment to the First Navigator to assist him in his work. If the radar failed, as happened on occasions, the First Navigator relied on dead reckoning calculations to lead them to the target. Then the Second Navigator would drop the bombs and/or the markers visually. When the radar was operating properly, the Second Navigator dropped the load by radar alone if the target was hidden from view.

In Cranswick's crew, Warrant Officer McRobbie looked after the radar and bomb-aiming. The two men had been together since starting with the Canadians on Halifaxes. Pilot Officer Hulme was now to join them as the other navigator, as a result of some crew changes in No. 35

Squadron at the beginning of May.

Cranswick, young and enthusiastic to an extreme, could be rather domineering in the air where navigators were involved, and there were times when he was liable to override the navigator on the way home.

'All right,' Alec would snap, 'I know the way.'

More often than not he did know the way, but such goings-on were apt to prove a little irksome to the navigator. When the navigator happened to be a non-commissioned officer, he was in an awkward spot if he objected to what his captain wanted to do. When Leslie Hulme, a commissioned officer, joined the crew, there was far less chance of Alec trying to bulldoze his own way. In fact, the two suited each other right from their first mission together on 4 May, an easy raid on Rheine, which gave them an opportunity to become accustomed to each other's ways without undue stress.

Hulme came to No. 35 Squadron from a Halifax Conversion Unit after flying in long-range Whitleys on U-boat patrols in the Bay of Biscay. He volunteered for aircrew at the beginning of the war, but at 31 he was too old. He joined the Equipment Branch of the RAF instead. When the age limit for navigators was eventually raised, he volunteered again, and this time he was accepted.

The really big raids were now beginning to build up and, on 23 May 1943, the greatest number of four-engined bombers ever to be sent out from Britain in a single night up to that time was engaged on the first major attack of the war on Dortmund.

Dortmund, in the Ruhr, was one of the chief centres of heavy industry in the Reich. With five 1,000-pound bombs and five target indicators in the belly of Cranswick's Halifax, they were off from Graveley that night in almost perfect weather at five minutes to eleven o'clock to spearhead the attack. Over the Dutch coast on the way out from Britain, two enemy night-fighters put in an appearance, sniffing around trying to find an opening to blaze away at Alec's lumbering Halifax.

In the words of Ivor Howard:

*We exchanged chunks of lead and then everyone cleared off. One was a twin-engined aircraft; I'm not sure what the other one was.*

*The secret of our success, you might say, was that I didn't like them to get too close.*

*The idea was for me to keep a watch out for fighters whenever there was a chance of them operating near us and when I spotted one I used to yell out to Cranswick what their position was in relation to the numbers of a clock – two o'clock, three o'clock and so on.*

*When I said 'GO!' he would turn us in towards the fighter. If you turned away you left yourself wide open for him to attack you and we wanted to make sure that didn't happen too often.*

That night many enemy fighters were sent up to hamper the raiding bombers in what was up to that date the heaviest air attack in history. The hour-long 2,000-ton assault brought the weight of bombs on Germany up to 100,000 tons and prompted Air Chief Marshal 'Bomber' Harris to send the following message to all his crews:

> In 1939 Goering promised that not a single enemy bomb would reach the Ruhr. Congratulations on having delivered the first 100,000 tons of bombs on Germany to refute him. The next 100,000, if he waits for them, will be even bigger and better bombs delivered even more accurately and in a much shorter time.

Marking for an equally heavy raid on Düsseldorf two nights later, during which more than five of the massive 2-ton bombs crashed down every minute, earned Cranswick's crew a prized distinction, although costing them some precious sleep.

They were back at Graveley at five minutes past four in the morning and were directed straight in to the interrogation session, where the Intelligence officers went through their inevitable probe to find out the results of the night's attack.

They had a quick meal and all anyone wanted to do then was to sleep. When you have been over Germany for most of the night, no one wants to be woken up after an hour or so with the raucous command to rise and shine. Anyway, that is what happened to Cranswick and his crew this particular morning.

The order was to get cleaned up, uniforms pressed, and be back on the airfield at ten to fly a new Halifax to Wyton, another of the PFF aerodromes, to represent No. 35 Squadron in meeting a Very Important Person – unspecified in fact but identified by rumour as the Prime Minister, Mr Churchill.

At Wyton, Cranswick and his crew – among them Leslie Hulme, McRobbie, Ivor Howard and 'Johnny' Johnson – lined up to await the arrival of the VIP.

It was one of those typically RAF swank shows – even the aircraft engine propellers had to be set at just the right angle to present a symmetrical picture of neatness and dazzling efficiency for the benefit of the visiting group of 'top brass' personnel.

Cranswick's crew were there to represent those in the squadron who had taken part in the great Düsseldorf raid the previous night, and their sense of pride gradually overcame their annoyance at having to forgo most of their well-earned beauty sleep to be paraded at Wyton before a personage whose identity was being kept so secret.

Suddenly a car swept towards them; here at last was the Prime Minister. The flag mounted on the front of the car was flapping about in the stiff breeze – but it was soon recognized as the Royal Standard.

The car eased down to a silent halt and out stepped King George VI and Queen Elizabeth.

It fell to Acting Squadron Leader Alec Cranswick, DFC – his promotion had come through less than three weeks previously – to introduce his crew to their Majesties.

These presentations are always supposed to go without a hitch, of course, and normally they do.

As it happened, however, Flight Sergeant 'Johnny' Johnson, the Canadian engineer, was so overwhelmed by the honour and the excitement of the occasion that he jumped the gun by a second or two.

He sprang forward with the precision of a guardsman and snapped up a most wonderful salute, proudly announcing his rank and name as he froze to attention before the Queen had reached him even, and before Cranswick had had time to introduce him.

It was a bit startling for the parade, but the Queen laughed and the tension was broken. She stopped to talk for some little while with Johnson before moving on. It was one of the more light-hearted moments of the 500-mile tour of seven RAF camps and two United States Army Air Corps bases that the Royal couple were undertaking.

The first action of 'Johnny' Johnson on the way back by road from Wyton to Graveley was to stop at a Post Office and spend fifteen shillings on a cable home to Canada to tell his folks: 'Have just had great honour of meeting the King and Queen of England.'

Whenever a new target was announced to the bomber crews at the briefing session four or five hours before take-off, an added interest was immediately displayed.

On one occasion, 29 May 1943, the senior briefing officer pointed to a map fixed within easy view of the assembled flyers and told them:

'Gentlemen, Wuppertal is our target for tonight.'

The name probably meant nothing at all to the majority of the air-men there because the town had escaped any real attention from the RAF, even though there were chemical works in the area as well as many other war industries. It had just not fitted so far into the bombing pattern.

Wuppertal had been created only as comparatively recently as 1929 by the amalgamation of the towns of Elberfeld and Barmen. It lay some 40 miles due east of Düsseldorf, which had been left smarting from a thorough blitzing only four nights before to bring the total number of attacks to more than fifty.

The two places did have one point in common – to get to either of them in an RAF bomber meant pitting yourself against Happy Valley.

Happy Valley was the RAF's name for the Ruhr, that great, sprawling industrial centre where the tools of war were being churned out by the thousands of tons.

Understandably the defences were just about the most ferocious to be found anywhere – not that you needed to go looking for them. They introduced themselves with first a huge white wall of searchlights and then a flak barrage that seemed to fill the whole sky.

The fact that the target was a new one this night, therefore, meant little when these facts had sunk into the bomber boys' minds, because, as far as everyone was concerned, it was still the Ruhr.

And the Ruhr was not a pleasant place to be with bombs bulging in your belly and Jerry waiting, menacingly, for you.

The briefing maps revealed that Wuppertal was strung out on either side of the River Wupper and stretched up a fairly narrow valley for some 10 miles – a slender target area packed with factories that were turn-ing out components to feed the big neighbouring industries of the Ruhr.

To reach Wuppertal, the bombers had to run right through that Ruhr defence gauntlet. The searchlights – criss-crossing the night sky – were one of the main dreads of Pathfinder Cranswick. And there were plenty in action that night. Those penetrating beams would flood the aircraft with artificial daylight, dazzling the eyes until they hurt. To slip from their grip required a major struggle, often a long and drawn-out test of man and machine. Navigator Leslie Hulme saw Cranswick fling off the broad straps that held him in his seat and start battling with the controls of the bomber while he did his utmost to toss the giant machine about the sky as if she were a tiny little single-engined aerobatic plane.

Cranswick's Halifax, once more leading the main force to the target, carried a single 2,000-pound bomb and fourteen canisters of incendiaries. Hulme remembered Wuppertal in these words:

*Everything that was dropped seemed to roll down the mountainsides into the valley. It looked as though the roofs were being lifted up to meet the aircraft when the bombs went down. I thought the roofs were going to hit us. I had never seen anything like it and neither had Alec.*

The incendiaries were showered down at a tremendous rate, and long before the attack was over the whole of the target area was studded by fires. In one vast explosion smoke plumed 3 miles up, and the entire neighbourhood was lit up. The sky erupted into man-made daylight for a while, and pilots were able to pick out other bombers silhouetted against the red glow of a blazing Wuppertal that had been fearfully blasted into near obliteration in that single sixty-minute attack.

One Scottish pilot managed to bring back his Lancaster safely after a particularly long ordeal. One of the four engines was put out of action by a heavy shell over the Ruhr, but he went on to bomb his target. A further hit stopped a second engine, and the plane floundered 6,000 feet downwards before he could bring it under control once more. Flying on two engines, he could not climb above 3,000 feet. Yet at this height he succeeded in coaxing the crippled bomber back to England.

There was one consolation for the crews who had to face the Ruhr barrage so many times. It was this: throughout that month of May 1943, the RAF despatched nearly forty bombers over Germany for each one that the Luftwaffe sent venturing to attack Britain. And most of the RAF's planes were the heaviest types in service. Since the early days of 1940 and 1941, the size of the bombers and the bombs had increased.

Some of the crews out raiding Germany had their own special sport utilizing an unofficial bomb load used particularly against troops in the garrison towns. There is no reference to these attacks in the bombing records of the RAF. They were beer bottle bombs, which often screamed down just as the troops were coming out of their cinemas at night to go back to the barracks. On account of their shape, the empty bottles used to sail down to earth with a terrifying shriek – one man who delighted in this sport explained: 'I can vouch for the fearful wail they made because we practised with them on our own airfield. Boy, you should have seen the lads run. A banshee's wail has nothing on our beer bottle bombs.'

But even the Ruhr had a rest at times.

Cranswick's crew soon found themselves detailed to attack factories and a transformer station at Le Creusot, 170 miles south of Paris, and Montchanin, 5 miles away from Le Creusot.

The bombing force, composed entirely of four-engined machines, found ideal conditions for the raid; roads, stretches of water and finally the tall works themselves made unmistakable landmarks, which stood out clearly when the Path Finder Force flares began floating down to reinforce the moonlight.

There was little opposition to disturb the bombers, so the crews were able to take their time in aiming, and the visibility was so good that members of one Halifax crew actually saw two bombs smash great holes in the roof of one of the main buildings.

It was what one might term a 'piece-of-cake' raid — except that Cranswick ran into that most irritating fault known as a 'hang up', which meant the bombs would not drop.

The reason could normally be put down to a failure in the electrical release mechanism, but no one quite knew what to do to overcome the problem. Usually the trouble developed only with the smallest high-explosive bombs.

If the bombs refused to budge at all, there was not likely to be any bother. You just went back home after one or two attempts to release them and then hoped for the best when you landed.

But the snag was that the bombs might easily be hanging suspended half-on and half-off in the bomb bay with the strong possibility of one dropping off on landing.

'It makes a nice hole in the runway if it drops when you're landing,' Hulme explained. 'Doesn't do the runway much good, let alone the aircraft and the lads inside.'

This was the problem facing Alec Cranswick that night over Le Creusot. Two of the smaller bombs simply decided to stay put. He could only let them go on some unsuspecting French farm or over the sea — if he was able to let them go at all.

He started an airborne rodeo show by waggling the wings and trying a spot of rough-riding, bucking the bomber up and down to see if the bombs would dislodge themselves.

At the umpteenth attempt over the sea, an obviously relieved bomb-aimer reported: 'It's all right, Skipper. Bombs gone — at last.'

Cranswick only frowned and made no reply, however. For the safety of his crew he had had to get rid of the jammed bombs somehow before going back to Graveley, but he hated the idea of wasting them in the sea. He believed there were only two places for all his bombs – in the bomb bay on the way to the attack or slapped down right on the target before turning for home.

Two nights later Cranswick's bomber was pathfinding for a force of more than 700 heavies, which were to drop one of the most colossal loads so far in a fifty-minute attack on the industrial town of Krefeld on the edge of the Ruhr at the western end of dear old Happy Valley – it was probably the most strongly defended area anywhere in the world.

The Pathfinders saw cones of searchlights from Duisburg and other centres probing the sky. Soon the guns opened up. Krefeld's own defences were slow going into action themselves, and within a short time they were being overwhelmed.

It was then that the night-fighters began flying into battle – the largest force seen for some time – and many combats were fought out in the moonlight over the Ruhr. Forty-four bombers failed to return from the raid.

The navigator 'Hulmie' was in continuous contact with his pilot over the intercom the whole time they were in the air, and the remainder of the crew were only supposed to cut in during an emergency. While working at his table in the nose, ahead of and below the cockpit, Hulme was unable to see anything of the outside world. So, to keep him in touch with what was going on, Cranswick used to give him a running commentary, and this probably helped relieve some of the strain on Cranswick.

*He used to go a bit quiet when he saw a lot of our planes crashing in flames or blowing up in the air* [Hulme said]. *They seemed to be suspended on a piece of rope, burning and falling so slowly before gradually disintegrating. Then there would be another whopper of an explosion on hitting the ground. Everybody would be subdued then. If there were a lot shot down before you reached the target that used to have a sobering influence. It used to steady you up. It's rather like seeing a motor accident – it makes you drive steadily for a while. If you missed the aiming point on the first run in for your target, and you had already seen thirty or forty planes going down, you might well be inclined to drop the bombs the first time. Cranswick would frequently go round a second or a third time, come what may. It was not like him to drop the damn things and go running off home.*

Flying was Cranswick's one great joy, and its perfection his constant aim – his prime reason for living. Yet, just as there were soldiers who sought nothing more exalted than to serve with unswerving obedience in the ranks, and sailors who were never happier than in performing menial but self-satisfying duties below decks, Alec showed no urge to seek a position of authority in the RAF. He appeared content to carry out other people's orders; he never showed any inclination towards giving orders of his own. He wanted to control nothing more than his own plane.

Cranswick's squadron commanders admired his flying capabilities, for he was beyond dispute a superb pilot, but some who flew with him regularly in Path Finder Force grew acutely aware that he was displaying neither the necessary administrative ability, nor even the interest, to control others on the ground. In the air, of course, Squadron Leader Cranswick maintained his position as aircraft commander – by virtue of his crew-place as pilot. In the main, he was always flying with people he knew well and whose skill and judgement he never had cause to doubt. The crew was a team, his team, but the commands that he gave probably seemed to him less like orders and more as decisions made on behalf of the team and backed by their unspoken agreement. Nevertheless, Cranswick became Flight Commander of No. 35 Squadron's 'B' Flight for a time that summer, so that he had to assume responsibilities for the efficiency of half the squadron on the ground as well as in the air. He abhorred the paperwork and organizing that went with the position of Flight Commander. He wanted to fly a plane and not a desk – he made that point abundantly clear to anyone who would listen to him.

As a pilot Alec was a master, but, some said, he failed to approach anywhere near the same peak in his interest or knowledge of such kindred subjects as aero-engineering and navigation. His comparative lack of proficiency here may well have retarded chances of further promotion. It was often remarked in Path Finder Force what a pity it was that Alec Cranswick did not find it possible to apply himself to other aspects of RAF work with the same vigour that he adopted when tackling flying. Most Pathfinder pilots possessed an unusually high standard of navigational prowess, but Cranswick was not quite so skilled; he felt satisfied to leave everything to his own navigator without question and without comment. 'We got on terribly well together and luckily we never came unstuck!' recalled Leslie Hulme, who was with him for much of 1943.

Cranswick never smoked, and he drank nothing with a stronger kick than lime juice. He was often asked why he would not drink, and the answer was always the same – 'I don't like the taste.' His favourite drink was fizzy lemonade and lime juice. Once another officer slipped some gin into Alec's glass in the Mess at Graveley and he exploded with anger when he realized that someone had been tampering with his drink.

Cranswick was neither severe nor particularly serious in his outlook, but jokes and pranks were not a part of his activities.

He found some relaxation in the company of an occasional WAAF, and both Ivor Howard, the gunner, and navigator Hulme were quick to pull his leg about these excursions into the realms of womanly charm. However, he laughed off their wisecracks and invariably took them in good part.

There was one rather pressing WAAF type who used to haunt him quite a bit. They had met at a camp dance and been out together a couple of times. Hulme and Howard decided to egg her on a bit and when they saw her approaching for news of Cranswick, Hulme called out: 'He's in the squadron office, waiting for you. Hurry up, he's been talking about no one else the whole time we were flying this morning.'

Cranswick, who by this time had decided she was not his type at all, fled in the opposite direction, but when, eventually, the eager young lady did manage to track him down he had to beg Hulme: 'For Heaven's sake tell her I've gone on leave, or gone to Group, or gone anywhere. But whatever you do, get rid of her.'

The fact that Cranswick was a teetotaller robbed him of much of the high-spirited camaraderie of the wartime RAF when periods of stand-down from ops were punctuated by parties in a variety of hostelries in Huntingdon and Cambridge. Some of these sessions, with a few drinks and a game or two of darts, were arranged by the flying personnel so as to repay the ground crews for their unselfish service in keeping the bombers in tip-top flying condition.

One night the squadron was already in the briefing room, receiving final instructions, when the raid was called off because bad weather had clamped down over the target area.

As the crews filed out, Hulme suggested to Howard: 'Let's give the ground crew boys a bit of a do when they've got the bombs off the aircraft. We'll go into Cambridge.'

The gunner turned to Cranswick: 'How about it, Alec?'

'Certainly. By all means.'

'Are you coming tonight?' asked Hulme.

'No, thanks,' replied Cranswick. 'It's not my line, you know. But here's five bob for the kitty. Have a good time!'

It was usually the Skipper's job to arrange these outings for the ground crews, but Alec always handed over the task to Hulme or someone else in his crew. Other teetotal captains went out with their crews, but Cranswick always excused himself and spent the evening playing classical records in his room or roaming the fields and lanes of Huntingdon with his dog, Kluva. The crew respected their Skipper's desire to be excluded from these parties, and no one ever pressed him to change his mind. Invariably, Cranswick would hand over the five or six bob per head, which would pay for the night's drinks and then slip quietly away to the loneliness of his room and his radiogram, with Kluva bounding along at his side.

Cranswick's persistent refusal to get himself involved in even the mildest of drinking sessions meant that he escaped the more exuberant of the high-jinks parties in the Mess at Graveley. He never came noisily home from Huntingdon like some – bearing as a trophy a lavatory seat removed secretly yet nonetheless proudly from one of the more select hotels in the town. He was reserved and withdrawn, restrained almost to timidity. Privately, Cranswick must have felt out of place, but he expressed no craving to join in the rowdy antics and wild abandon of his colleagues.

When the squadron returned one night from a bombing operation, the crews found that the Mess was in the hands of the decorators. The sight of the ladders and pots of paint in the deserted room was too much for the flyers who were now seeking some way to unwind from the tension of the night's raid. They leapt upon the pots and scrambled up the ladders to paint every window in the Mess. Squadron Leaders, Flight Lieutenants, Flying Officers and the most junior Pilot Officers joined in the prank, but next morning, when calmed into a more reasonable frame of mind by a long sleep, everyone apologized and expressed a willingness to put right the trouble that had been caused by their thoughtlessness.

Cranswick found it difficult to enjoy such tomfoolery – nor did he derive pleasure from other Mess antics like flinging billiard balls through the windows, piling every stick of furniture in the room on top of a rug to form a bonfire, or heaping chairs and tables on top of each other and persuading someone to climb to the summit so that the whole edifice could be brought crashing to the floor with the crafty dislodging of the lower supports. These high-spirited displays may seem rather foolish now, but at the time they provided an essential outlet for young men living under a tension that was beyond the comprehension of an outsider.

Alec spent a lot of time tinkering about with motor cars when he was at Graveley. He had a car of his own and, when some trouble developed, he enlisted the aid of his gunner, Ivor Howard, who had worked in the motor trade before joining the RAF. The enthusiasm of these two men for cars was probably more instrumental than any other single factor in bringing them close together for a long and lasting friendship.

There was quite a craze for owning cars at Graveley at that time, and someone asked Cranswick if he could get one for him. Cranswick put the problem to Howard, with the result that in a builder's shed in Buckden they found and bought an apparently unserviceable Morris 10, which the two men pushed down to Howard's cottage. Repairs were then started to allow the car to be sold to Cranswick's prospective client. Howard, assisted by the less knowledgeable but equally enthusiastic Cranswick, took out the batteries, saved the acid and pitch, cut new plates to size with a rough pair of scissors and even made a blowlamp to help in their endeavours. The newly restored batteries seemed to turn out a first-class job. The two flyers put the cleaned and rejuvenated car behind Howard's own car and after a few anxious minutes the engine sprang suddenly into life. Then the car had to be run for a couple of hours on rationed petrol in order to charge the batteries. The car had cost the two men little more than the proverbial song, but Howard insisted they could not accept a penny less than £180 when reselling.

*Alec was a bit chicken at that figure* [Howard said afterwards], *so we decided on £150 and the deal was completed. The following morning the chap who bought it was on to Alec complaining bitterly that the car would not start. Alec was petrified. He visualised all sorts of trouble and came to me in quite a state to ask what we should do. I told him to tell the chap that all that was needed was for the batteries to be charged. The purchaser did as we suggested and went off a happy man, apparently highly delighted with the car.*

That was the beginning of a partnership and a succession of car deals that provided Alec Cranswick with a slightly adventurous outlet from the rigours of operational flying. It was perhaps the nearest he came to experiencing the tingle of excitement to be gained from an act of bravado, for the deals were occasionally laced with the element of surprise.

**The last formal portrait of Alec Cranswick, he is wearing his second medal ribbon, the DSO, which came in July 1943, in recognition of 'a very large number of sorties' and 'excellent and sustained efforts worthy of the highest praise'.** (Print belonging to the St Edward's School Archive and reproduced with their permission)

Each fresh purchase of an apparently unusable vehicle was a gamble; each business deal after rejuvenating the car was a challenge. The pilot and his gunner were contented men – and so, apparently, were their customers. They were fulfilling a demand from those without cars – but more importantly, perhaps, they were keeping their minds clear of the anxiety of further gruelling bombing missions that were still to come.

Squadron Leader Cranswick's façade as a quiet, rather shy, nonsmoker and non-drinker, lover of poetry and classical music, gave no hint of the valour he was continually displaying in the flak-spattered night skies over Europe. Yet appearances were so often violently deceptive in those times of stress when death rode with the bombers to claim the careful and the reckless, the timid and the bold. Cranswick was entirely alien to the more usual conception of a hero. In truth, however, bravery in the air stemmed from no set mould – for there has never been a pattern for courage.

In some measure there was recognition of his prowess in the award of a second medal – a DSO in July 1943, to add to the DFC awarded in April 1942. There came, too, a letter from Air Chief Marshal Sir Arthur Harris, Air Officer Commanding-in-Chief, Bomber Command, recording his warmest congratulations on the award of his DSO, the citation for which declared:

> This officer has taken part in a very large number of sorties, involving attacks on targets in Germany, occupied territory, Italy and in the Middle East. He has always pressed home his attacks with vigour, obtaining much success. His excellent and sustained efforts have been worthy of the highest praise.

A very large number of sorties.

It was already a formidable tally, indeed, but there was no stopping Cranswick. Each additional sortie brought new hazards; fresh perils to be surmounted in order to survive. Every mission became a further battle against the increasing weight of countless adversities. The flak was growing even fiercer, and the night-fighter force was gaining strength. Yet that was not all. Frequently the bombers had to combat another enemy of equal ferocity and with the power to smash an aircraft to bits. This unrelenting foe was the weather. When the skies became alive with the crash of thunder amid the heaving, lightning-seared storm clouds, that was the time a real pilot would prove his worth.

# Chapter 9

# Bull's Eyes out of the Sky

August Bank Holiday 1943: a pleasant enough day early on, which gave no hint of the savage change in the weather ahead. At Graveley, Cranswick had been along to the Flight Office, found he was down to fly and then gone to collect the two navigators, two gunners, the wireless operator and the flight engineer from their respective offices to get ready for the morning air test on their Halifax, *K-Katie*.

This was the customary forty-minute trip before lunch to check the aircraft, armament, radar and wireless equipment in readiness for the night's mission. Often the crews would hold a sweepstake on the likely meteorological forecast, but this time the weather looked too settled to arouse undue interest.

The air test and lunch now over, No. 35 Squadron crews rested during the afternoon, confined to camp as usual on security grounds so as to avoid the risk of anything leaking out about the preparations. They knew that, unless there was a surprise cancellation, the time was their own until the briefing session around 6 p.m. It was then that the target was revealed for the first time – Hamburg's massive Blohm and Voss aircraft works. Sitting at the stark wooden tables in the long, low briefing hut across the road from the Officers' and Sergeants' Mess, they listened intently to the met. forecast and instructions about the attack – the final blow of a devastating series of raids against the great port. In ten days and nights, Hamburg had reeled beneath an enormous tonnage of bombs, as many as had smashed down on London during the whole Luftwaffe batterings of 1940 and 1941. At one end of the permanently blacked-out and closely guarded room, white tape zigzagged across a huge map and disclosed the bombers' routes; after everyone else had gone, the navigators had to remain behind to receive their complex detailed orders about routeing, marking and bombing.

Meanwhile, Cranswick had gone back alone to his room. On these occasions, between the briefing and the take-off, he rather avoided company. He wanted nobody near him; he would isolate himself in the solitude of his room, playing some of his favourite pieces of music on the radiogram or composing a poem.

Nine o'clock came; Cranswick joined his brother officers in the Mess for the interminable operational supper of eggs, bacon and chips before picking up flying clothing and parachute and walking over slowly to the briefing room once more, where the crews were assembling. While the Medical Officer was doing his rounds, ensuring everyone was fit for flying and issuing tablets to anyone with a tendency to feel drowsy in the long night ahead, the gunners were drawing the rations – a flask of coffee apiece, slabs of milk chocolate, tinned fruit juice and malted milk tablets.

One of the gunners, returning without a tin opener, quipped: 'There's no opener again, chaps. You'll have to shove the can outside and let the flak knock a hole in it!'

The trucks were ready now to transport the crews out to the dispersal sites where the aircraft, fuelled and bombed up, were undergoing the final inspections at the hands of the fitters and armourers. It was gone 10 p.m. now, and the flyers, quiet but for an occasional exchange of banter with the ground crews, sat on the grass waiting for the word to enter the Halifaxes some thirty minutes before the time arranged for take-off. Then, led by Cranswick, his crew began filing aboard through the door low in the port side of the rear fuselage. The last man still smoking passed back the cigarette for each of the others to have a last puff before going inside the bomber. Almost a ritual, that last smoke.

Hulme, in his mid-thirties and comfortably chubby, usually experienced more difficulty than the others because of the bulky flying clothing and Mae West lifejacket, plus the fact that he had to struggle with his parachute and the awkward green satchel that contained his navigation documents. From inside the plane someone stretched out a gloved hand and a jocular voice boomed:

'Come on, Dad. Let me help you up.'

As the engines roared into life, one after the other until all four were warmed up and running perfectly, Ivor Howard picked his way down the fuselage into his tail gun turret and the mid-upper gunner settled himself into his position. The second pilot, Flying Officer Muller, a new man on the squadron, sat alongside Cranswick with the engineer standing between them. The other three, McRobbie and Hulme, plus the wireless operator, whose crew stations were all forward and below the pilots' compartment, always sat on the floor with their backs pressed against the main spar, knees up and feet braced against special supports; getting a bomb-laden thirty-ton Halifax off the runway was made easier if as much weight as possible was concentrated aft of the nose. At 500 feet, when these three men had moved into their normal flight positions, Cranswick adjusted the trim of his bomber and began climbing towards the east coast.

Even now there was no suggestion of any deterioration in the weather, but over the North Sea he felt his controls stiffening and he was finding difficulty in gaining height. The engineer, eyeing the gauges carefully in case the engines were giving trouble, was warned: 'I think we're icing. Get a torch and shine it on the wing for me, will you.'

There was immediate confirmation of Cranswick's fears. In the torchlight beam the leading edge of the wings glistened with a covering of ice. The speed dropped back as the coating of ice began creeping across the wings and over the whole plane, first tracing spiders' web patterns and then forming into dangerously thick layers that dragged down the struggling aircraft and threatened to freeze up the controls. The ice, too, was hampering the engines, and they began spitting and spluttering. *K-Katie* was in the grip of the most fearsome cloud formation that aviators can ever face – Cumulo-nimbus, the Flyers' Dread.

There were close on 750 bombers in the assault force, but, because the various squadrons were spread out over a large area of the North Sea, the extent to which each plane became involved in the storm depended on its placing in the flight plan. Some of the main force were lucky; Cranswick and the Pathfinders were far from fortunate. The 'cu-nimb' masses soared up to an anvil top at 25,000 feet, an impossible height for the aircraft to reach, but Cranswick had to keep trying to get up higher in the faint hope that the next 50 feet might take them clear of the storm cloud. For there was no means of telling just how high was the summit of the cloud, nor was there any method of estimating the lower limits except by dropping right down through it.

It required superhuman skill to save the giant bomber from being torn right out of the sky. As cool as the ice that he feared would choke the life from his strained engines, Cranswick maintained a cautious climb, waiting each moment for the slackening air speed and tell-tale signs of a stall from which there could be hardly a chance of surviving. He dared not dive to try and get down under the cloud, because the rising speed would increase the rate of icing. The struggling *K-Katie* might have parted with her two tons of high explosives, of course, but not when her pilot was Alec Cranswick. He was going on, onwards to Hamburg; onwards through that turbulent mass of cloud and the violent upward- and downward-sweeping currents from which there seemed no haven.

Ice was shooting off the tips of the propellers and spattering against the fuselage, with a noise like hailstones bombarding a window. The flying chips of ice were not sufficient to cause serious damage, but the efficiency of the propellers was greatly reduced – and that all added to the troubles of handling the plane. Ice also formed in the carburettors, cutting down the engine power and bringing with it a distinct possibility of total engine failure. Saint Elmo's Fire flickered around the propellers, too – a form of lightning that was rather alarming to those in the aircraft but rarely dangerous.

In the teeth of the storm, Cranswick's bomber stood out in startling relief against the brilliant, eerie flashes of sheet lightning bathing the clouds. Hail lashed against the cockpit, but Cranswick was oblivious to the clatter as the storm raged on with no signs of easing.

Over the intercom he ordered: 'Jettison all the ammunition. We've got to keep our height.'

And out of the flare chute aft of the mid-upper gun turret slid belt after belt of machine-gun bullets. The bomber was now defenceless if any night-fighter should come within shooting distance in the event of an improvement in the weather.

At his H2S set McRobbie was peering into the face of the cathode ray tube, the size of a tea saucer, and watching the islands off the North German coast forming with fascinating realism rather like an X-ray picture. From the clarity of the images of these islands it was hard to realize that layers of heavy storm clouds, thousands and thousands of feet thick, blanketed them. Trying to ignore the buffeting that the Halifax was receiving, McRobbie and Hulme kept supplying Cranswick with information to get him over Germany and then turning for their run across the dock area of Hamburg, which contained their special target.

The temptation to drop the bombs quickly and turn back to Britain must have been almost irresistible. With the aircraft lighter by a couple of tons, she would be easier to control in the grip of the storm. Cranswick felt he owed at least that to his crew. With the engines behaving erratically, *K-Katie* was plunging lower and lower and for once Cranswick was all for getting rid of the bombs as fast as he could in order to maintain a safe enough height to limp back to Britain; as captain of the aircraft he had the final say, but he also respected the opinions of those who had been flying with him so long.

McRobbie was ready for action at his bombsight and stretched out flat on his stomach on the floor of the nose. When he reported that Hamburg was only 5 miles away and urged that they must carry on, Cranswick decided to keep going and hang on to the two tons of high explosives that the Graveley armourers had hoisted aboard earlier in the evening.

McRobbie rapped out over the intercom: 'We've come this far, we'll deliver them. We'll drop the blasted things in a glide if we have to. We're losing height anyway.'

Cranswick, pulling almost every knob and handle in sight to coax the ice-choked, failing engines into some semblance of orderly operation, called out: 'This is it. Stand by to bale out. We'll have to go if the engines keep playing up like this.'

The crew fastened on their parachutes, waiting for the word to go, and Flying Officer Muller, the second pilot, opened the emergency escape door in the nose. By now all four engines had cut and the bomber was actually gliding towards their target. The only sound was the rushing wind and the flapping of Hulme's maps being whipped from his table and scattered about the nose by the slipstream. Muller, an instructor on Tiger Moths before joining Path Finder Force for his very first operational experience, clearly viewed with some alarm his prospects of completing a 60-ops tour, for he commented dryly: 'Sixty of these trips and I'll be finished completely!'

The stout-hearted McRobbie remained all this time stuck by his bombsight. From some 14,000 feet up, *K-Katie* had slumped down to about 9,000 feet and was still going down. But McRobbie, aware that Cranswick was doing his best to retain the unswerving run that would carry them over the Hamburg docks, swung his hand down across the bomb-selection panel at his side so that all the switches were now turned on for a simultaneous drop. He gripped the bomb release push, which resembled a bedside electric lamp switch on the end of a length of flex, and prepared to press the mechanism the moment the target slid into his sight.

But the engines stayed silent.

McRobbie saw a reddish tinge amid the clouds ahead and guessed that the plane must be almost through the cloud base. The red hue would be the flames ravaging Hamburg, set ablaze by the main force bombers, which had managed to avoid the worst of the storm. Such were the vagaries of the weather this August Bank Holiday night that the roles of the bombers had been reversed and someone else had lit a path for Pathfinder Cranswick. Muller's legs were dangling through the escape door and Howard was out of his tail turret, axe in hand, ready to smash his way through the fuselage side if Cranswick ordered the crew to quit the lumbering plane. Yet even now that might not be necessary. The drop in height during the silent glide had brought the Halifax out of the dangerous ice belt and the engines suddenly picked up in quick succession.

Cranswick yelled: 'Hold it! We're going to be all right.'

Helping Muller back inside, Leslie Hulme muttered: 'We nearly lost you that time!'

McRobbie pressed his switch and down screamed the bombs, the 1,000-pounder and the six 500-pounders, all at the same time, to create further destruction among the crippled and burning docks of Germany's second city. Freed of the lethal load, *K-Katie* shot up like a lift for a couple of hundred feet before roaring away for the coast.

The skill of Cranswick had got *K-Katie* to Hamburg; the dogged de-votion of McRobbie had put their cargo of devastation down smartly on the objective. Hulme had the homeward course ready for his pilot, and there was no time wasted in getting on to it. This was the stage, almost the only stage, when Cranswick would become the 'bus driver' and fly automatically, straight and level, until they were over the English coast.

Commenting on that raid later, Hulme said: 'I was never, ever worried with Cranswick. I had complete confidence in him.'

Only one in two of the bombers that had set out on that fateful trip reached Hamburg. Thirty failed to return – several of them falling victim to the savage, snarling storm clouds. Flying in those conditions was very different from bus driving, and the physical strain involved in heaving a four-engined, bomb-carrying plane was enormous. Even in more favourable circumstances a pilot soon became exhausted handling such a huge machine, because, apart from the first few miles from their base in Britain, the bombers had to be constantly weaving through the sky and changing direction at intervals, in order to stay out of the way of the enemy defences.

Some men chose to fly considerable distances on the automatic pilot – a device that can be set to keep the plane on a steady course without

the captain having to handle the controls all the time – but Cranswick
rarely took advantage of this aid for fear of leaving his bomber wide
open to fighter attack. He would use the automatic pilot on the closing
stages of the journey back to base, however, so as to reduce the strain.
An odd point about these return flights, incidentally, was that, although
the plane would usually be at a much lower altitude than on the way to
the target, everyone on board would feel much colder. They would start
shivering, too. It was all put down to the after-effects of the raid – the
same thing that would make them huddle round the fire when they got
back safely to camp, relieved that once more they had looked death
straight in the eye and cocked a snook.

A week after the drama over Hamburg, Cranswick's crew found themselves in a similar predicament when their plane, *P-Peter* this time,
suffered a dose of engine trouble at 17,000 feet near Luxembourg; they
were on their way to Mannheim under the now lengthening period of
darkness. First one engine failed, suffering from fuel starvation; then a
second engine cut completely. When one of the remaining two engines
began cutting spasmodically, the future was definitely none too bright.

Still 90 miles short of Mannheim, Cranswick ordered the bombs to be
dropped and warned the crew to prepare to jump. Lurching drunkenly
downwards, *P-Peter* had only one of the engines working properly with
the other three intermittently cutting out. Cranswick fought to keep the
bomber from plunging steeply away in a dive from which they might
never recover. At about 5,000 feet one of the faulty engines picked up
again to give enough flying speed to keep going and maintain height.

Ivor Howard, who once more had been ready to chop his way through
the fuselage and take to his parachute, explained: 'We had an understanding, Cranswick and I. He told me he would always hang on to the
last minute in case he could keep the aircraft flying. He said that the last
minute would not be any lower than 3,000 feet. We were pretty near that
height when he pulled us through on that occasion.'

It had been Cranswick's 86th bombing mission and the second in
succession during which he had had to battle for all he was worth to
maintain his plane in the air in the face of a critical situation; had he
failed to keep his head, there would have been little chance of the bomber
getting home to Britain. What worried him most, however, was that he
had had to waste his bombs.

The next time, he told himself, he would make up for the wasted effort. And that chance came over an almost unknown target called Peenemünde.

To score a bull's-eye in a game of darts the player must have a sharp eye to fix on the target, a firm stance from which to throw and a steady aim to speed the dart on its way.

Dropping a bomb on the bull's-eye of the target is not quite so easy.

In the bombing game one is dependent upon so much more, above all else on the accuracy of the instruments that help the bomb-aimer find the target area, the skill of the aimer in identifying the target correctly and the ability and nerve of the pilot to keep the plane on an even course in the face of enemy opposition.

The bombs will fall wide if the pilot fails to stick exactly to the aimer's direction instructions or if he jerks the plane about when an ack-ack shell bursts uncomfortably near. And, if the aimer tries to hurry the release of his bombs, the chances of hitting the target are much less. All in all, it is a very tricky business.

It was on 17 August 1943 that a powerful force of bombers was ordered to Peenemünde to carry out the heaviest moonlight attack on a German target so far that year.

Cranswick's own section of the target was given the code name: Aiming Point 'E'.

Peenemünde was Germany's largest and most important centre of its kind, specializing in aircraft, radar location and armament development and experiments that particularly concerned the V1 flying bomb and V2 rocket secret weapons programme.

It was because of the news of Germany's progress in their buzz-bomb and rocket programme filtering through to Intelligence sources in Britain that the Peenemünde raid was planned.

The Baltic coast establishment of Peenemünde consisted of buildings and assembly shops scattered and cunningly hidden among the woods along a strip of seashore $4\frac{1}{2}$ miles long by a little more than 1 mile wide – rather like a long, narrow finger, viewed from $2\frac{1}{2}$ miles up, where the Pathfinders were flying in the midst of stiff opposition from the ack-ack guns blasting away at what were the first raiders ever to fly against Peenemünde.

Aiming Point 'E', Cranswick's target, was centred upon the barracks area on the southern tip of the finger that was Peenemünde.

Ignoring the flak, Cranswick held the plane as steady as a rock while the bomb-aimer called out the instructions for the correct course throughout the bombing run towards Aiming Point 'E'.

Below the woods were black smudges and the barracks were little tiny lighter blobs interspersed among them.

Down went the target indicator from Cranswick's Halifax to blaze a brilliant green on which the bombers coming up behind were to release their high explosives. The natural impulse was to swerve hurriedly away the instant the run was ended, for that offered the best chance of avoiding the flak that usually became increasingly accurate the longer the bomber kept on a straight and level course. To do so, however, meant failing to secure photographic evidence of the positioning of the target indicator. It was necessary to stick rigidly to the same course and height for a while longer to give the indicator time to drop and for the bomber's camera to catch the moment of ignition. These extra, tense, dragging seconds were frequently the most nerve-racking of the whole raid, and the pilots, particularly, would find themselves drenched in sweat when at last they were free to break off the level run.

The nervous exhaustion was certainly worthwhile on this occasion, for, as Cranswick's target indicator burst into life, the camera recorded a beautiful example of target pinpointing. They had hit Aiming Point 'E' all right – a bull's-eye as nice as the Intelligence officers had seen for a long, long time.[1]

During the Peenemünde raid the Pathfinders had been employed in a rather different technique. The attack was split into successive phases, with each group tackling a separate section of the research establishment. Each phase was led by a Pathfinder, and the entire operation was under the control of a Pathfinder Master Bomber, Group Captain J. H. Searby, Commanding Officer of No. 83 Squadron, who won the DSO for what the citation described as 'executing his difficult task with consummate skill, displaying faultless leadership, great courage and resolution throughout the raid'.

Well over 1,500 tons of high explosives and incendiaries were dropped accurately within the area of Peenemünde – some of them from such a low level that the bombers were buffeted by the bursts of their own bombs. Buildings were gutted and fires gained such a firm hold that they were visible from the Danish coast. It was a masterpiece of pinpointing, for Peenemünde was not a huge and sprawling industrial area, but a comparatively tiny target where, for the raid to be successful, the bombs had to go down on specified groups of buildings. That the attack achieved its objective was another victory for Path Finder Force, which had led the way in each phase of the raid.

By now Cranswick's crew had a new plane, *L-Leather*, and on the side of the fuselage, just beneath the cockpit, one of the ground staff NCOs had painted Cranswick's family crest. There was an enormous amount of pride attached to having one's own aircraft, and whenever a Halifax

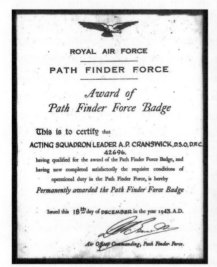

Certificate marking permanent award of the Path Finder Force Badge; and the Cranstoun family crest. (Author's Collection)

came to the squadron from the factory, there was keen competition for it. This was especially fierce if the Halifax had come off the production line of the works that had formerly made London's buses, for these had seats covered with green leather to give additional comfort and they also had superior riveting, which was reckoned to boost the airspeed by 10 or 15 knots.

After Peenemünde, Cranswick's crew were going from strength to strength in Pathfinding efficiency. So considerable was their success that, in the next raid, against Berlin on the night of 23–4 August 1943, they had the dubious privilege of being the first aircraft over the target: the leading planes over any target carried a heavy responsibility. The cardinal principle for the Pathfinders was never to drop the target indicators unless there was absolute certainty about the exact pinpointing of the target. If the Pathfinders erred and let their markers go on some green open fields miles away from the nearest signs of habitation, it was there and there only that the bombs would be sent crashing down. And the knowledge that some 700 aircraft had completely obliterated a huge chunk of German greenery simply because one had aimed badly would be understandably terrifying; one dared not even hazard the slightest guess at the dire reception that would await one on return to base.

However, fresh from the triumph of the Aiming Point 'E' bull's-eye at Peenemünde, Alec's crew were going to make darned sure that the right target was hit again this time – right slap on the nose once more.

Again there were those unnerving few minutes while the bomb-aimer instructed the pilot along the run-in and the crew hardly dared to breathe for fear of upsetting the gentle trim of the aircraft at this most critical time of the whole raid. Across Berlin, almost 4 miles up, droned their Halifax. McRobbie, carefully watching the aiming point drift into his sight, gave his instructions to Cranswick: 'Left, left – steady – bombs gone!'

In conjunction with those of his fellow Pathfinders, who were follow- ing the proven pattern of illuminating, finding and marking the objective in central Berlin, Cranswick's target indicators burned brightly – a cascading mass of tiny stars, almost like a dazzling waterfall of vivid colour when viewed from close quarters – and presenting an un- mistakable pointer for the main stream of bombers still a few minutes away from the capital. Some searchlights lazily probed the sky and presumably there were a few night-fighters around, too, but no one came embarrassingly close to Cranswick's bomber. The fighters pounced soon afterwards – in an ambush that claimed No. 35 Squadron's old CO, Group Captain Robinson, as one of the victims among the fifty-six planes that failed to get back home.

From way up there at 19,000 feet, the quickest way to avoid trouble now that the job was done was to go into a dive to get as far away as possible. The problem was that, if you dived too sharply, you might never pull safely out of the dive.

Cranswick's way round this danger was to have a piece of rope handy that he could tie onto the control stick so that another pair of willing hands could hang on and help to haul the great plane out of its earth- ward plunge. Now that the target was left behind, he had the rope fastened to the control column, and the flight engineer took tight hold of the other end. At the word of command – 'Heave!' – the engineer would heave for all he was worth to augment Cranswick's frantic efforts to pull back the stick and bring *L-Leather* out of her hell-for-leather dive.

It was a deliberate manœuvre on Cranswick's part to swoop away from the target after a bombing run, but on this occasion, flying considerably higher than usual, the wings were fairly creaking from the strain as the Halifax went down, down, down ...

'If the wings don't drop off now,' Cranswick shouted, 'they jolly well ought to!'

They were only some 5,000 feet up now and shooting across towards Denmark with all haste as the bomber shuddered and groaned to level out rather shakily after the screaming dive. They were saved – by a piece of rope.

The return trip was uneventful from that point on, and when the photos were developed back at Graveley the sight was enough to delight the most critical eyes. There was the marker right in the middle of the aiming point. The achievement was all the more important because this particular assault on the German capital was the heaviest up to that time. Some 330 Lancasters, 250 Halifaxes and 120 Stirlings had thundered through the sky, their throbbing engines shaking the heavens and their bomb bays bulging with 1,200 tons of high explosives and fire-bombs. It was also one of the most concentrated raids carried out by Bomber Command – the attack was all over in fifty minutes. The weight of bombs was roughly twice that dropped in the most severe blasting of Berlin previously on 27 March, and about eighty times as much as was dropped in Berlin's first raid of all three years earlier, almost to the night. A day or two later Cranswick's crew received a personal letter of congratulation and commendation on their Berlin target-marking from no less a person than Air Chief Marshal Sir Arthur Harris, Bomber Command's boss. It was framed and hung proudly over the dressing table in Cranswick's quarters at Graveley – a tribute to the proficiency of the bomber crew he was leading and a reminder of his ninetieth mission against the enemy. It was his fourth crack against the capital of the Reich.

By now the nights were growing longer and the bomber offensive was being stepped up still further. Every few evenings Cranswick's crew was out in the spearhead of the attacks: Nurnberg; Berlin again; Modane – the frontier town at the northern end of the Mont Cenis tunnel linking France with Italy; Mannheim; and Kassel.

Their bomber did not always return unscathed. Alec hated to have his plane tattered and torn; a scar was still a scar, however honourably received. He recalled those ugly duelling scars on the faces of all too many students at German universities in pre-war days. And he thought, too, of the scars left now on the face of many of Europe's finest cities as a result of the bombing deluge. Yet such was the price of war, and bombing was his job.

Over Nurnberg, for instance, roaring through a seething curtain of ack-ack fire, red-hot fragments smashed into the starboard inner engine and shattered one of the propeller blades. The crew thought a cannon shell from a night-fighter had hit them and exploded. Cranswick switched off the damaged engine and flew home on the remaining three. The Halifax was not the easiest of planes to land on three engines, however, so he cautiously switched on again when he saw the Graveley beacon flashing out a welcoming message and he found there was enough power left for him to effect a satisfactory touch-down. He made a habit of taking the return flight rather sedately, so as to avoid having to join the general melee over Graveley of queuing bombers circling over and over again until their turn came to land. Cranswick was often kidded about his comparatively leisurely journey home, because this effected quite a saving on petrol and the wags would chide him:

'What are you up to, then? Anybody would think you had to use your own petrol coupons and pay the bill yourself!'

The personal strain was mounting with every raid. At the thirtieth Pathfinder op from Graveley he knew that, unless he could do a wangle, he would fall due for a compulsory rest. That thirtieth mission with Path Finder Force was against Frankfurt on 4 October 1943. It would bring his personal score up to ninety-six and he badly wanted to get his century.

The plane was *L-Leather* again, the one he had flown for the previous eight ops. He was thinking of this particular Halifax as '*L-Lucky*'. It had brought bull's-eyes on Peenemünde and Berlin, survived a number of maulings from flak and treated him well in that death-defying dive from close on 4 miles up over Berlin. Surely he would be all right this time?

He was quiet during the trip. It was the RAF's first big attack there and came less than twelve hours after a daylight blasting from American Fortresses and Liberators. Thick cloud hid the raiders until some 50 or so miles off the city. Then, as the bombers came out into clear sky, a massive belt of searchlights stretched for miles across the area. But Cranswick had seen all this many times before. First there were the lights and then the flak barrage. Then the gunfire would die out so that the fighters could close in for the attack.

The concentration needed over the target area was so intense that he had no time for wayward brooding thoughts of being grounded, of flying a desk instead of his beloved bomber, but the long, lonely trek back to Graveley allowed plenty of scope for silent meditation.

Soon the Halifax was over its base, unscathed by the fury of the flak and the fighters, and Alec let down the wheels for the landing. There was the familiar bump as the tyres touched and screeched momentarily on the concrete runway, and *L-Leather* was home – again she had proved to be '*L-Lucky*'. For once in his life Cranswick was close to tears.

Leslie Hulme still had five more trips to make to complete his operational tour of forty-five missions, however, and Cranswick anticipated he might use this fact as a lever to keep on flying. He told Hulme when they got back: 'I think they'll let me get my century and then I can do an extra one to see you through to the finish. I'd hate you to do them with anyone else after we've been together for so long.'

In the Officers' Mess, Hulme mentioned this arrangement to the Squadron Commander, Wing Commander 'Dixie' Dean, and came away convinced that there would not be any objections.

A little later, however, Dean broke the news to Hulme: 'I'm afraid that won't now be possible. Group Headquarters say that Cranswick must rest. You can do your remaining five when you like and with whoever you like.'

And that was quite final.

What sort of a man had Alec Cranswick become after three bombing tours? Paul Blagrove, his old school chum, who was an officer in the Royal Tank Corps and home from an arduous spell of duty in the Western Desert, judged him to be as nervous as a kitten. He was jittery; he was fidgety.

Bluntly, Blagrove warned him that he was a liability to the rest of the crew. He cracked down heavily on Cranswick, snapping that he did not have only himself to worry about when he was flying his bomber. He was holding in his hands the lives of five or six men each time. Blagrove told him he must stop thinking about himself and spare some thoughts for the men in his crew. Alec's answer was that he was as right as rain when he was in the air.

Certainly Cranswick's operational record supported the plea that he was coolly efficient, fast-thinking and resolute in his intentions when he was flying his bomber.

In his talks with Paul Blagrove, Cranswick admitted that he experienced fear when he was taking part in a raid. It was a strange kind of

fear. He was not so much frightened for himself as frightened that he
might be letting down other people. It seemed to Blagrove that this
particular sort of fear was really Alec's guiding spirit. He was so scared
that his comrades might think him frightened that he would purposely
carry out actions that he would not have considered in less pressing
circumstances. Cranswick was not being reckless; he was merely driving
himself further than the normal limit. He was forcing himself into
accomplishing deeds of bravery rather than have people stamp him as a
frightened flyer.

With ninety-six operational missions behind him, Squadron Leader
Cranswick had more than proved his point. Statistically he was ahead of
the whole field, outstripping by far the majority of these airborne jockeys
who rode the heavy bombers over the many hurdles to enemy targets
and back home again to their stables in Britain. If we take into account
the odds-on survival for bombing crews, Alec's dogged enthusiasm had
put him into an unenviable situation. He lived for flying and, as he told
his chum Paul Blagrove, he found peace of mind only when he was in
the air. He could not bear to pursue any other function than that of a
bomber pilot, yet he was forced to concede that he had overrun his time.
Cranswick's mother had been begging Paul Blagrove to appeal to him to
quit flying. The two friends had been separated by their respective service
overseas, and Mrs Cranswick fondly hoped that the resumption of their
close contact might provide a chance for Paul to steer her son away from
wanting to continue operational flying. It was a forlorn hope.

Alec answered simply: 'The only time I have peace of mind is when
I'm flying. I can't stop now.'

Cranswick's obstinate refusal to heed the plea came as no surprise to
Paul. They had been close friends since their schooldays at New College
Preparatory School, Oxford, when Alec was 8 and Paul was 10.
Cranswick could never be easily swayed.

Alec was fully aware that every time he took a bomber over enemy
territory he was carrying a cargo of potential death. He hated killing; he
was appalled at anyone suffering. He used to say about bombing: 'What
a stupid way of killing people! It is all so futile.'

With Path Finder Force, however, Alec viewed his war work in a
different way – he was engaged more in lighting the way for others to do
the killing that he knew could not be avoided as long as Nazism ruled
Germany. Even so, he would not be budged when Blagrove urged him to
consider calling a halt.

Inevitably Alec Cranswick was accused of being a medal-hunter. The jibe was tossed in his face, or behind his back, as his personal tally of ops grew more and more impressive and he graduated to the position where he held what was considered on the squadron to be the operational record for a heavy bomber pilot. Yet Cranswick reasoned that he was only doing his job. He would fly whenever he was called upon to do so; he never argued, even though there were times when he could have dodged out of some of the raids.

There were others who were more forthright, however, and once Cranswick found himself in an unfortunate and painful situation; a member of his own crew refused to fly. The crew had been engaged in a protracted series of bombing trips crammed into the space of only a few nights, and during the briefing for yet another raid one of Cranswick's gunners went up to the squadron commander and announced that he did not intend to fly that night. He pleaded that the whole crew was unusually fatigued because of the number of operations that had been sandwiched into the past few nights. They had had insufficient rest, claimed the gunner. Cranswick, astonished by what he was hearing, maintained an embarrassed silence. The threatened refusal to fly made the crew member, a young officer, liable for a court-martial, yet he was prepared to face such proceedings rather than prejudice the lives of the crew through taking part in an attack when he sincerely believed that he was too tired to be able to do his work properly.

No such thought of rebellion had entered Squadron Leader Cranswick's head, although he was clearly under the same strain. He was prepared to carry out the order with complete obedience until he dropped; he simply took the view that he had been told to fly – so fly he must. Fortunately there was no court-martial after all. The raid was cancelled and the awkward incident faded into a forgotten past.

Cranswick was convinced that each fresh mission he flew was one step nearer the end of the war. Leslie Hulme, the navigator, discounted any suggestion of gong-hunting and contended that sheer patriotism kept Cranswick flying.

'He had an intense hatred of the Germans. He loathed them. He was incensed over their treatment of the Jews. He thought it was the end of the world that people should be gassed for their religious beliefs. He regarded the whole Nazi regime as something wicked,' declared Hulme.

Even Hulme's completely plausible explanation drew critics who were quick to pose the question: 'Why commit suicide yourself as a gesture against mass-murder?' For by flying as much as Cranswick was doing, he was virtually on the way to committing suicide on account of the odds on survival that were piling heavier and heavier against him.

Alec and the older Hulme had the opportunity for many talks together, and these gave the navigator a clearer glimpse into his Skipper's thoughts. He decided that Cranswick's achievements in war were accomplished to give him a substantial grounding in peace. He assessed the young squadron leader not as a show-off – indeed, he was quite the opposite – but as a person striving whole-heartedly to amass all the flying experience that was possible in order to ensure himself a suitable post in civil aviation after the war. Cranswick believed that, the harder he drove himself and the more flying hours he could show in his logbook, the better would be the job he hoped might be waiting for him when he could put aside his RAF uniform and join one of the airlines for the peace time career that he was thinking about.

Another remarkable member of Path Finder Force whose logbook was filling steadily was Wing Commander J. C. MacGown, MD, Ch.B., Senior Medical Officer of No. 8 (Path Finder Force) Group, whose love of flying was equalled only by his devotion to his career in medicine, which he had begun shortly before the outbreak of the First World War.

John MacGown enlisted in the Royal Flying Corps and trained to be a pilot. When he won his wings, he joined No. 41 Squadron, and, while flying single-seater de Havilland fighters on the Western Front, he brought down two enemy aircraft. Amid the rigours of war, strapped into the little open cockpit of the de Havilland that sent the wind whipping roses into the cheeks and a tingle of exhilaration bubbling through the whole body, Doc MacGown first tasted the excitement of flying that never faded with the passage of the years.

He resumed his medical studies when the war was over and qualified as a doctor of medicine in 1922. The following year he went out to Hong Kong and, as a member of the Volunteer Defence Air Squadron, he put in several hundred hours in the air. Three years before the start of the Second World War, Dr MacGown returned to Britain, and in 1939 he joined the RAF Volunteer Reserve Medical Branch as an ophthalmic surgeon.

He made a study of night vision in the air and soon realized that to see an object clearly in the darkness meant looking at the object sideways instead of directly at it. The discovery became particularly useful for the Allied night-fighter crews. As the war progressed, Doc MacGown developed a system of night vision training, and for a time he was in charge of an RAF school to teach bomber personnel how best to see in the dark. Besides his ophthalmic qualifications, and the experience of some 2,000 hours as a pilot, Dr MacGown was a skilled navigator, so that, when Path Finder Force was formed, RAF Bomber Command had little hesitation in deciding he was the person best suited to fill the post of Senior Medical Officer. Among other requirements, Pathfinder crews were expected to have a very high standard of night vision and navigation, so someone with Doc MacGown's combined medical and aeronautical capabilities was obviously going to be a wonderful asset to the Force.

There was already quite enough routine work for him to do at Path Finder Force Headquarters and on the various airfields connected with the Group, but Wing Commander MacGown refused to be content with carrying out only these duties. He always had to learn what conditions were like on night bombing operations at second hand; he could talk to the crews and he could see films and photographs brought back after the Pathfinder missions, but this was not enough. There was only one really adequate way of gaining a sound appreciation of the complex variety of optical problems facing the night raiders – and that was to go on a bombing mission himself with one of the Pathfinder squadrons.

He wanted to experience personally the effects of dazzle and glare from the flares and target markers dropped by the PFF bombers and to judge for himself the way that various landmarks stood out in the darkness many thousands of feet beneath the spearhead force's aircraft searching for their aiming points.

So Dr MacGown, a familiar figure with greying hair – for he was in his late forties and twice the age of most of the flying personnel – received permission to fly in one of the aircraft detailed for an attack on the submarine base at Saint-Nazaire. From the point of view of operational hazards the trip was fairly uneventful, but regarding the real purpose of the flight he came back with some worthwhile knowledge that was to prove useful in his programme of optical research.

Wing Commander MacGown did not stop at that one trip. He went on to carry out a total of fifty-two operational flights, accompanying crews from each one of the Path Finder Force squadrons and normally joining them in the role of second pilot or assistant flight engineer. He chose his flights for the usefulness of the medical information he expected to gain on the way to, and over, the chosen target.

There was never any question of shirking the targets where exceptional dangers were likely. Doc MacGown flew on some of the longest and most difficult Pathfinder missions – among them those to Berlin and the famous Peenemünde rocket research station assault – as well as on some where the RAF losses were exceptionally heavy.

His own ability as a navigator was a great help in one aspect of his work, for he could tell the crews the landmarks to watch and then, while flying over them, check just what could be seen of these guiding points. Sometimes a crew might have difficulty in spotting the target, so the doctor had an opportunity on his return to tell them where they had gone wrong.

The Pathfinder bomber boys had tremendous respect and admiration for their Flying Doctor. It would have been so easy for him to sit tight and do only his own optical studies on each operational flight, but he consistently took his turn at the irksome job of keeping watch for enemy attacks. Once over Nurnberg the doctor's bomber was caught in the searchlights while he was standing in the astrodome looking out for night-fighters. He kept up a competent non-stop spate of instructions, telling his pilot how to evade the defences, and each change of direction that the doctor ordered was obeyed instantly and without question. Back at base, Doc MacGown said to the pilot: 'So you heard my instructions, then?'

The pilot looked puzzled – 'I didn't hear a thing!' he answered.

The pilot had been under such immense strain and tension while taking the evasive action that he had acted entirely subconsciously on every order so that he had to admit when the plane was safely home that he had not the slightest recollection of hearing a single word from his spotter, Doc MacGown.

Wing Commander MacGown, who received a DFC from King George VI for going on these bombing trips, which were clearly far beyond the normal limit of his duties as a doctor, always spoke highly of the way that the Pathfinder crews stood up to their exceptionally dangerous tasks. Occasionally there was a weak man, but generally the rest of the crew would be able to help him recover the lost confidence and so master his nerves.

The conclusion of this chapter of unusual courage in the pursuit of medical knowledge came while flying over Germany with one of No. 35 Squadron's pilots, Squadron Leader Danny Everett – a mission for which the young pilot gained his third DFC within fourteen months for gallantry and devotion to duty. Everett, in the role of Master Bomber, was in a head-on collision with another plane while making his first run over the target.

Danny Everett had had a good deal of ill-luck in the air. Once an incendiary bomb released from another aircraft on a bombing run dropped straight through the fuselage of his Lancaster during a night attack. It left gaping holes in the top and bottom, but fortunately did not ignite. A few nights later there was a similar incident, only this time the bomb was a high-explosive. Although this also did not explode, it sliced off the end of the fuselage, and the rear gunner fell with the smashed turret.

On the occasion when Doc MacGown was aboard, Everett lost a 4-foot section of the starboard wing when it was sheared off in the head-on crash. At the same time the starboard inner engine burst into flames, and the plane plunged momentarily out of control. Cool as ever, Everett managed to resume level flight and feathered the propeller of the burning engine. Although the flames were quelled, he could not tell how badly his plane was damaged. Despite this handicap and with one engine useless, Squadron Leader Everett made several further runs over the target. Only when he was perfectly satisfied that the operation had proved a success did he make for home.

Wing Commander Bill Bromley, who became one of the Flight Commanders of No. 35 Squadron, said of Everett:

*He was one of a very few people who didn't seem to turn a hair when he was on ops. He had the right temperament and he probably loved it. He was a most likeable chap and he had done a hell of a lot of ops. One night we were having a drink together and I suggested he had done enough bombing trips and might well have a non-operational spell. He became quite umbraged. He said: 'Why? My nerve is perfectly all right. I know it gets a lot of people down but it is not getting me down. I'm perfectly all right.' He liked to have a few drinks and a game of darts for his relaxation – it gave him an uplift to help forget about bombing for a while. Very often bravery and courage come from the men who are really frightened. The man who is scared stiff and still hangs on has a lot more courage in my opinion than the chap who sits there without realising he is sticking his neck out.*

Alec Cranswick's own brand of bravery was perhaps rather like that shown by Everett. Cranswick well knew the feeling of fear, but he reckoned on having acclimatized himself to the more normal conditions of operational stress by using his almost overpowering love of flying as an umbrella against acknowledging the existence of danger. A pilot from the start of war, Cranswick saw no reason why he should not finish it in the cockpit of a plane. Bombing was his job and staying alive was a most important means towards that end. It was an art to be mastered.

Although he was a dashing figure, tall and slim, well groomed and imposing in appearance, Cranswick came to be known as 'the Flying Tramp'.

The title gave the complete lie to Alec's normally impeccable air even when in moments of welcome relaxation he lapsed into boyish informality so that his hat would stray towards the back of his head and his hands would fidget to be thrust casually into his uniform trouser pockets. The style of dress that brought him recognition as the Flying Tramp was never seen away from the airfield; it was reserved for special occasions – those times when he would be shepherding his crew into a bomber to go winging across the Continent. It was, in fact, Alec's bombing uniform – the clothes he wore whenever he flew on a raid – that earned Cranswick the title that was so out of keeping with his usual character.

Alec had an absolute horror of becoming an enemy captive. His one driving purpose in the RAF was to do his utmost to bring about a speedy end to the war. He thought that could be best achieved by flying as often as possible and with the maximum efficiency. Now, if he should fall into enemy hands, he would be of no further use as a bomber captain. He must, therefore, take active steps to ensure he never became a prisoner.

Every trip that he made over the Continent laid him open to capture, of course. If he should have to bale out over enemy-occupied territory, Alec was at least going to be equipped to dodge capture from the very outset. The essence of the escape game was never to be caught at all. Two friends from his own squadron, Carter and Sale, had both successfully evaded being taken prisoner when their planes went down the first time, and Cranswick was determined to try equally enthusiastically to get back to Britain if his bomber was hit over the Continent.

Cranswick considered that he required a combination of four aids: one, reasonable fluency in the continental languages; two, some adequate form of disguise; three, an ability to find his way from place to place; and, four, a fair share of luck. He could not do very much about the luck, but he could make quite sure of the other points.

First, languages – both at school and from the students staying with his mother, Alec had acquired a working knowledge of French and German and formed a lesser acquaintance with Dutch. He had spoken them all on pre-war visits to the Continent and once he had even addressed a German school in their own language. Disguise? – he would have to wear some sort of civilian clothing, for the RAF flying kit was a dead giveaway to the enemy. As far as getting from place to place was concerned, he had to make sure that he had a compass and that he had maps covering the particular portion of the Continent where he landed. With a great deal of careful thought, Alec reckoned on being suitably prepared before too many raids had taken place.

It was the outcome of these deliberations that was to gain him the title of 'the Flying Tramp'.

The disguise was comparatively easy. Beneath his flying suit Alec decided to wear crumpled old civvies – underclothes, shirt, jumper and trousers; he would have to take a chance on being shot as a spy if the Jerries picked him up. A beret was an almost indispensable item of dress in Western Europe – at least among the class of people with whom he was likely to come into contact as he furtively crossed the hostile countryside – so he knew he must have one of those; so much for the disguise.

Obviously he could have no idea whereabouts he was going to land if he should be shot down, so he would require an almost unwieldy collection of maps to be fully prepared for a cross-continental hike. He might be in a position to cut down the amount of maps slightly by adjusting his requirements to suit the geographical location of each particular night's target. However, Alec was still going to be faced with the necessity to carry a cumbersome bundle of maps. They had to be placed where he could reach them when the time came to jump for his life from the plane, so he chose to keep them in a rather battered black box. This he could fasten to his parachute harness by means of a piece of rope strong enough to prevent the box snapping free when he baled out. In the box, too, Alec would be able to store his iron rations to keep him going until there was food available for him. Newcomers to the crew called it his Mystery Box.

He did not believe in keeping all his maps in one place. He also had some special maps on silk, which he had stitched into his flying helmet, his trousers and his jacket; he reckoned that ought to be enough.

Cranswick believed in doing a thorough job. He was going to make quite sure he never got himself lost; he must obviously carry a compass if the maps were to be put to use with the minimum waste of time and accuracy. Hidden compasses were normal issue for aircrew for use in an escape, but, as Cranswick wanted to be really sure he was never without one, he arranged to equip himself with several extra ones. He had one behind his pilot's wings and another in a tunic button – these were on the uniform jacket he sometimes wore when flying. He had another inside a comb and another in a pipe – a pipe he carried with him on ops for just this purpose, although he never smoked. A further compass was hidden in a seam in his trousers. Alec Cranswick was almost a walking direction-finder.

With his rough clothes and the beret, Alec could be said to justify the description of a flying tramp. For good measure he added a knife, slipped down inside one of his socks. There were plenty of good uses for a knife when a man was on the run – in the last resort, perhaps, it would come in handy for a killing, if that had to be done. One more item was carried by Cranswick on ops. It was a revolver. If he was ever caught in a tight spot while escaping, he swore to use that revolver.

Alec Cranswick knew it was his duty to try to avoid capture if he should be shot down over enemy territory, but as the months slipped past that was not his only reason for carrying such an extraordinarily complete escape kit.

For, with his posting away from Graveley at the conclusion of his third operational tour, Squadron Leader Cranswick discovered a new reason for living.

Chapter 10

# Pathway to Romance

However violently Alec Cranswick hated leaving No. 35 Squadron for No. 8 (Path Finder Force) Group Headquarters at Huntingdon, he had to concede later that there was a bright side to his enforced six-month rest from operational flying. It was there, among the teleprinters chattering out code messages to the Pathfinder squadrons, that Alec found romance.

When the orders for the move came through, Alec took up his ruler, pens and bottles of blue and red ink and compiled in his flying logbook a statistical summary of his experience as a bomber pilot. The figures were remarkable for he had survived no less than 96 operational missions totalling 606 hours 30 minutes' flying time – only a little less than half of the entire length of time he had spent at the controls of a plane since he first learned to fly at Desford in July 1939. His grand total now stood at 1,323 hours as first pilot or second pilot in single-engined and multi-engined aircraft.

After the Frankfurt raid of 4 October 1943, which was his thirtieth with Path Finder Force, Alec made only one flight before moving to PFF Headquarters. It was a fifteen-minute air test on one of the new Halifax Mark IIIs with Air Commodore Donald Bennett, founder and leader of Pathfinders, sharing the controls. They were in a privileged position, for the first production Halifax III had made its maiden flight little more than a month earlier. It was the first of the Halifaxes to change from Merlin engines to Hercules radials, which gave a higher performance. There was another noticeable contrast, in that later production Mark IIIs had their wings increased from 98 feet 8 inches to 104 feet with the introduction of rounded tips.

Alec pestered to be retained on operational flying – he could not see why he should be compelled to stay on the ground when there were bombers for him to fly against Germany.

In that damp, foggy October the thoughts of many people were turning to the cessation of hostilities. Mr Geoffrey Lloyd, MP, declared that everyone was agreed that the first priority was to win the war quickly, and he suggested Britain's next priority should be to arrange to get our living as a nation in the post-war world. While Cranswick was in the midst of preparations to leave the bomber base at Graveley, there came a report that looked fairly and squarely at the end of the world fighting. It was the recommendation for a points scheme to determine priorities for the demobilization of men from the Forces after the war.

These were encouraging views, but the war was still to be won. News was reaching London of more Dutchmen facing trial for sabotage and resistance activities. German opposition was stiffening along the battlefront in Italy. London was again under attack from the Luftwaffe, although the weight of the assault was pathetic when compared with the fresh peaks of intensity that RAF Bomber Command and the United States Eighth Air Force were marshalling against targets as far away as Danzig and Gdynia.

The Prime Minister passed on the War Cabinet's congratulations to bomber chief Sir Arthur Harris, saying that these growing successes had been achieved only by the devotion, endurance and courage for which Bomber Command was renowned. His message went on: 'Airmen and airwomen of Britain, the Dominions and our allies, have worked wholeheartedly together to perfect the mighty offensive weapon which you wield in a battle watched by the world.'

One vital component of that mighty offensive weapon was Path Finder Force with headquarters in the market town of Huntingdon, to which Squadron Leader Cranswick was now appointed as a member of the Air Staff. He was to assist in the planning of the raids, carrying out his duties in the Operations Room at a time when preparations were in hand for launching the Battle of Berlin. This was due to open shortly after the existence of the fire-raising Path Finder Force was made public on a singularly appropriate day, 5 November, Guy Fawkes' Day. With Bomber Command's striking power at least a dozen times as strong as at the outbreak of war, Path Finder Force proved its worth over and over again and made the bombers largely independent of the weather. The Air Minister, Sir Archibald Sinclair, pronounced in a vigorous speech: 'We

shall continue to hammer the enemy from the skies till we have paralysed
their war industries, disrupted their transport system, and broken their
will to war. Then, at last, the road will lie open to Berlin.'

The PFF squadrons themselves were all set to pave the way along the
aerial road to Berlin.

Many of the bombing plan details from PFF Headquarters were
circulated in code on teleprinters linked with the squadrons comprising
the group – No. 8 Group in Bomber Command. Among the skilled team
of nimble-fingered operators was a blonde WAAF, Leading Aircraftwoman Val Parr, a girl of 21 from North London who had been at Headquarters for about a year. Soon after Cranswick had joined the
Headquarters staff he was introduced to her by another WAAF whom
he had already met there in the course of his work.

The next night Alec took the two girls to the cinema. In those moments
for frank assessment when she was alone after the cinema visit, Val came
to the decision that she did not like him very much. It was difficult to find
a reason, so she chose to reserve final judgement until after another
meeting with him, if such a chance came along. There was, after all, a
second meeting. Then came a third; and a fourth. The friendship of Alec
and Val was strengthening with every evening spent in each other's
company.

Inevitably there were instances of friction between them.

He hated her in uniform, and he did not like her to wear make-up; he
loathed lipstick. These annoying trifles were first the fuel to kindle minor
squabbles, but then ways were found to quell these irritations. Officially
barred from wearing civilian clothes by regulations, Val took to leaving
her ordinary clothes in a nearby grocery shop, and she changed out of
her uniform in a back room there whenever she had a date with Alec. In
a town as compact as Huntingdon, there were numerous occasions when
Val must have been recognized by WAAF officers from Headquarters,
who were normally particularly strict on the rules. Much to Val's surprise,
she was never once pulled up for being in plain clothes. The officers
sympathized with the turbulent paths of wartime love and continually
turned a blind eye.

On camp she had to wear her long hair scruffed up beneath her
Service cap, and this also upset Alec, so that when he met her he used to
pull out the pins and allow the hair to tumble freely down her back.

She always waited for him outside a side gate of the Headquarters,
known to the girls working there as the Concentration Camp. The only

time she wore lipstick was when he was late. The longer she had to wait, the more thickly she put on her lipstick. He could not be blamed for his late arrival, for the Battle of Berlin was about to be opened by Bomber Command, and Path Finder Force's nerve centre was becoming a particularly busy spot.

This assault on the German capital opened on the night of 18–19 November 1943, when a new record was established with the mounting of two major raids simultaneously. In one terrifying half-hour more than 350 two-ton blockbuster bombs sledge-hammered Berlin, while a second smaller force of RAF planes struck against Mannheim-Ludwigshafen.

For the next four months Berlin was to wilt beneath sixteen major attacks from Bomber Command, when as many as a thousand aircraft in a night blasted the city with high explosives and showered down fire bombs in their thousands, which sent walls of flame raging unchecked across vast districts with monster palls of black smoke pluming 4 miles high. In that time more than 28,000 tons of bombs thundered down upon the Nazi citadel in a spate of crushing blows largely inflicted in dreadful weather when crews had to bomb through unbroken cloud with nothing to guide them but the Pathfinders' skymarker flares.

With such complete reliance upon the skill of the Pathfinders for a successful raid, planning for all these operations had to be done with exaggerated care based on a combination of practical experience and theoretical judgement. For these reasons a selected nucleus of operation-ally qualified pilots such as Cranswick were drawn from the PFF squad-rons from time to time to join the Headquarters Air Staff. Cranswick himself had been over Berlin five times – on the last two occasions as a Pathfinder.

In one spell in November 1943, RAF bombers pounded Berlin on five consecutive nights with 5,000 tons of explosives.[1] In the vanguard of the assaults flew seasoned Pathfinder crews fulfilling their role with complete thoroughness and refusing to allow anything to prevent them from illuminating the target area throughout the length of the Main Force's stay over the crumbling, burning city. Light ack-ack guns peppered the falling flares, but the Pathfinders' controllers merely ordered in their backer-up planes to replenish the fading markers on which the bombers were to aim. About 300 aircraft were lost during the Battle of Berlin – a rate of some $6\frac{1}{2}$ per cent – but the Pathfinders themselves suffered a percentage of loss on one occasion that was twice as heavy.

During that winter of 1943–4 a new instrument of air warfare was forged when the Tactical Air Force entered the field of aerial operations in Europe as a weapon to support the invasion scheduled for 1944. Fighters, fighter-bombers and medium bombers were drawn into the force with the prime intention of softening Germany's coastal defences and then providing close cover for the Allied land forces.

By now the plans for the invasion of Europe were well ahead. Now, too, Alec Cranswick had plans of his own – plans far removed from activities of war. Alec and Val's friendship had been blossoming into romance in their few leisure hours away from the Ops Room and the Signals Section where the couple were engaged on their respective commitments for PFF. It was on Christmas Eve 1943 that he saw his hopes fulfilled.

They both succeeded in getting leave over Christmas, so Alec took Val across to Oxford to meet his mother. Alec delighted in teasing her, and he proceeded to build up an alarming picture of his mother.

'She is a terrible ogre who will pull you to pieces. Probably she'll hate the sight of you,' warned an apparently serious Alec, his eyes revealing not the slightest hint to contradict the dead-pan look on his face.

She paused with apprehension on the threshold of the Cranswick home in Polstead Road, Oxford.[2]

*I knew I was not the first girl Alec had taken home, so I fully expected his mother to give me an old-fashioned glance. I was absolutely horrified – petrified! He bounded up the steps to the front door and sang out 'M-O-T-H-E-R' at the top of his voice. When she came into the hall I realised at once that Alec had been kidding me. She was no ogre – she was as sweet as anything.*

He cooked Val an enormous omelette for supper and then led her hand in hand down into his den in the basement of the house. The couple had spent some little time talking there together when suddenly Alec strode over towards the door leaving Val still in her chair. The lights went out and a startled Val cried out: 'Hi! What do you think you are doing?'

'I've got a surprise for you.'

Bending down, the young pilot took a gentle hold of Val's left hand and without a word slipped a three-stone diamond engagement ring onto the third finger. They sealed their engagement with a kiss before going upstairs to break the news to Alec's mother. For a short while the war was wiped clear from their thoughts by the happiness of the moment and contemplation of their joint future.

The engagement came almost as much of a surprise to Val herself as to Alec's mother. She had realized their engagement was imminent, but Alec had not mentioned anything about buying the ring.

By the time the couple returned to Huntingdon, the names had been announced of the senior Allied officers to take charge of the campaign for the liberation of Europe. The invasion date was drawing nearer. Yet for Squadron Leader Cranswick and LACW Val Parr only one date really seemed to matter: the date to be fixed for their wedding.

After a full month of bliss in the expectations of marriage, Val and Alec found a crisis threatening their romance even before they had been able to decide on the date for the wedding. A quarrel pitched their marriage plans into jeopardy for one whole dreary weekend towards the end of January 1944.

It came at an unfortunate time, for only a week earlier the couple had gone over to Oxford to buy the wedding ring. The row was over a mis-understanding involving Alec and another WAAF from Path Finder Force Headquarters – the girl who had first introduced them. Val suspected that his love for her was less warm and that he had become keener on the other girl. Angrily Val returned all Alec's photos and broke off the engagement. It was a sad Saturday.

Worrying whether her actions were perhaps short-tempered and hasty, Val was experiencing grave misgivings by the following day, Sunday, for she had to be honest with herself and admit she still loved Alec with all her heart.

The end of the crisis came suddenly next day when Alec telephoned her and made her realize she had been unjust towards him. Over dinner at a table for two in The George Hotel in Huntingdon, Val had their engagement ring back once more on her finger.

A day later the couple were in London ordering the wedding dress. It was ready within a week and at the same time that she collected the dress she also bought the veil. Her trousseau was now almost ready. All that remained was to decide the essential details of where and when the wedding was to take place. These were points that could not be settled for a few more weeks.

The pair stole every available moment to be in each other's company both off camp and on duty. Cranswick was working in the Operations Room only a stone's throw from the Signals Section in the grounds of the Path Finder Force Headquarters camp. One of his jobs was to fill in various documents, which were then taken across to Signals, where the

WAAF teleprinter operators, one of whom was his fiancée, relayed the messages to Bomber Command Headquarters and to PFF squadrons at Graveley (35 Squadron), Oakington (7 and 627), Wyton (83 and 139), Bourn (97), Warboys (156), Gransden Lodge (405 Canadian Squadron) and Marham (105 and 109).[3]

Alec's imperfect handwriting provided a plausible excuse many times for Val to slip away from her machine in the Signals Section on the ground floor of the house that formed the main building of the Head-quarters and nip across to the Ops Room annexe pretending she could not read her fiancé's writing.

As winter blossomed into spring, Alec's old unit, No. 35 Squadron at Graveley, became non-operational for a short period while the Halifaxes they had been flying in the previous three years were replaced by the more powerful Lancaster bombers. By 15 March 1944, No. 35 Squadron had completed their conversion training on the new aircraft and were roaring across Stuttgart laying a succession of target indicators on which a large bombing force unloosed some 3,000 tons of high explosives. It was the first time more than 1,000 four-engined bombers had been out in a single night. Cloud banks towered 3 miles high along the route, and Stuttgart itself was almost completely hidden beneath a 5,000-foot mass of cloud. The attack was so severe that soon the glow of big fires sweeping the target area was seen even through the clouds.

The knowledge that his former squadron was entering a further phase in the offensive against Germany was fresh encouragement for Cranswick to set about pestering his superiors to allow him to resume operational flying. It was now five months since he had left Graveley. He had made less than a dozen flights in that period, to keep his hand in, but these were mainly in light planes, and only once had he been up in a bomber. He was itching to grip the control column of a bomber again, but each request drew only a refusal. He could only wait.

During an evening together in Huntingdon, Alec and Val completed their arrangements for the wedding. The date was to be 14 April 1944, and the place Holy Trinity Church, Brompton, Kensington.

Val had been to a wedding there once and she had decided she loved the splendid old church so much that she would choose it for her own wedding.

Next morning, 24 March, when she was off duty until 11 p.m., Val caught a train for London to put up the banns. In the rush of attending to all the details, coupled no doubt with the excitement of the moment, she reached the railway station to find that the only train that would get her back to camp in time for duty had already gone. Frantically she enquired if there was any other way of getting back to Huntingdon. The station staff shook their heads sadly. Now she was really in trouble.

. Forced to wait until 1.30 a.m. before there was any train she could catch, Val stayed at King's Cross with her thoughts darting between the happiness of her fast-approaching wedding now only twenty-one days ahead and the uncertainty of her fate when eventually she arrived back in camp, many hours late for duty at PFF Headquarters.

Shortly before midnight the air raid sirens swelled into their mournful wail, and soon Luftwaffe bombers were droning across London to be greeted by a heavier ack-ack barrage than had ever been known over London. Their flares hung suspended like brilliant gleaming white balls of light blazing against the backcloth of the sombre night sky. For a few moments she was acutely aware that she had been caught in much the same position as the people in Germany when her own fiancé was releasing his flares to mark the way for our bombers, often at least ten times as large a force as those now flying over England.

The guns boomed, crashing out their thundering chorus as their bursts peppered the sky around the eighty to a hundred raiders who were trying to level the score for the RAF's assault that evening on Berlin. Was there never going to be peace? Val asked herself.

At Cambridge there were no buses running, and the sole hope of reaching Huntingdon before daylight seemed to be to hitch a ride in a truck drawn up outside the station to take American servicemen to their camps close to Huntingdon. Although Val was carrying WAAF identification papers, she was wearing civilian clothes, and she was unable to persuade the Americans to let her travel with them: 'They probably thought I was a spy,' she explained to Alec when the couple next met. In desperation she almost sank down on hands and knees to beg the Americans to allow her on the truck. At last they relented, and once in Huntingdon she slunk in through the main gate of PFF Headquarters, where next morning she faced a series of charges relating to her absence without leave.

She confessed to being a bit scared when she had to stand before the officer conducting the hearing of the charges. She fully expected at least fourteen days Confinement to Camp; in fact she was given only seven days. With Alec still working at the camp himself, she was able to go out

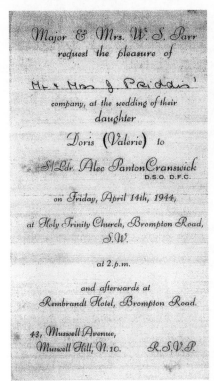

Major & Mrs. W. S. Parr
request the pleasure of

Mr & Mrs J Priddis'
company, at the wedding of their
daughter

Doris (Valerie) to

S/Ldr. Alec PantonCranswick
D.S.O. D.F.C.

on Friday, April 14th, 1944,

at Holy Trinity Church, Brompton Road,
S.W.

at 2.p.m.

and afterwards at
Rembrandt Hotel, Brompton Road.

43, Muswell Avenue,
Muswell Hill, N.10.    R.S.V.P.

David Priddis, grandson of the Reverend James Humphries, who conducted the marriage service, came across this 'rather faded' wedding invitation among his late mother's possessions, kindly agreeing to its publication. (David Priddis)

with him as usual in the evenings. It meant that almost the only hindrance to their meeting came when she had to report at regular intervals to the Guard Room or to the Cookhouse supposedly for penal chores – 'A girl friend of mine was in charge so I never did any work there at all. I used to sit and eat – didn't do anything but that!'

Shortly after Val had been given her seven days, all WAAFs on the camp were ordered into the Mess Hall one night for a lecture by one of the Squadron Officers, during the course of which she looked straight across at Val and announced the blunt warning:

'Any of you girls who want to get married would be best advised to get leave – don't just "Take off"...' Poor Val; she blushed to the roots of her long blonde hair when the Squadron Officer's withering glance fastened sternly upon her.

The great day was drawing closer with every message she sent ticking away on her teleprinter. By now Alec had received news of his posting from PFF Headquarters. He was going back to No. 35 Squadron at Graveley – on a date of unusual significance, the fourth anniversary of his starting operational bomber training, the third anniversary of his promotion to Flying Officer and the second anniversary of both his promotion to Flight Lieutenant and the award of his DFC.

Within three days of returning, he was piloting a Halifax bomber again – the very plane in which he had carried out three bombing raids in a row a year ago and the one he had flown from Graveley to Wyton to introduce his crew to the King and Queen after the devastating Düsseldorf attack of 25–6 May 1943. Cranswick was the happiest person in the world when he learned he was to be allowed to fly again. As soon as he had gone into the Ops Room at the end of his first Pathfinder tour,

On the way to the wedding, the Reverend James Humphries, his wife, Elsie, and their son, John, a Lieutenant in the 33rd Field Regiment, Royal Artillery; early on D-Day he would drive a tank onto Sword Beach. Wounded in an attack by German aircraft near Caen on 10 July 1944, he was shipped home, an X-ray on 15 July in Harefield Hospital, near London, revealing – lodged in his right loin – an unexploded cannon shell, safely removed by the surgeon Mr Alan Hunt. Sixty-one years later, John returned to Normandy – finding exactly where he landed at La Brèche d'Hermanville and visiting the sea front memorial dedicated to the five artillery regiments of the 3rd British Infantry Division. (David Priddis)

he had tried all the time to get back to flying. Now to crown Cranswick's immense joy there was the delight of his approaching marriage to a lovely girl he might never have met had he not been to work in the Ops Room. For Alec and Val, 14 April could not come soon enough.

In an ivory satin gown and attended by three bridesmaids, Val Parr walked proudly up the aisle of Holy Trinity Church, Brompton, on the arm of her father, Major W. S. Parr, RAMC, to where her bridegroom in RAF uniform waited with the best man, Paul Blagrove. The service was conducted by Val's uncle, the Revd James Humphries, Rector of Bushey, Hertfordshire.

The wedding was small and quiet. The guests were almost exclusively members of the two families and their closest friends. The reception, too, was unpretentious and took place at a hotel in Brompton Road, Kensington.

The drive up to Cheltenham, where they were to spend their honeymoon, was not entirely without incident. As their car was surmounting one of the more severe Gloucestershire hills, Val began sniffing suspiciously. There was an alarming smell of burning, and smoke was puffing gently through chinks in the floor of the car. It was too much for the bride.

'Hi! Stop!' she demanded. 'We're on fire!'

Alec consented to draw in to the side of the road, but without showing much concern. Val jumped out – terrified that at any moment the car might disintegrate in a mass of flames. Alec climbed from the driver's seat to reassure her. He told her not to worry and said that in any case this was not the first time it had happened to the car. It had not blazed before, so there was no reason to think it was going to blaze now. Val was not quite so sure. She waited for the first tongues of flame, but they did not come. So Alec was right! She settled into the seat beside him in a less anxious frame of mind and away they went to the Rising Sun at Cheltenham.

When the honeymoon was over, Alec Cranswick went back to his room in the Officers' Quarters at Graveley and his wife returned to her dormitory billet at PFF Headquarters in Huntingdon, 5 miles away. Not for them the chance of a cosy home together, for in the cold, official unsympathetic eyes of the WAAF, Val Cranswick remained a Leading Aircraftwoman – an 'Other Rank' who could not be allowed to sleep away from camp.

In the shadow of war and under these stringent and exasperating conditions, Alec and Val Cranswick began their married life.

One morning in April 1944, a few days after returning from his honeymoon, Cranswick found a letter from one of his pals wishing him all the very best on his fourth tour of bombing operations, the fourth tour on which he need never have embarked.

Cranswick's normal practice was to shrug away without comment all enquiries seeking an explanation for his pressing, almost fanatical, determination to resume bombing ops. His wife knew that he was accepted because so many Pathfinder pilots were being lost; their places had to be taken and he had the experience to fill one of the gaps.

'He was distressed because so many of his friends had been shot down,' his mother explained. 'He was a very loyal friend to all of them. He felt he must go back. He considered they had to be revenged yet he could have got off that fourth tour so easily. He insisted he must go back to his squadron.'

Neither Alec's wife nor his mother wanted him to return to flying. Both realized that he had already amassed a greater number of operational flights than possibly any other heavy bomber captain, but they accepted the fact that he must make his own decision. There was no sense in arguing. To do so must obviously make him unhappy, unsure. In the air, particularly on active service, there was no room for a pilot with doubts.

Once, when Alec and his mother were together on the banks of the River Cherwell, she was about to try to persuade him against any more operational flying. The intense bond between them provided an almost telepathic link, so that there were times when mother and son could read each other's minds. Alec turned suddenly and looked at his mother. She smiled but said nothing, for now she realized she could not ask him to stop flying. Sometime afterwards Alec told his mother he had known what she had intended to ask him on that occasion beside the Cherwell and he was grateful she had not done so.

In the single month of April 1944, RAF and USAAF planes dropped double the weight of bombs on Germany than the Luftwaffe sent crashing down on England in the whole of 1940. It followed another record-breaking month of night bombing, when more than 8,000 bombers flew off from their bases in Britain – over three-quarters of them heading for targets inside Germany. The raids were mounting in fury, but the losses were rising, too.

In February when almost a thousand bombers were sent out, mainly against Leipzig, seventy-nine failed to return home. On another night, in March, seventy-two bombers were lost. There was worse still to come when, at the end of the month, Nurnberg was battered in one of the heaviest onslaughts of the war at a cost of ninety-five RAF planes. There was a pressing need for replacements for the lost crews.

Accepted again for operational flying, Cranswick badly wanted to have his old crew with him on his fourth tour. He set about trying to round them all up. They were scattered over various airfields, so the task was difficult. Meanwhile, Alec's wife had been posted to RAF Station, Warboys, which was one of the Pathfinder Group dromes, so when he was visiting her one day he made use of the opportunity to try to talk one of his former navigators, Leslie Hulme, into rejoining him at Graveley. Hulme had still had five more trips to make to finish his tour when Cranswick was given his enforced six-month rest. While Cranswick was on leave before going to PFF Headquarters, Hulme completed the five trips in five nights out of seven and then went on leave himself before his posting came through as a navigation instructor at Warboys. The two men did not meet again until the day Cranswick was at Warboys visiting his wife.

Alec found out where Hulme was working and poked his head round the door of the room. Hulme was standing at a blackboard taking a class of forty people. Alec grinned broadly and beckoned Hulme across to the door. He told him he was going back to start another tour of ops and claimed he had been able to get all the rest of the old crew to rejoin the squadron. Hulme must come too, insisted Alec. Hulme refused an immediate answer. That night he rang up each of the men Cranswick had stated were willing to resume ops with him. Each one agreed that Alec had spoken to him about flying again, but only Ivor Howard, the tail-gunner, had accepted. A week later Cranswick again went to see Leslie Hulme.

'I've been spruced. They won't come,' admitted a dejected Alec Cranswick.

While Cranswick was still a Pathfinder Headquarters Air Staff officer, Ivor Howard had been posted to Silverstone to be an instructor, but he preferred to go back to No. 35 Squadron. He made two telephone calls to Path Finder Force Headquarters to see what he could do to arrange the transfer. The first call was to Alec Cranswick, and Howard learned that Alec was already pulling every string possible to get back to the squadron himself. The second call was to the Postings Officer to discover the prospects – only to be told: 'We'll see what we can do.'

The tail-gunner was living in a furnished cottage at Buckden, quite close to Graveley, and one night shortly after he had made the two telephone calls he heard Cranswick's sports car roaring up to the front door. Alec took Howard and his wife to dinner at the Lion and asked the gunner if he would go back in the crew. Howard needed no encouragement, but his wife was a different proposition. The two friends pointed out to Mrs Howard that they were seasoned aircrew members, skilled in Pathfinder techniques, and that, because they were experienced people, everything that they did in the air was a step nearer the end of the war. As a further prod, Cranswick tossed in the inducement that he and Ivor had come through together quite safely so far and why shouldn't they continue to do so?

'Alec was very loquacious, very convincing,' Howard recalled later. 'If I had not known him better I would have thought he had been drinking!'

For Alec Cranswick it was a mission completed satisfactorily: the way was now clear for his friend to rejoin him at Graveley.

He was so keen to make an early start on operational flying again with No. 35 Squadron that he resolved to try a short cut by recruiting his own crew. Hulme was able to assist over the choice of an air-bomber. In the class Hulme had been instructing at Warboys when Alec Cranswick visited him was Philip Burt, whom Hulme knew well. The two men had trained together at Jurby on the Isle of Man in 1941. Burt had completed thirty bomber trips as a navigator with Main Force and he was going through the Path Finder Force School to fly his second tour with Pathfinders. He won the DFC in September 1943 with No. 158 Squadron for gallantry and devotion to duty in the execution of air operations. To help Cranswick, Hulme now recommended Philip Burt to him, and with Alec's consent the posting to No. 35 Squadron was arranged, with the result that he was crewed up with Cranswick.

Almost the last position to be filled was that of wireless operator, and Alec made his way across to a row of offices at Graveley, where the wireless operators' section was situated. It was a single room with, on this occasion, a single occupant, Flight Sergeant Wilfred Horner. Cranswick asked to see the section leader, and when Horner replied that he was out, Cranswick announced that he had just returned to the squadron to do another tour of ops and he was looking for a wireless operator.

Horner was familiar with Cranswick's reputation as an ultra-enthusiastic and zealously capable bomber captain. It happened that Horner had no regular crew, because his own captain had developed sinus trouble and been withdrawn from flying duties. Here was Horner's chance to regain a regular place in a bomber crew.

He asked Cranswick if he could go with him – providing there was room for his special mate, Flight Sergeant Alf Wood, with whom he had been crewed up straight from the Operational Training Unit. They had been together throughout their service with No. 78 Squadron at Breighton, near Selby, Yorkshire, before joining No. 35 Squadron together towards the end of 1943.

There was one hitch still to be overcome.

Wood was a tail-gunner and there was no vacancy, because Cranswick had already arranged for Ivor Howard to occupy that position. However, Cranswick agreed that Horner and Wood could join his crew if Wood would fly as mid-upper gunner. With Wood's instant acceptance, Cranswick now had a full crew. It was going to be like old times again.[4]

For Alec and his wife, their separation ordered by wartime regulations was becoming an increasing strain. There was something ludicrous about their detached existence brought about exclusively by the fact that Alec was a commissioned officer and Val was a lowly Leading Aircraftwoman. Their only chance to be together was when their off-duty times coincided. An evening at The George Hotel in Huntingdon or a visit to the cinema stood out among their few pleasures.

Squadron Leader Cranswick took up his crew in a Lancaster for the first time on 27 April. It was the beginning of the concerted training programme that must come before sufficient proficiency was reached to join the squadron's operational strength. Throughout the first fortnight in May, Cranswick's crew continued bombing, gunnery and radar practice, and then on 15 May Lancaster ND846 *J-Johnnie* was handed over to them. It marked the end of training and the start of ops.

Four nights later came their first attack – a raid on Boulogne. It was an appropriate occasion for Alec Cranswick's resumption of operations against the enemy. That night's activities were the prelude to a new record in Britain's air offensive, with almost 5,000 bombers and fighters swarming across the Channel in a dawn-to-dusk series of attacks on twelve railway centres, nine airfields and other installations in France and Belgium.

In the next four nights Cranswick carried out three more raids – Duisburg, Dortmund and Aachen, which were respectively his 98th, 99th and 100th operational missions.

Each was a blistering assault. Against Duisburg, Germany's biggest inland port, Cranswick's *J-Johnnie* bore one of the two-ton blockbuster bombs plus a formidable load of incendiaries. Seven minutes after the Pathfinders' flares had bathed Dortmund in artificial daylight, there was a violent explosion every thirty seconds for three minutes, and many ravaging fires followed the concentrated bombing. At Aachen, where three marshalling yards were handling the bulk of traffic from the Ruhr and western Germany into occupied territory in the west, Cranswick's aircraft had to shake off an attack by one of a large force of enemy night-fighters while on the way to the target with 12,000 pounds of high explosives stacked in the bomb bay.

It was a night of desperate opposition from the fighters, and Cranswick was jubilant when he reached Graveley at 2.45 a.m. after blitzing Aachen. In his logbook he wrote the figure '100' against the Aachen entry and permitted himself to add the comment in red ink:

| SINGLE-ENGINE AIRCRAFT | | | | MULTI-ENGINE AIRCRAFT | | | | | | PASS-ENGER | INSTR/CLOUD FLYING [incl. in cols. (1) to (10)] | |
|---|---|---|---|---|---|---|---|---|---|---|---|---|
| DAY | | NIGHT | | DAY | | | NIGHT | | | | | |
| Dual | Pilot | Dual | Pilot | Dual | 1st Pilot | 2nd Pilot | Dual | 1st Pilot | 2nd Pilot | | Dual | Pilot |
| (1) | (2) | (3) | (4) | (5) | (6) | (7) | (8) | (9) | (10) | (11) | (12) | (13) |
| 27.00 | 51.00 | | | 39.00 | 641.55 | 34.00 | 8.00 | 518.40 | 40.00 | 84.00 | 15.20 | 35.00 |
| | | | | | .45 | | | | | | | |
| | | | | | 1.40 | | | | | | | |
| | | | | | 1.00 | | | | | | | |
| | | | | | | | | 2.20 | | | | |
| | | | | | | | | 4.30 | | | | |
| | | | | | | | | 5.00 99ᵈ | | | | |
| | | | | | | | | 3.45 *Whoo!! Whoo!!* | | | | |
| | | | | 1.35 | | | | | | | | |
| 27.00 | 51.00 | | | 39.00 | 644.56 | 34.00 | 8.00 | 534.15 | 40.00 | 84.00 | 15.20 | 35.00 |
| (1) | (2) | (3) | (4) | (5) | (6) | (7) | (8) | (9) | (10) | (11) | (12) | (13) |

A page from Cranswick's flying logbook with his annotation confirming the 100th op; a unique document, it was released by the Air Ministry to the Cranswick family at the request of the author, becoming an unrivalled source for this biography. (Author's Collection)

*Whoo!! Whoo!!* For now an ambition had been realized, and he was a 'centenarian' among the RAF's heavy bomber pilots.

In the early hours of D-Day, No. 35 Squadron despatched sixteen Lancasters against coastal batteries that could have greatly imperilled the landing forces, reporting a good concentration of bombs on their marker flares, while later two planes were provided as Master Bomber and Deputy Master Bomber to control a raid on a railhead at Saint-Lo.

By now Cranswick was terribly worried about his wife, who had gone into hospital on 1 June for an operation. She was at Ely, in the neighbouring county of Cambridgeshire, and he drove over to see her as often as

he was able. For ten days all went well, and there was considerable
improvement. Then Val had a sudden haemorrhage, which threatened
her life. She was so critically ill that an RAF padre was called. He knelt
in prayer at her bedside as an SOS went out to Alec, who was spending
the day with his mother at Oxford, in the belief that Val was so much
recovered that she was about to be discharged from hospital. Somehow
he must get to her bedside. It was some 80 miles from Oxford to Ely. The
message summoning him urgently had already been delayed, so every
fresh moment lost brought Alec added pain. The quickest way he knew
was to fly.

Squadron Leader Cranswick raced by car to Kidlington Aerodrome,
Oxford, but a storm was blowing up, and, even though he succeeded in
talking his way into being allowed to use a spare aircraft, Cranswick was
warned he must not attempt to fly unless there was an appreciable
change in the weather. Frantic with anguish, Alec scoffed at the warning
and took off for Witchford, close to the hospital, in a flimsy little single-
seater run-about plane. Three-quarters of an hour later he was landing
safely and hurrying over to the hospital with his arms loaded with cherries
and a mass of flowers.

His hat was perched unsteadily on the back of his head and falling
petals trailed behind him. 'I couldn't believe my eyes when I saw him
coming along the ward,' Val recalled. 'There was I, feeling like death,
and Alec looking as though he was bearing all the worries in the world.'

That evening Alec Cranswick stayed at Graveley and, after spending
the following morning with his wife, he returned the borrowed plane to
Kidlington. When his leave was over, he went back to Graveley, where
his squadron was engaged on an arduous series of attacks upon flying-
bomb sites and targets in support of the Allied invaders struggling for a
hold in Normandy.

Cranswick knew when he returned to No. 35 Squadron that he would
be allowed to reach a total of 120 missions before he was withdrawn
completely from operational duties. He had flown his first twenty-nine
missions with No. 214 Squadron at Stradishall, a further thirty-two in the
Middle East with No. 148 Squadron, five with the Canadians and thirty
on his first Path Finder Force tour. By the end of June he had flown nine
of his second PFF tour.[5]

However, what he did not know was that a surprising course had now
been taken by his senior officers; they had deliberately and secretly
reduced that maximum figure of 120 ops to 110 ops. It was done when

Val revealed that she was going to have a baby.

There was a just cause for keeping the decision from Cranswick. It was appreciated that, if Cranswick had learned his operational service was being slashed – whether for this or for any other motive – he would have refused to accept it. Already Val had pleaded with him to think of their baby and quit now for ever. The more she pleaded, the unhappier he became. In the end there was no other course for her – she had to let him have his way.

When sixteen planes from his squadron were pathfinding for a big assault on the Oisemont flying-bomb site, Cranswick was the Master Bomber. This was his 106th mission – and his very first in daylight. Everyone in *J-Johnnie* that afternoon felt almost naked now that they were stripped of the protective cloak of darkness. One of the crew summed up their reaction to the switch from night bombing to daylight bombing: 'There were Lancs to be seen all around us. At night we rarely spotted another bomber. It was rather like someone who is used to living in the country suddenly moving into a town. I don't think any of us would admit to enjoying that daylight op.'

Val Cranswick was still in hospital as the month of June turned into July. It was only in the last week in June that she was able to get out of bed for the first time. She felt weak, her legs powerless.

On the afternoon of Tuesday 4 July, Val eased the boredom of hospital routine by reading over and over again a letter she had just received from Alec. It discussed at some length the baby they were expecting, and contained the hope that, if the child was a boy, he could be brought up in exactly the same way as Alec, with the same sort of home life and a similar education. There was someone to plan for now, and life seemed sweet that particular afternoon.

Val herself was growing stronger and soon she would be out of hospital. Soon, too, she would be out of the WAAF, for now that a baby was on the way she would be granted a compassionate discharge. It meant that she and Alec could be free at last to have a home of their own. No more of that ridiculous existence with Alec living in one camp and Val in another, meeting only when duty spared them.

Each time Alec returned from a bombing raid his wife ticked off the total number of ops he had flown. It was 106 so far, and she guessed that tonight he would be off on another trip. That would make the total stand at 107, and there would only be 3 more after that before he would be grounded for all time. At the rate the bombers were flying now, he might easily finish off those remaining raids by the weekend.

Meanwhile, Squadron Leader Alec Cranswick walked alone to his room on the airfield at Graveley to rest through the aggravating, inactive hours before he was to take off in Lancaster *J-Johnnie* for the Villeneuve-St.-Georges marshalling yards on the edge of Paris.

As the evening wore on Val fell into an undisturbed sleep in her hospital bed at Ely. It was going to require much more than the throbbing beat of *J-Johnnie's* powerful engines to jar her dreams of the handsome pilot who had them running faultlessly beneath his practised care.

Chapter 11

# The Last Command

Sleep came easily to Leading Aircraftwoman Val Cranswick that night of 4–5 July 1944, while her husband of eleven weeks droned across France on his 107th operational mission as an RAF bomber pilot.

A variety of factors were merging to form a wonderful tonic towards swift, peaceful sleep. She had been a patient at Ely for more than a month, but she was fit again and in the morning Alec would come sweeping up to the hospital in their car to whisk her off home to Oxford. By the weekend he was almost certain to have completed the maximum 110 missions he was to be allowed to fly before entering into compulsory retirement as an operational pilot. Her own release from the WAAF was imminent now that she was expecting a baby. She was happy, gloriously happy.

After one of the best night's sleep in weeks, Val had breakfast and then busied herself with preparations for discharge from hospital. By now Alec would have rested briefly after the night ordeal and be driving over from Graveley. In the hospital ward a wireless chanced to be switched on and for a moment Val's heart thumped furiously with apprehension when the announcer started speaking of the previous night's bombing attacks by the RAF. Relaxation came only when her pounding heartbeats of anxiety were calmed by the assurance that all the planes had returned safely.

Soon Val was sitting on her bed and waiting for Alec. It would not be too long, now.

Minutes later a nursing sister walked over to say that there was an RAF padre asking to see Val. Instinctively she guessed something was wrong with Alec. Why else should a padre wish to see her now? But it could not be about Alec, for she had heard that all the bombers were safely home.

Even as the sombre-faced padre moved towards her, she knew now that he had come to tell her about Alec – she knew, too, that Alec was not going to come to pick her up and take her home after all.

Gently the padre explained that two bombers were now known to have gone down in the Villeneuve-St.-Georges raid last night. The crew of one of the planes had been able to escape by parachute, he told her, but no one knew yet which of the crews were saved.[1] She must be patient; she must be brave.

With only three more bombing trips to face, Squadron Leader Alec Cranswick, together with the rest of the eight-man crew of Lancaster *J-Johnnie*, had been officially listed as missing.

Nothing further had been heard from *J-Johnnie* since Cranswick sent the bomber speeding down the Graveley runway at 11.16 p.m., one of a fourteen-strong Lancaster Pathfinder force from No. 35 Squadron chosen to spearhead a raid on the Villeneuve-St.-Georges marshalling yards, which were handling the hurried transfer of German troops in a bid to hold the Allied advance in Normandy.

With the powerful coloured marker flares blazing persistently across the great yard, *J-Johnnie*'s load of high explosives was unloosed with deliberate and precise care upon the target. Almost immediately navigator Reg Kille called out a course for Alec to follow to fly clear of the attack area. For *J-Johnnie* these were to be the last moments.[2]

Flight Sergeant Wilfred Horner, wireless operator in Cranswick's crew, thought those closing seconds seemed almost uncanny. The crashing bursts of enemy gunfire throbbed inside Horner's ears, yet he heard none of the evasion instructions he expected to pass between the gunners and the pilot over the intercom so that Cranswick might dodge the relentless pursuing guns.

At such times as these, except when on the actual bombing run, Cranswick never flew straight and level. He adopted a practice of flying a slow corkscrew so that the enemy gunners could not predict the bomber's course. The 'Cranswick Corkscrew' was one of the first features of Alec's flying habits that Horner had noticed and that made his operational tactics differ from those of other pilots with whom Horner had flown his previous twenty-four bombing raids.

The intercom system was an internal telephone link between all members of the crew. The sets had been checked before take-off and found to be working correctly, but something could have gone wrong at

one or more crew positions to account for the unnatural silence. There
was another possibility. The two gunners, Davies in the mid-upper turret
and Wood in the tail, might have had no chance to warn the Skipper.
Before Horner had any opportunity to reason out any sort of
explanation, he heard enemy shells thumping into the bomb bay and
Cranswick was shouting that the plane was on fire.

Through an inspection port Horner now saw that the fuselage was
ablaze behind the bulkhead door on the starboard side, just to the rear
of where he was standing. The bulkhead door gave access not only to the
walkway leading to the mid-upper and tail gun turrets, but also to a door
in the starboard side of the fuselage, immediately forward of the tail,
which provided Horner's emergency escape route. He yelled out to
Cranswick that the back was on fire. The shells that had found the
Lancaster must have been incendiaries, for the bomb bay where the
shells had struck was now swept by a torrent of flames and Cranswick
was giving his last command:

'Bale out! EMERGENCY! J-U-M-P!'

There was diminishing hope for Davies and Wood, trapped in the
blazing aft section, but Alec battled with the heaving controls to hold the
bomber steady so as to give the surviving crew members a chance to
jump. He had drilled them over and over again in the escape procedure
to drive each man into instant and automatic action. The one vital factor
he was powerless to give them was sufficient time to carry through the
escape drill.

With Horner's normal escape route to the door near the tail cut off,
he had now to take his turn at the front escape hatch with the two Air
Bombers, Burt and Gibson Taylor, Navigator Kille, Engineer Jock
Erickson and Cranswick. At the terrifying rate the raging flames were
leaping the length of the doomed aircraft Horner could not count on
even the most slender hope of getting through the hatch.

He had two, perhaps three, seconds to register that Reg Kille was
standing up beside the chart table prior to fitting on his parachute and
that bomb-aimer Mike Gibson Taylor would be lying flat in the nose
close to the escape hatch where all he needed to do was to clip on his
parachute and drop out. The rest must then follow, one after the other in
regulation order, with Horner the last to leave the plane before the pilot.

By the time Horner's eyes had taken in the scene and his mind had
seized the awful finality of the situation, *J-Johnnie* must have already
broken up in the air.

Unaware for more than 50 years that such a photograph existed, the author was able to locate this one – taken by local resident Jean Marson at the Villecresnes crash site of Cranswick's Lancaster, ND846, *J-Johnnie* – through one of the foremost French photo-journalists specialising in Second World War aviation, Claude Archambault.[5] (Claude Archambault)

The blazing fuselage snapped free at the main spar just aft of wireless operator Wilfred Horner's position. The end came so swiftly that he had no chance to start moving the few paces to the nose of the bomber ready to make his escape. The two separated portions of the fuselage spiralled towards the French countryside near the village of Réau, some 10 miles from *J-Johnnie's* target for the night, Villeneuve-St.-Georges.[3]

Horner had the most incredible luck...

If he had started going towards the nose, he must surely have been trapped, but he had no time to do anything but find and secure his parachute. When the plane broke its back, he was pitched right out from where he was standing, so that he dropped clear of the crumbling, burning wreck of Lancaster ND846. Though luck had thrown him free, obedience saved his life. His actions in those last seconds could not have been more automatic. He had never before been faced with such a desperate situation, but at least he had been drilled into a robot-like state of preparedness that relieved him of any need to think what he must do. He did not remember pulling the D-ring across his chest to jerk the parachute open, but this he must obviously have done. It would have been one of those involuntary actions prompted purely by the instructions drummed into him constantly throughout his aircrew training and operational duties with his two bomber squadrons.

Wilfred Horner has no recollections whatever of the period between realizing that he must make his way towards the front escape hatch in the burning bomber and regaining consciousness some few minutes later on the cinder path of a German radar post. He thought how quiet everything seemed after hearing the noise of the engines for so long. Still in a state of shock, Horner was sprawled out flat across the rough track, where he became engaged in an unsuccessful struggle to raise his back off the ground. Each time he managed to shift his shoulders clear of the cinders he was sent reeling back again sharply by some unknown force. For a while he was too dazed to appreciate that a huge Alsatian guard dog was restraining every attempt he made to move.

Horner was in a pitiful condition when the Germans found him and ordered off their menacing guard dog. The leaping flames had caught the young wireless operator before he was tossed mercifully out of the plane. His hands and legs were badly burned; his heavy trousers, flying boots and thick white woollen socks were gone. He had been gripping the parachute D-ring fiercely when he fell from the bomber and, despite the gloves he was wearing, Horner's right hand was so severely burned that the shrivelled flesh was moulded round the metal ring. As the Germans wrapped him up to take him to a clinic in a nearby village, he lapsed once more into the blessed relief of unconsciousness.

He came round to find a French nurse holding his hand and he tried to ask her what had happened to the watch he had worn in the plane. He could not remember the French word for watch, but he knew that 'small' was petit, so he asked about the 'petit clock', and she seemed to understand. She could not tell him, so he guessed the watch had perished in the blaze.

For the rest of the night Wilfred Horner remained in the clinic under guard. At that time he had no idea whether there were any more survivors from *J-Johnnie*. It was many months before he knew for certain he was the only member of the crew to escape with his life.

While Horner was having his wounds treated at the village clinic in the few hours left before daybreak, German troops were bringing in the bodies taken from *J-Johnnie* and putting them in the Town Hall at Réau. At *J-Johnnie*'s base, meanwhile, No. 35 Squadron waited and wondered.

The news that *J-Johnnie* was missing filtered almost casually around the airfield at Graveley, passed on from mouth to mouth, but no one on the camp could have been more stunned than Sergeant Kluva – Alec's Alsatian, his near-inseparable companion who waited eagerly beside the runway on each night of ops to welcome back his master.

His keen ears would quiver as he picked up the faint yet distinctive hum of the bomber engines. The moment Cranswick's plane was down and safely positioned at the dispersal point, Kluva would be released from the grip of the RAF Police NCO in whose care he had been placed for the night to go leaping across to his advancing master. It was always a touching scene, this airfield reunion between Alec and the dog he was compelled to leave behind, because, much as Alec wanted to have Kluva with him in the plane, he put the safety of the crew above the disappointment of separation from his dog.

That night of 4–5 July 1944 was the first occasion Kluva had ever waited in vain for his master. One by one No. 35 Squadron's Lancasters settled down on the runway, but there was no *J-Johnnie*, and neither was there any way to tell Kluva what had happened to the missing crew.

At that time, in fact, no one had any idea what had befallen *J-Johnnie*. It was always a slow process finding out the fate of a missing bomber, for there might be several explanations to account for the fact that the plane had not reached base after a raid. This was why the news of *J-Johnnie*'s failure to get back to Graveley was slow to go round the camp.[4]

Cranswick's bomber might have made a forced landing at another drome in Britain because of shortage of fuel or through damage from enemy action. For the same reason, it could have gone down in the sea with an opportunity for rescue. If the plane had been hit over enemy territory, there was still a fair chance of the crew getting out with their parachutes. If the crew had managed to escape, there was still a possibility of one or more evading capture. For some appreciable time, therefore, the inevitable anxiety over the disappearance of a bomber was tempered by the often justified hope that those in the plane were still safe.

There was no means of easing Kluva's worried mind, however, and when Flying Officer Howard went next morning to the office at Graveley that he shared with Cranswick, Kluva was sprawled out disconsolately on the floor and showing no inclination either to fuss over Howard or to go out onto the airfield. It was pathetic – almost as if he already knew that his master had died in the blazing bomber over the south-eastern outskirts of Paris.

Ivor Howard, who had missed going on the raid only because the doctor would not pass him fit on account of a cold, first knew that Cranswick had been posted missing when one of the squadron personnel entered the office to gather up Cranswick's personal effects to be stored away until there was confirmation of his fate. As he invariably flew with Alec, Howard now understood why, while walking to the office earlier in the morning, a navigator from another crew had stared at him as though he was seeing a ghost and then shuffled off muttering: 'Christ!'

Meanwhile, the padre was telling Val Cranswick that her husband was missing. She had been expecting Alec to arrive at the hospital within a few minutes to take her to his mother's house in Oxford, where she was going to stay until they were able to set up their own home. Her demobilization from the WAAF was due within a matter of days.

If she had still been at Pathfinder Headquarters, she might have had to face on duty the shock that he had failed to return from the night's attack. With their hearts in their mouths, the girls in the Signals Section where she worked used to crowd round the ticker-tape teleprinters as the squadrons reported the names of the missing crews.

Val's release from the WAAF was rushed through on compassionate grounds and the formalities were attended to at Warboys, to which she had been moved from Path Finder Force Headquarters a fortnight after her wedding.

The usual procedure before leaving an RAF camp on posting to another camp or on release from the Service was to get a Clearance Chit signed by an officer or NCO from each of perhaps twenty or more different sections throughout the camp to indicate that there were no Service debts incurred, no borrowed property still outstanding or miscellaneous requirements unfulfilled. The often exasperating job of collecting so many signatures might take as long as a whole day on some of the bigger airfields.

Val Cranswick's smouldering fury erupted when she was ordered to get her Clearance Chit signed at Warboys. It meant walking from section to section round the great drome until she had secured each signature on the sheet. Only then would the camp demands be satisfied and she would be able to leave for Oxford. It was clearly no task for anyone in her position. She protested that she had only just been discharged after more than a month in hospital and on top of that she had just learned her husband was missing. She remonstrated with the officer who insisted she must get her Clearance Chit signed, but only when she saw a senior officer who was more sympathetic was Val excused the formality and someone else took the chit round Warboys for her in order to comply with the camp regulations.

Alec's mother drove down to the airfield to collect Val and pick up Alec's personal gear at Graveley. It was a visit crowded with memories of happier times. In these tragic circumstances the two women collected the treasured possessions of the missing pilot whom they both loved – one with the tender warmth of a wife, the other with the guiding care of a mother.

For the last time Val turned her back on her husband's airfield and went with her mother-in-law to Oxford, where she was to live until the birth of her baby. The seldom-admitted fear of every flyer's wife had to be acknowledged with painful finality as Val wrote in her diary: 'I knew it would come. I must be brave for his sake. I loved him so much.'

# Postscript

Once the bodies of the crew of Cranswick's bomber were recovered and transported to Réau Town Hall, the villagers were not allowed to go near them for fear that anti-German outbursts might be sparked off in the district. There was already an energetic Resistance group in the area, and the Germans exercised such caution to avoid risking fresh incidents of open hostility.

For the same reason, too, villagers were forbidden to join in the funeral held for the bomber crew next day, when a German guard of honour fired a salvo of rifle shots in their honour. As a further mark of respect the Germans placed wreaths and laurel-leaf crosses upon the coffins before Cranswick and his crew were laid in separate graves in the parish cemetery. Perhaps to forestall the chances of the French people indulging in sympathetic scenes at the gravesides, no names or crosses were placed on the graves. The efforts to hide the identities completely were to no avail. As soon as the villagers learned the positions of the graves of the Royal Air Force men, they began to shower flowers upon them and did all in their power to tend each grave with devoted care beneath the angry eyes of the occupying troops.

At Graveley, meanwhile, telegrams had been sent out to the next-of-kin of those who were on board *J-Johnnie*. They reported each flyer missing as a result of air operations – the first tragic step that had to be taken in a series of formalities, which was next followed by a personal letter to each of the next-of-kin from Wing Commander S. P. Daniels, Commanding Officer of No. 35 Squadron. The letters said that it was with profound regret that he found it his unhappy task to confirm the telegram and went on to give brief details of the operation from which *J-Johnnie* had failed to return.

These letters spoke particularly highly about Cranswick's crew. The one sent to Wilfred Horner's mother told her: 'Your son had been doing exceptionally well and he and his crew had proved themselves to be one of the most efficient and reliable in the Squadron and it will not be easy to replace them.'

The letter to Val Cranswick said: 'As you probably know, your husband is one of the most experienced operational captains in the Command. His loss is deeply felt by the entire Squadron; both officers and men have always had great admiration for his exceptional skill and ability as a pilot.'

Wing Commander Daniels pointed out that the usual source of news was the International Red Cross Committee, which would advise the Air Ministry, which would then send a telegram direct to the next-of-kin. In other cases, where the aircrew concerned was a prisoner of war in enemy hands, frequently a letter was received direct by his family before the telegram.

The Wing Commander told Horner's mother:

*There are, however, always a proportion of missing crews who escape by parachute or make a forced landing and I, the Squadron as a whole and your son's brother aircrew share your impatience for the good news that he is safe though a prisoner of war. Meanwhile we wish you to know that you have our deepest sympathy in this period of anxiety.*

It was eleven weeks before Val Cranswick learned, through the International Red Cross Committee, that her husband was believed to have lost his life. Then, in her diary, she wrote these words:

*Had the telegram I had been expecting. Alec 'believed killed'. Not really definite but... Please God keep him safe. He was everything to me. If he's gone I have nothing but his baby. Thank God I have that. My life will never be the same without him.*

Failing to return from his 107th mission, the entry in Val Cranswick's diary on 21 September 1944, that Alec was 'believed killed'. (Author's Collection)

When the news was passed on to his old school there appeared this tribute in the St Edward's *Chronicle*:

*No day boy entered more whole-heartedly into School activities than did Alec Cranswick. He was always happy and always on the go. He left rather young and after a promising start in the Police Force joined the RAF, where his outstanding qualities were soon recognised. He had done brilliant work as a Pathfinder and seemed destined for bigger things. But the chances of war have deprived the RAF of a very gallant officer and all who knew him of a charming and loyal friend.*

The letter confirming the telegram to Val Cranswick came on 26 September 1944, saying that the Committee's telegram quoted official German information that her husband was killed, but there was no information regarding the place of his burial. It went on: 'Although there is, unhappily, little reason to doubt the accuracy of this report, the casualty will be recorded as 'Missing, Believed killed' until confirmed by further evidence or until, in the absence of such evidence, it becomes necessary owing to lapse of time to presume for official purposes that death has occurred'.

Even for the family and friends of the sole survivor, Flight Sergeant Wilfred Horner, there was a long, nerve-straining period of anxiety. It was not for close on three months after the blazing *J-Johnnie* had crumbled out of the night skies that Horner's mother learned he was safe.

Finally, from the new Officer Commanding, No. 35 Squadron, Group Captain D. F. E. C. Dean, came a letter in which he quoted news that had come through the International Red Cross Committee. The Group Captain wrote:

*It is with the greatest pleasure that I have received a telegram from Air Ministry giving information through the International Red Cross Committee stating your son has been reported safe though a prisoner of war, in Germany.*

*Please accept from the whole of the Squadron our heartfelt congratulations on your son's survival. We share with you the feeling of relief that this news brings after so long a period of anxiety.*

*I can assure you that our aircrews receive good treatment in the German prison camps and there is no cause for worry on that account.*

The prayers of Horner's mother, and those of the girl he was to marry, had been answered at last.

When the Germans found Wilfred Horner he was carried to a clinic in a village near the radar post where his parachute had borne him – safe yet burned badly in the closing moments before he was somehow catapulted out of the disintegrating bomber. As a gesture of appreciation towards the airmen and airwomen in the Parachute Section at Graveley who had packed and checked his parachute and so helped to save his life, Horner wrote to his sister from prison camp asking her to make a gift of some money for them.

After receiving first-aid treatment, he was moved to St Denis Hospital in Paris, where he stayed until shortly before the liberation of the French capital in August 1944. He was then transferred to two hospitals in Germany and finally to Stalag Luft 7 at Kreuzburg, only some 10 miles from the Polish border. As the Russians surged forward into Germany, the prisoners were ordered out of the camp and forced to march towards Berlin – 230 miles away as a direct line on a map but many more miles off along the hard, twisting, unfriendly roads. After a trek in which time lost all meaning, Horner and the men of Stalag Luft 7 were bundled onto a train and eventually reached Luckenwalde, which lay to the south of the German capital. The end of their captivity came strangely. One morning the camp was swarming with Germans; the next morning there were none. Into the camp soon afterwards came advance groups of the Russian army to liberate them.

The first thoughts of Wilfred Horner when he reached home in May 1945 were to see if there was any way he might ease the anxiety for the families of the other members of the crew of *J-Johnnie*.

He wrote a letter the first night he returned to Britain in which he gave Val Cranswick a short account of what happened when the bomber caught fire. He went on to say:

*I made numerous enquiries about the rest of the crew but was unable to learn anything definite. A German interrogation officer told me that your husband, Flying Officer Kille and Flight Lieutenant Burt had been killed. I shouldn't take this too seriously as the Germans often used this method in the hope of squeezing a little extra information out of their prisoners.*

*I'm afraid this is very unsatisfactory to you but if we could meet sometime and I could be of any help to you in any way, please don't hesitate to ask. I'm sorry I have no better news but don't give up hope.*

Not for many more months did Val Cranswick learn that her husband lay buried in a flower-decked grave, without a cross and without a nameplate, alongside his crew in the parish cemetery at Réau, some 20 miles south-east of Paris. Only then did she throw away the last cherished hope that he might come back.

By those who knew him, Squadron Leader Alec Panton Cranswick, DSO, DFC, has been acclaimed as one of the most outstanding bomber captains of the Second World War. Statistics compiled by Martin Middlebrook and Chris Everitt for *The Bomber Command War Diaries*, on RAF Bomber Command's role in the war against Germany, would show that he was one of 55,573 aircrew members who lost their lives; that the eight-man crew on board *J-Johnnie* that night were engaged on one of 387,416 operational sorties flown by aircraft of Bomber Command; and that theirs was one of 8,953 aircraft that it lost in action.

He made just one more journey from the tiny, tree-shaded burial ground in Réau. When peace had returned to the village of Réau, American Graves Unit personnel carefully removed the bodies of Cranswick and his crew and bore them through the French capital to the town of Clichy on the northern boundary of Paris.

There, in the New Communal Cemetery, between the Town Hall and the River Seine, Alec Cranswick and his comrades were delivered to their final resting place. It is in a plot of British Commonwealth graves of the Second World War cared for by the Commonwealth War Graves Commission. There are 226 graves – 162 of them the fallen of United Kingdom Forces, the remainder Canadians, Australians, New Zealanders and South Africans.

On the plot stands a Cross of Sacrifice, and in Row 13, Grave 16, lies one unquestionably valiant man who spared nothing and then ultimately gave himself in the supreme sacrifice: Squadron Leader Alec Panton Cranswick, DSO, DFC.

I began Alec Cranswick's story by telling of the theft of his DSO and DFC. These stolen medals turned up later – deposited in a pawnshop by the thief in exchange for a few shillings. The medals have since been given to Alexander – the son he never lived to see.

What happened to the principal characters in Alec's life story? Both Alec's mother and widow remarried. Alexander, in many ways almost a carbon copy of his father, went to Alec's old school, just as he wanted him to do. Alexander's mother was happy that he went into the RAF Cadet Corps at school, where he enjoyed the thrill of flying as well as gaining some insight into the kind of life his father led in the RAF. The blue Alsatian, Kluva, bought as a puppy when Alec was back from the Middle East, spent his final years with Alec's mother.

It was from Path Finder Force's founder and sole chief, Air Vice-Marshal Donald Bennett, that I first learned about the brilliant wartime career of Alec Cranswick. Bennett wrote in his autobiography *Pathfinder*, which he dedicated to Cranswick, that, despite Cranswick's record, the public have never heard of him. I felt that the public ought to know about him. In gathering the facts about Alec Cranswick I have enjoyed the close cooperation of his family and of many who flew and worked with him.

From the outset I have had the personal encouragement of one of the Air Ministry's Senior Information Officers, C. C. H. Cole, as well as the most valued assistance from Air Ministry Librarian and Head of Air Historical Branch, L. A. Jackets, and his ever-helpful library staff in the wealth of research necessary to present an accurate picture of life in the RAF in the Second World War.

Air Vice-Marshal Bennett considers that the contribution of an aircrew member of Bomber Command who completed a single operational tour, or who died in the process, was far greater than that of any other fighting man, RAF, Navy or Army, when measured in terms of danger of death. He goes on to say in his autobiography: 'The contribution of a Pathfinder in the same terms of intensity and duration of danger – and indeed of responsibility – was at least twice that of other Bomber Command crews.'

Alec Cranswick was on his fourth operational tour when he was killed. He must have realised he had very little chance of staying alive when he was facing such odds. Hardly one man in three could expect to survive his first tour of thirty bombing missions, yet Cranswick won through to complete a second and then a third tour. He could have quit a number of times. He refused. He was surely an extraordinarily brave man or else a fool; and there was no place for a fool in a Pathfinder squadron.

If I have succeeded in making Alec's name familiar to some of the public I shall be proud. He must have been a remarkable man.

*He lived as a gallant flyer. He died as a hero unknown...*

Appendix

# 1. Alec Cranswick: The Name Lives on

Since the original *Pathfinder Cranswick* came out in 1962, bringing Alec Cranswick's name to prominence for the first time, the RAF itself has taken a dominant step to perpetuate his name in an unexpected yet altogether fitting manner, when, at the turn of the century, RAF Station, Wyton, where Path Finder Force was headquartered throughout its existence, chose to name a building after him, Cranswick House.

Air Vice-Marshal Donald Bennett's words for the Foreword to the book were included in explanatory text displayed within the building, and most appropriately it was his widow, Mrs Ly Bennett, who unveiled the name plaque during a formal ceremony where former Pathfinders were present. This was one of a number of occasions when I have been able to refresh my half-century and more of association with Alec Cranswick's family and his wartime service – fortunately being in a position, then, to provide the RAF with a rare pristine copy of the 38-year-old *Pathfinder Cranswick*.

I well remember the first of many visits to the Cranswick home in Oxford, this wartime address somehow having come into my possession in the autumn of 1958, though I recall being apprehensive about the prospects of finding anyone there with personal knowledge of the family. It did not seem at all hopeful; checking the electoral roll had confirmed that there was no one listed named Cranswick, so there would be a need for caution when the front door opened in response to my knock. I asked if someone in the neighbourhood might know the whereabouts of the Cranswicks, explaining that I was trying to locate anyone who might be able to tell me about an RAF pilot of that name. The response was immediate – and it was astonishing, given the circumstances. 'You'd better come in,' said the lady in the doorway; 'he was my son.' It was indeed Alec Cranswick's mother, now with a different surname from a second marriage.

To the mother and to the widow, in those early conversations, it was clear that I was in a position to relate much about Alec's experiences that would be fresh to them; and of course I recognized that, if they chose to do so, as fortunately they were prepared to do, this would be an invaluable opportunity to share many of their personal memories of Alec for the exclusive feature articles that would soon appear in what was then one of London's three evening newspapers, *The Star*.

I was able to recount Air Vice-Marshal Bennett's words to me about the choice of person to whom he would dedicate his autobiography (the decision, when I saw the name in print, sparking instant intrigue in Cranswick). Bennett was not, he explained, interested in dedicating the book 'to a glamour boy'; he wanted it 'to be a tribute to one whose record I do not think can be surpassed', judging Cranswick to have done 'a remarkably good job, very quietly and well'. Yet, as he told me, the public have never heard of him. As for the reason for that anonymity, it is evident that this particular Pathfinder would have baulked at anything to bring him into the limelight; and certainly he would have done nothing himself to attract attention when – as I wrote in the paper – Cranswick never even told his wife why he had won his medals. She knew nothing of the reasons for the award of first the DFC and then the DSO until I read the citations to her when we met.

It transpired that the last letter Alec's wife and mother had from him told them that he was leaving behind a note for them to open if he did not return from a raid. The note contained Cranswick's last wish – that, if the child his wife was going to have was a boy, he was to be brought up like his father. As we have learned, Alex became a pupil at St Edward's School in Oxford, as was his father pre-war; Alex was in his final year when, on the publication of *Pathfinder Cranswick*, I was privileged to introduce him to Air Vice-Marshal Bennett. It was an occasion that saw two of Cranswick's crew members reunited: survivor Wilfred Horner and the regular air gunner who had not flown that night on doctor's orders, Ivor Howard.

With mother and wife having passed on and Alex born after the death of his father, the ability to obtain meaningful personal detail about this remarkable person has long gone; fortuitously this has not been the case with regard to sources of information about contemporaneous events as a pilot. Such occasions and various opportunities have arisen, over the

**At the naming ceremony for Cranswick House, left to right are Mrs Lillian Horner, Judith and Alex Cranswick, and their son, Peter.** (Author's Collection)

years, to facilitate further editions of this biography, both in print and in digital format, demonstrating fulfilment of a declared intent to service a continuity of availability to the definitive account of the life and the times of Alec Cranswick, produced with assistance from many individuals who knew him so well.

The successive possibilities that facilitated updates to the Cranswick biography have been developed, here, to produce the Appendix encompassing both further detail about particularly significant episodes in his career as an operational pilot in RAF Bomber Command and events post-war that have done much to uphold his name. For events during his time in the RAF, this has meant many fruitful hours spent at The National Archives in Kew and also delving into Luftwaffe records to establish how his Lancaster was shot down, the latter being a particularly challenging experience that produced its reward with some surprising answers to questions raised without response many years ago.

Naturally, every operational flight in those wartime years brought its hazards – an aircraft failure, the effect of weather or enemy action being the most obvious. But in Cranswick's case there was a unique incident – touched upon in the original text though necessarily lacking in detail – that shows how the unexpected, occurring at an early stage in his career as a bomber pilot, could have considerably shortened the lifespan of this outstanding man.

# 2. A Dummy Airfield and a Near-fatal Crash

When I was engaged on the original research for *Pathfinder Cranswick*, scant information existed in the public domain concerning dummy airfields, one of which caused Alec Cranswick's Wellington bomber to become a write-off and might well have brought an untimely end to all six occupants when it touched down on the 'runway' – a turnip field, no less!

Since then, however, much of the secrecy that inevitably surrounded these and other deception measures has been put aside, and it has become possible both to identify the location of this illuminated fake landing ground and to include details, here, about the purpose, creation and achievements of these 'Q' sites, as they were called, besides mentioning the various other components of what was a vital defence strategy in wartime Britain.

It was at Crostwick in Norfolk, some 10 miles inland and 50 miles short of their home base at Stradishall in neighbouring Suffolk, that this No. 214 Squadron crew made their forced crash-landing after a flight of 7 hours 22 minutes. The Schœneberg marshalling yard was bombed from 13,000 feet at 22:14 hours, the primary target in the German capital (a power station) not being located owing to bad visibility. The radio transmitter having become 'unserviceable over Berlin', the aircraft was 'unable to ascertain its position over England on returning' and 'ran short of petrol' – to quote the Station Operations Officer at RAF Station, Stradishall, when writing about the attack and its aftermath in the Operations War Diary, which the author found in The National Archives.

By the time of this incident (it happened in the early hours of 8 October 1940), there were already more than sixty 'Q' sites in use – each one set up with the express intention of fooling the enemy into the belief that it was actually the 'parent station', functioning as if illuminated to despatch and receive aircraft during routine night operations. Besides 'Q' sites, there were their daytime equivalents, known as 'K' sites and sometimes at the same location, as well as 'QF' and 'Starfish' sites (diversionary fires), 'QL' sites to simulate urban lighting and a number of dummy factories and other buildings. It was a complex yet a rapidly developed deception programme.

The 'Q' and 'K' sites each shadowed its parent station, their location generally being between 5 and 6 miles of the active airfield and in the direction of an enemy's anticipated line of approach. Crostwick was some 3 miles north-east of its parent; this was Horsham St Faith, built pre-war, opened officially on 1 June 1940, used by the RAF and the US Army Air Force and transformed post-war into Norwich International Airport.

The common components of a 'Q' site were flare-path lights, obstruction lights and/or recognition lights, motor headlights and a night shelter that would house the lighting, switchgear, communications and other equipment. The shelter would also be a refuge for those staffing the site – generally a two-man team from the parent station, whose Operations Room would issue the orders for the decoy airfield to be brought into use.

The indications are that Crostwick's lighting was on when Cranswick's Wellington was nearing home shores, the strategy being to lure any enemy aircraft in the area into thinking that here was the real Horsham St Faith aerodrome; it was a ruse that, up to 31 October 1940, drew as many as 135 attacks on 'Q' sites compared with the 65 against their parent airfields. These figures come from *Bombing Decoys of WWII*, which is volume III in the Council for British Archaeology series *20th Century Fortifications in England*, by C. S. Dobinson, published in 1996. Subsequently in a television programme – *The Decoy Men*, shown on BBC2 on 5 March 2002 (in which a former airman who served at Crostwick emphasized how secrecy about these 'Q' sites was maintained) – Colin Dobinson described them as 'magnificent'. They drew some 440 attacks, which was 'an enormous amount of wasted effort on behalf of the Germans'.

An Essex County Council project to survey the composition of Second World War defences in the county noted that an 'extraordinarily imaginative' range of bombing decoys had been set up to try and confuse enemy bombers. The eventual 171 'Q' sites were 'the backbone of the airfield decoy defence'.

Unfortunately, it was friend not foe, that night of 7–8 October 1940, that was lured by the decoy drome at Crostwick. If Cranswick's aircraft was perchance the first to land on a 'Q' site, believing this to be an actual airfield, it was certainly not alone in so doing – though apparently for Crostwick this would go down as a never-to-be-repeated experience.

Documents in The National Archives show that – notwithstanding new precautions and updated procedures – pilots continued to be hood-winked in the same manner. At one point the Air Ministry called for the figures as to how many times this had happened (taking the period June–September 1941); Bomber Command reported seven such landings on its 'Q' sites, while Coastal Command, with a nil return, reported one in April 1941. The following January the Air Ministry department responsible for setting up its decoy airfields would refer to 'isolated instances' when friendly pilots landed on 'Q' sites 'in mistake for RAF aerodromes', though without indicating the time frame in which these landings occurred.[1]

Procedures were in place that required all the lights on a 'Q' site to be turned off should a friendly aircraft approach to land, the pilot being 'warned off' with a red signal and expected to 'go elsewhere' – the assumption being not only that would the pilot be aware of the presence of such sites, as well as their means of operation, but that a suitable opportunity would exist for him to seek an alternative landing facility.

Yet in Cranswick's case the crew apparently had no prior knowledge of dummy airfields nor, for that matter, could they have diverted safely. The fuel gauges were showing 'Empty' – some of the fuel that normally would have remained to get them back home had been lost through the punctured tank; and apart from the darkness there was low-level fog, which further limited visibility in an already critical situation for the homecoming bomber.

Interesting details about Crostwick have since emerged in a Norfolk & Suffolk Aviation Museum publication – *Airfields of Norfolk & Suffolk*, com-piled and edited by Huby Fairhead and Roy Tuffen – which refers to a second instance of a friendly aircraft seemingly being deceived by the realism of this decoy; this time it was what was believed to be a crippled American B-24 four-engined bomber, trying to get back to Horsham St Faith. However, it abandoned an attempt to land and flew off when the decoy crew began sending up some red flares as a warning to stay away.

That publication describes the decoy site at Crostwick as being 'a large field on Church Farm'. As a 'Q' site, there was a dummy flare-path running across it for night-time use; and when serving as a 'K' site for daytime use, dummy aircraft were deployed to simulate the Blenheims operating from Horsham St Faith. Crostwick attracted the attention of the Luftwaffe on 'a number of occasions', one including a stick of about twenty bombs. In serving its purpose, Crostwick emerges as having been one of the most successful 'Q' sites, in one period taking 11 attacks compared with the 3 on its parent, there being 135 and 65 attacks respectively on all the 'Q' sites between their creation and the end of October 1940.

When its flare-path beckoned a welcome to Cranswick's fuel-starved Wellington, approaching through the murky darkness, the glimpse of an apparent runway must have seemed like salvation – a miracle, even. With the crew unaware of the purpose of Crostwick, it promised, surely, a safe haven for all aboard the otherwise doomed bomber – provided that Cranswick himself stayed cool in those desperate final seconds. This he did – as with consummate skill he exercised masterly control over the aircraft, despite the tumult of the unexpected crash-landing that left it 'very severely damaged'.

A much-needed bomber was lost – a much more needed crew saved.[2]

# 3. Remembering Fallen Comrades:
## No. 35 Squadron and Path Finder Force

Though the events described in these pages took place so long ago, for those who experienced them – or were aware of them either then or subsequently – it must have been an unbelievably traumatic period.

For some, it was a time to forget; others felt a desire, a compulsion perhaps, to perpetuate those memories, acknowledging that, while there was sadness, there was enjoyment too.

Former aircrew and others who served with No. 35 Squadron during the Second World War, together with members of their families and friends, have reunited year after year in the post-war period – a time to exchange news and views, a chance to look back upon the war years and above all a fitting occasion to assemble together in remembrance of fallen comrades.

Positive steps have been taken, too, to establish permanent reminders to keep alive the location and the purpose of this squadron and all squadrons in Path Finder Force, first with a marker stone at the site of No. 35 Squadron's base and later with a memorial window in a nearby church.

The marker stone at the entrance to Graveley Airfield, now in the county of Cambridgeshire, was laid in 1992 to commemorate the 50th anniversary of the founding of Path Finder Force. The memorial window in All Saints Church, Offord Cluny, was installed in 1998. It was designed and installed by Gordon Monaghan and unveiled by Mrs Ly Bennett, whose late husband was in command of PFF, which began with four squadrons and ultimately comprised as many as nineteen operational squadrons, No. 35 Squadron, one of the founding foursome, being there to the end.[1]

As is now to become evident, particular events further afield have centred upon an individual Pathfinder – the subject of this biography, Alec Cranswick – and upon members of the last crew to fly with him: Philip Burt (Air Bomber), Eric Davies (Air Gunner, occupying the mid-upper turret), Charles Erickson (Flight Engineer), Mike Gibson Taylor (Second Air Bomber), Wilf Horner (Wireless Operator), Reg Kille (Navigator) and Alf Wood (Air Gunner, occupying the turret at the rear of the aircraft).

## At RAF Station, Wyton, and at Villecresnes

As the twentieth century has drawn to a close and with the beginning of the twenty-first century, events in Britain and in France have added poignancy to the memory of Alec Cranswick: at RAF Station, Wyton, in the spring of the year 2000 – where Path Finder Force had been founded as a component of the wartime Bomber Command – and at Villecresnes, near Paris, year after year on VE-Day, 8 May – where towns-people erected a memorial post-war to commemorate RAF and USAAF aircrew who lost their lives when their bombers came down in its vicinity during the Second World War.[2]

At Villecresnes in France, a memorial erected by the townspeople to the crews of Allied bombers that crashed in the vicinity – one of them Cranswick's Lancaster. (Author's Collection)

At Villecresnes, Lillian Horner, whose late husband was Crans-wick's wireless operator on that final mission, twice attended com-memorative events held in the town, the first time with Wilf himself; family members associ-ated with others in the crew have also been present, among them navigator Reg Kille's children. Susan, who travelled with her husband from their home in Tennessee, USA, was 16 months old when her father was killed; Stephen was born 12 days after his father's death.

Visiting Villecresnes provided an unexpected opportunity to meet townspeople who were there when the Lancaster crashed; these included a fireman who was first on the scene – he saw the plane coming down – and the daughter of a doctor who tended Wilf when, severely burned, he had been found after landing by parachute. Ex-Servicemen in this part of France have honoured Wilf with their Croix de Mérite; a posthumous award, it was received by Lillian at the commemorative event in 1999, Wilf having passed away on 25 May 1998.

At Wyton, on 17 March 2000, staff of the Equipment Support (Air) organization were joined by PFF veterans, by Donald Bennett's widow, by Wilfred Horner's widow and by Alex and Judith Cranswick with their son, Peter, Alec's wife having died in January 1992. The occasion was to name a newly refurbished headquarters building as Cranswick House, in honour of Squadron Leader A. P. Cranswick, DSO, DFC.

There, Mrs Ly Bennett unveiled a plaque at the entrance to the building where just inside another plaque included Don Bennett's personal tribute to Pathfinder Cranswick – the words, in fact, that he wrote for his Foreword to this book, about the 'boy-man so simply courageous and so selfless in his sacrifice'. The inscription also recalled details of the flyer's last mission, to the moment the burning plane broke up and Wilf Horner was the sole survivor.

The recognition given to Alec Cranswick in this most fitting manner is in context when it is seen that four other buildings on the site have a name connection with Path Finder Force, one being named after Don Bennett, who died in 1986, aged 76, and the other three named after the only members of Path Finder Force to be decorated with the Victoria Cross: Ian Bazalgette (No. 635 Squadron), Robert Palmer (No. 109 Squadron) and Edwin Swales (No. 582 Squadron), all three being posthumous awards.

In peacetime, a Pathfinder Museum has been created at Wyton, continuing with pride its dedicated work to maintain and foster awareness in Path Finder Force; annually, the RAF Station itself has taken much pleasure in hosting a reunion for former members and their families. While no doubt best known as having been the Headquarters of Path Finder Force (and, incidentally, the airfield from which the RAF carried out its first and its last operational sorties of the Second World War[3]) it is important to recognize that Wyton has a long and distinguished history on either side of this exceptional chapter in the annals of aviation. Indeed, that history goes back to the Royal Flying Corps in 1916, and, latterly, with its Nimrods, Victors and Canberras gone, it has continued with distinction in the provision of a base to carry out the many and varied needs of the 'air pillar' of the Defence Logistics Organization.

In this function, Wyton became the principal home of the Director General Logistics (Strike) organization, the DLO then merging with the Defence Procurement Agency on 1 April 2007, to become Defence Equipment and Support (DE&S), control of the Station moving to HQ Air Command. It has not given way entirely to 'office-bound' activities, however; its airfield has remained in use over the years, with Wyton becoming a home for No. 2 Squadron of No. 1 Elementary Flying Training School, the University of Cambridge Air Squadron, the University of London Air Squadron and No. 5 Air Experience Flight.

Interestingly, since the late 1990s RAF Station, Wyton, has also been home to the county police force's helicopter, its function being both crime-fighting and supporting the life-saving activities of the Mid Anglia General Practitioner Accident Service – a far cry indeed from the myriad of roles performed by the innumerable fixed-wing aircraft that have used Wyton's runways to help write aviation history for close on 100 years.

# 4. End of a Life – End of a Riddle

At RAF Station, Graveley, on 5 July 1944, the mood must have been especially sombre, as there were two Lancasters from No. 35 Squadron reported missing as a consequence of the night's attack on Villeneuve-St.-Georges, neither having made any contact with Graveley since take-off. Cranswick had been immediately behind the other in the runway queue and airborne two minutes later, both planes having the same role – that of Backers-up – with the squadron also providing ten Illuminators besides Master Bomber and Deputy, respectively Squadron Leaders Creswell and Chidgey. With the job done, Cranswick's Lancaster crashed a matter of minutes after the one that preceded him; the captain of that Lancaster was Squadron Leader G. F. Lambert, DFC, who had already 'gone missing' once before, when on a raid against Frankfurt on 10 April 1943, with this same squadron. On that occasion his Halifax was shot down by a night-fighter and crashed in the Ardennes, Lambert evading capture, although four in his crew were killed and two became prisoners of war. This time, however, it would emerge that, although four members of his crew survived to become prisoners of war, Lambert and three fellow officers lost their lives, being laid to rest in Emance Communal Cemetery, some 30 miles south-west of Villeneuve-St.-Georges. Overall that night, eleven bombers were lost on the Villeneuve-St.-Georges raid,[1] with a further three in an attack on the railway system at Orleans and thirteen more in an attack on a major underground flying-bomb storage and assembly area at Saint-Leu d'Esserent, taking the total to twenty-seven.

It can be determined that the two Lancasters from No. 35 Squadron, now starting to head for home, both fell victim to the night-fighter force comprising mainly Bf.110s, Ju.88s, Fw.190s and Bf.109s belonging to groups of Luftwaffe units based in the Netherlands, Belgium, France and Germany. Its pilots, that night, claimed as many as four dozen 'kills' among the RAF squadrons engaged in those three operations. Luftwaffe High Command documentation attributed to the Jagd-Flieger-Führer II puts a precise time and in most cases a specific map reference to each of those 'kills' – the fascinating speculation being that it might now be feasible to end any doubt as to how Cranswick's Lancaster was brought down – by pinpointing which night-fighter (or night-fighters) fired the shells that struck it, causing the fatal blaze. Most claims can be set aside for reasons of time-of-attack or distance from the crash site, though this has left two seeming to warrant due consideration. If substantiated, this would mean two aircraft from the same British bomber squadron being downed by two aircraft from the same German night-fighter unit, both claims being from pilots in No. 6 Staffel in No. 2 Nachtjagdgeschwader (NJG).

Building upon information contained in the Nachtjagd War Diaries, the meticulous work produced by historian and author Dr Theo Boiten, based in the Netherlands, it has now become possible to establish, as far as remains practical so many years after the event, that both Lancasters from No. 35 Squadron were indeed destroyed by Ju.88 night-fighters from No. 6 Staffel flying out of Coulommiers, a Luftflotte 3 airfield some 30 miles east of Paris. The indications are that these Ju.88s were the newly delivered G-I version, purpose-built as a night-fighter and equipped with four forward-firing 20 mm cannon capable of a mix of armour-piercing and incendiary rounds and a single 13 mm machine gun in the rear cockpit, though the weaponry aboard the aging C-series was not lacking in destructive capability.

Boiten was able to provide the serial number of the Lancaster that was the subject of each claim (ND846, flown by Cranswick, and ND731, by Lambert) and it is his assessment that, at 01.32 hours, when Unteroffizier (equivalent to Corporal) Heinrich Schultz claimed a four-engined aircraft it was 'either' Lambert's Lancaster 'or a Lancaster from No. 419 Squadron'; and that, at 01.36 hours, when Leutnant Fischer claimed a four-engined aircraft, it was 'probably' Cranswick's Lancaster. Notwithstanding, in the comfort of knowing that there was no one else laying claim to the destruction of one of the RAF bombing force within the relevant space of time and in the requisite portion of sky, the author concludes that no longer is there any question as to how Cranswick's plane was hit – gunfire from the ground now discounted – and that it was the fire-power of Fischer's Ju.88, no doubt including incendiary rounds, that set this Lancaster ablaze – pilot and crew doing their duty for Germany as were Cranswick and his crew for Britain. In likelihood, those aboard the Ju.88 were watching intently to be able to justify their jubilation when back again at Coulommiers, the fiery fuselage of the Lancaster having split in two to give the sole survivor his open door to safety by parachuting to the ground.

With the emergence of this new material, it is intriguing that, with what appears to have been Fischer's one and only 'kill' (at least during service with No. 6 Staffel), he himself – as well as any Luftwaffe colleague, family member or friend now reading *Pathfinder Cranswick* – would realise that it was he who put paid to the RAF bomber in which this remarkable flyer was returning home from his 107th operation. Fellow night-fighter pilots may well have brought down more aircraft but none a heavy bomber with a pilot at its controls who had established such an exceptional operational record – unbeaten then, unbeaten since.

Before we leave the aerial activities that tie-in the attack on Villeneuve-St.-Georges with those at Orleans and at Saint-Leu d'Esserent, it is pertinent to look at the wider picture with regard to the opposition that the Luftwaffe mounted and to the claims of RAF bombers destroyed that were submitted by the pilots in Nachtjagdgeschwaders (NJG) 1, 2, 3, 4 and 5 – each the equivalent of an RAF wing, with a 100-plus aircraft capability – and by those in the smaller JG 301 and SKG 10 units.

The NJGs were equipped mostly with twin-engine Ju.88 and Bf.110 aircraft though NJG 1 was alone in having a comparative rarity too, the He. 219. Also twin-engined, it was a purpose-built night-fighter of advanced design bringing improved speed and range as well as updated radar. Both JG 301 and SKG 10 had single-engine Bf.109 and Fw.190 aircraft. Pilots, crews and planes that night were drawn from each of the five NJGs and from the other two units to form the Luftwaffe night-fighter force tasked with hunting-down the RAF bombers participating in the attacks on all three targets.

Pilots in one of the five Nachtjagdgeschwader wings put forward seventeen claims – almost one in three of the total submissions; it was NJG 2, whose Geschwaderkommodore in overall command at that time was Oberstleutnant Günther Radusch, a proven specialist in this form of air warfare who, just four nights earlier, demonstrated his personal prowess by achieving two more of his eventual sixty-four 'kills' by night (which included fifty-seven four-engined bombers). It was one of the Staffeln in Radusch's 'wing' that brought down the two aircraft from No. 35 Squadron – No. 6 Staffel in Major Paul Semrau's No. II Gruppe.

There was, indeed, 'considerable night-fighter activity', as Bomber Command acknowledged, with several pilots claiming more than a single 'kill' in an intense period of activity that lasted just shy of one-and-a-half hours. No. 6 Staffel pilots claimed a further four bombers in addition to those of Lambert and Cranswick – three of them by Leutnant Erich Jung in the space of eight minutes, adding to his five previous claims with NJG 2 and contributing towards what Tom Kracker's Luftwaffe Pilot Archive lists as an eventual thirty 'kills', all of them with this same unit. Though, that night, no one surpassed Jung's individual accomplishment of a trio of victories, it was a feat that was nonetheless equalled – NCO pilot Wilhelm Glitz (Stab/NJG 2) claiming the wing's first, second and third bombers of the night, all within six minutes, while patrolling an area south of Dieppe. For the record, research on behalf of the Aircrew Remembrance Society has shown that Oberfeldwebel (equivalent to Flight Sergeant) Glitz survived the war with a total of twelve 'kills' to his name.[2]

# 5. Assessment

Now that the last vestiges of doubt over the cause of the destruction of *J-Johnnie* have dispersed, it is logical to return the focus to its pilot, Squadron Leader Alec Cranswick, DSO, DFC, and to strive for a perceivable motive behind his determination to continue as an operational pilot with Path Finder Force when there was no longer any need to do so. Pathfinder leader Donald Bennett provides the layman with some inkling of the risks Cranswick was facing when he assessed the contribution of an aircrew member of Bomber Command who completed a single operational tour, or who died in the process, as being 'far greater' than that of any other fighting man, RAF, Navy or Army, when 'measured in terms of danger of death'. As for the contribution of a Pathfinder, in the same terms of intensity and duration of danger, it was, he asserted, 'at least twice' that of other Bomber Command crews.

With his first, second and third tours behind him and now into his fourth, if Cranswick had returned from his 107th op, he would have anticipated carrying on towards his 120th before being withdrawn, albeit reluctantly, from further bombing operations (knowing nothing of the newly imposed order restricting him to just three more ops). Against this background of intensity and duration of danger, what was it, this unseen force, that drove him on so relentlessly? Was it something to do with the 'adrenalin rush', to use a term more familiar today than was current in those bygone times? Was it, as his mother indicated to the author, to avenge the ever-mounting death toll among his flier friends? Or was it, quite simply, that Cranswick kept going because he regarded operational flying as 'my job': a job – the only job – in which he could enjoy what he called 'complete peace of mind'.

Far more likely is the compulsion that was so dominant in the summer of 1944, that, with the Allies having secured a foothold on the Continent of Europe, it called for an even greater individual contribution on the part of Servicemen and women everywhere to help maintain the momentum – a concept that Cranswick would have translated simply into meaning that, the more ops he flew, the more he was doing for 'the war effort'. Yet, even as he neared his 100th, his closest chum outside the RAF – a friend from childhood – warned Cranswick that it was not merely his own life that he was putting in jeopardy but those of his crew. The reaction was much as anticipated, that Cranswick considered himself 'as right as rain when he was in the air'. It must be acknowledged that, ever the consummate captain, he would not have permitted anything or anyone to prejudice peak performance.

Had he survived his 107th operation and gone on to achieve 110, Cranswick would probably then have been in line for a second DFC or even a second DSO, the simple yet unfortunate fact being that he had matured too early as a bomber pilot... passing the 'magic' 100 before the chain of command came to realise its significance as a benchmark in human endeavour.

There is a timeline that reinforces this view. He carried out his 100th op in May 1944, unmarked by formal recognition. Four months later, when the incomparable Leonard Cheshire was awarded the Victoria Cross (its citation recognising that in four years of fighting 'he maintained a standard of outstanding personal achievement'), that citation went on to include a specific mention that Cheshire 'has now completed a total of 100 missions'.

Then in December 1944, on a day when as many as thirty-four awards of a second DFC were announced in the *London Gazette*, Path Finder Force pilot Robert Palmer's marked his completion of 100 operational sorties, the citation noting that he 'continued to operate with unremitting zeal and enthusiasm'. Among fellow recipients, ten were similarly serving on either of the two *Oboe* Mosquito squadrons. Palmer's 'century' combined his *Oboe* ops on No. 109 Squadron and pre-PFF ops flying 'heavies'.[1]

With the confirmation, as we have now seen, that *J-Johnnie* succumbed to the deadly fire of a German night-fighter, the unanswerable question is this: would this Lancaster bomber have fared differently had it not been for the crew-switch earlier in the day that was demanded by unarguable medical reasons, Cranswick's long-time air gunner Ivor Howard having picked up a cold and been barred from participating in the night's air operations. They had been together for eighteen months; Cranswick had never been on ops without Howard in all their time with the Pathfinders. They were, it is evident, more than just bosom pals; they implicitly trusted their lives the one to the other.

Ivor Howard's prowess had earned him the DFC the previous October for the 'utmost skill and coolness in directing his captain in evading enemy night-fighters, searchlights and anti-aircraft fire', the citation also singling out his 'fine fighting spirit'. Add competence to kinship, and surely no one would have expected Cranswick to think or to act differently when confronted abruptly with the revelation that Howard would not be a crew member this night.

So, it was hardly surprising that the pilot's 'knee-jerk' reaction was to say that he would contact the MO and 'get you on'; then, when that approach failed, to say that without his customary air gunner he would not be flying at all. The sense of stalemate ended when the stand-in was named, and it was apparent that his experience was beyond question: he was just one short of the forty-five ops needed to complete his tour with Pathfinders. Sensibility overcame initial impulse, with professionalism winning the day, Cranswick certainly being far too judgemental an individual to permit bravado to rule his head.

In the air, flying the same aircraft, ND846, *J-Johnnie*, that he had used on all ten previous ops when back with No. 35 Squadron for his fourth tour, Cranswick warned his crew that 'the night-fighters will be up tonight', recognizing their presence as the biggest menace to survival. It demanded collective human effort on top of that provided by Fishpond, the radar system designed to give early warning of German night-fighters approaching within 30 miles: a heavy responsibility upon the air gunners in their swivelling turrets, yes, but everyone with eyes-on-the-skies needed to be extra-vigilant to assure timely warning for the pilot to take evasive action. There would be 'blind spots', as may have been the case, for there is no doubt, now, that the shells that struck the Lancaster's bomb bay, immediately engulfing it in flames, came from a night-fighter. Lone survivor Wilfred Horner had no knowledge as to whether or not anyone on board became aware of an imminent attack, the resulting inferno being so sudden; for their part, the enemy crew would have done all in their power to creep up unseen, to strike and then to withdraw to safety.

In this 107th operation as the pilot of a heavy bomber, Cranswick had successfully transported his crew and a bomb bay filled with markers and bombs to the target; now, with the job done, it was 'homeward-bound' – though risks remained and danger persisted. Alert to the tasks in hand and no doubt trying desperately to keep it from his mind, he must have accepted that, one night, fortune could yield to adversity – though he would have been inclined to the view that, if the plane was hit by enemy gunfire, whether by a night-fighter or flak from the ground, there was the prospect of escape by parachute and the opportunity to evade capture as 'the Flying Tramp'. This was not to be; the bomber was ablaze too quickly, too fiercely and too extensively for any of the eight on board to escape in a planned manner.

Above the commune of Villecresnes, just outside the French capital, in the early hours of 5 July 1944, Alec Cranswick and six members of his last crew on his final operation came to the end of their young lives, as did so many more from this Squadron, from this Group and in this Command within the Royal Air Force in the Second World War. It could be said that he was 'just one man' – *but what a man he was, this Alec Cranswick.*

# Notes

### Prologue

1 Besides being one of the 110,000 men engaged on heavy bombing operations with the Royal Air Force in the Second World War, Alec Cranswick was one of the 55,573 members of Bomber Command who lost their lives in that period.

2 Readers with more than a passing interest in this most famous of bombers in the Second World War have an ever-expanding wealth of information open to them. Suffice here to record the dates that encompass its service in the war in Europe; that the first operational mission by Lancasters was on 3 March 1942, when No. 44 Squadron carried out four minelaying sorties off the German coast, and among the last were 'mercy ops' ferrying back to Britain between 26 April and 7 May 1945 some 75,000 prisoners of war liberated from camps on the Continent and, between 29 Apr. and 7 May 1945, dropping 6,672 tons of food to civilians approaching starvation in occupied Holland.

### Chapter 1: Mission at Midnight

1 Quoted by permission of the Controller of HM Stationery Office.

2 It is only with this 50th Anniversary Edition of *Pathfinder Cranswick* that there has come confirmation to demolish the 'flak' theory that persisted during and long after early research for this biography. For example, even when this book was in the early stages of production, a chance visit to the French website France-Crashes 39–45 (which details Allied aircraft going down on French soil during the Second World War) showed the cause of this Lancaster's demise as 'Hit by flak at 8000 feet', the same explanation appearing on Aérostèles, a listing of aviation memorials, when giving information about the location and purpose of the Villecresnes tribute to Allied bomber crews. Prior to this, however, Path Finder Force documentation made available to the author at The National Archives in Kew had gone some way towards resolving the manner in which *J-Johnnie* was brought down; while anti-aircraft fire was only 'slight', there was in fact 'considerable fighter activity', making this the more likely cause.

Out of sixty-two Lancasters and sixty-four Halifaxes detailed for this raid, six Lancasters and five Halifaxes were reported as missing – most, if not all, no doubt falling victim to the groups of Luftwaffe night-fighter units based in the Netherlands, Belgium, France and Germany as a significant and strategically positioned component of Generalfeldmarschall Hugo Sperrle's Luftflotte 3.

During those early hours, their crews claimed a total of forty-eight four-engined bombers destroyed, each of them a participant in one or other of RAF raids on three separate targets south of the French capital – at Saint-Leu d'Esserent and at Orleans in addition to Villeneuve-St.-Georges. As for this latter attack itself, Bomber Command's assessment was that the bombing was 'very concentrated'; however, smoke quickly obscured the Pathfinders' target indicators to such an extent that Master Bomber, in the later stages, must have accepted he could do no better in the interests of pursuing the desire for utmost precision than to instruct the incoming Main Force crews to 'Bomb column of smoke'.

### Chapter 2: Groomed for Gallantry

1   It is an historical coincidence that the uncle served for a time with No. 35 Squadron in the year of its formation, 1916, this being Alec Cranswick's squadron in Path Finder Force. Flying Officer (Observer) Cranswick did not return from a mission on 18 November 1917, when serving in France with No. 23 Squadron.

2   St Edward's School, Oxford, has developed significantly since the era of Alec Cranswick (1933–7) and even more so since that of his son, Alexander (1958–62). With some 360 pupils in Alec's time at the school, the intake has grown considerably to about 660 in 2010. The first girl joined the school in the Lower Sixth in 1982 and St Edward's became fully co-educational in 1997.

The Combined Cadet Force (CCF) continues to flourish, its stated aims being 'to develop a young person's powers of leadership through training, to promote the qualities of responsibility, self-reliance, resourcefulness and a sense of service to the School'. Pupils join in their 4th Form year, choosing either the Army, Navy or Air Force section and meeting in the much-used sporting complex called Esporta – the Douglas Bader Centre; this was built on a site where the now long-gone Air Hut used to stand.

It is the aim of the CCF to provide background knowledge about the three Services, with the RAF section offering particularly wide-ranging activities, including drill, shooting with the .22 rifle, principles of flight and navigation, airmanship, first aid and command tasks. For air experience, there is powered flight at RAF Station, Benson, as well as gliding.

### Chapter 3: School for Heroes

1   Ninety-nine as a fighter pilot.

2   In one rare instance, a wartime gallantry award to a St Edward's Old Boy who served in the RAF marked not a demonstration of conspicuous actions while in the air but courage displayed while directly in the face of enemy forces on the ground. This distinction goes to Arthur Banks, whose posthumous George Cross was for his courage and endurance when held captive in Italy. A member of the RAF Volunteer Reserve, he was serving with No. 112 Squadron in the Desert Air Force when, engaged on armed reconnaissance over north-eastern Italy in a single-seater Mustang in the summer of 1944, he was brought down by ground fire. Having managed to negotiate a successful crash-landing, he came into contact with a partisan group, becoming what the citation for his George Cross – announced post-war, on 5 November 1946 – would describe as being 'an outstanding figure' among them, advising and encouraging the group in actions against the enemy. With the misfortune to be captured in an ambush in December 1944, apparently as the result of betrayal, Arthur Banks was brutally tortured yet remained silent, eventually being shot in the back of the head. The Common-wealth War Graves Commission records his death as having occurred on 20 December 1944, and his grave as being in the Argenta Gap War Cemetery.

3   Long gone, the Air Hut site has been transformed latterly into the much-used sporting complex called Esporta – the Douglas Bader Centre.

### Chapter 4: Enthusiast with Wings

1   Further details about this particular dummy airfield and about deception measures in general have been encompassed in a separate section in the Appendix, in the section entitled 'A Dummy Airfield and a Near-fatal Crash'.

### Chapter 6: Posted to Path Finder Force

1   Quoted in the original hardback of *Pathfinder Cranswick* by permission of the Controller of

HM Stationery Office.

2  Published in 1958 by Frederick Muller.

3  Published in 1947 by Collins.

4  *Oboe* was carried in the twin-engined Mosquito, with its considerable speed and ceiling advantages over the aircraft operated by the heavy bomber squadrons of PFF, using signals from coastal wireless stations in Britain to keep these Pathfinders on a set course. However, the fact that the signals were transmitted from ground level meant that there was a range limitation of some 200 miles – sufficient, nonetheless, to embrace key industrial targets in the Ruhr. Pilot and navigator picked up their separate signals in earphones, the pilot using his to follow a course to the target and the navigator using his to trigger the moment for bomb/target indicator release. Many years after *Pathfinder Cranswick*, the author met a number of those pilots and navigators when researching and writing *Beam Bombers: The Secret War of No 109 Squadron*, its central theme being the development, introduction and use of *Oboe*.

5  It is worthy of note that Miss Sonnica H. Godden, owner of Kentwood Kennels, where Cranswick bought Kluva, went on to achieve distinction in 1965 when a German Shepherd Dog (GSD) she bred and owned – Ch. Fenton of Kentwood – became 'Best in Show', in other words the Supreme Champion that year, at the internationally renowned Cruft's. Ch. Fenton of Kentwood was the first of a trio of representatives of this breed to take that title in the space of just seven years. In present-day parlance, Kluva would have been a German Shepherd; however, to Cranswick and others in those days, Kluva was an 'Alsatian', the reintroduction of the synonymous breed name 'GSD' (which dates back to the end of the nineteenth century) awaiting a change in attitude to the 'German' connotation in the post-war era. Cranswick's choice for such a dog is understandable; it is a popular breed recognized for loyalty, intelligence and obedience, often being described as a 'one-man' dog – certainly so in this instance. Inevitably, Alsatians are regarded always as 'big dogs', both in size and in weight, so there is an important point to be made: it has to be recognized that the Kluva making as many as eighty-two flights in an aircraft totalling 106 hours 50 minutes with Cranswick at the controls was then just a puppy (these remarkable statistics, incidentally, coming from 'Sergeant' Kluva's own 'logbook' that the author was able to examine). At that time, therefore, Kluva was a long way from adulthood, which would be reached at 18–24 months, and probably no more than half the likely adult weight of between 75 and 100 lb. Cranswick missed so many wonderful years with Kluva, who, with an average life expectancy of twelve years for this breed, survived well beyond that span, the author meeting him on a number of occasions in the late 1950s – Cranswick's mother then caring for Kluva just as he himself would have done.

### Chapter 8: Captain Courageous

1  An opportunity for the author to view the relevant reports in The National Archives subsequently revealed that – for PFF overall – the operation had gone 'right' (if 'wrong' for Cranswick and his crew). The first Pathfinder 'arrived punctually' and dropped its target indicators 'quite accurately', as a prelude to a 'very successful raid'.

### Chapter 9: Bull's Eyes out of the Sky

1  Martin Middlebrook's extensive research considerably later for his book, *The Peenemunde Raid*, which benefitted from more and more material having come into the public domain, appears to conflict with personal recollections gathered towards the end of the 1950s when Michael Cumming was interviewing aircrew who flew with Cranswick. Where the contention was that 'the camera recorded a beautiful example of target pinpointing'... 'a bull's eye as nice as the Intelligence officers had seen for a long, long time', Middlebrook indicates that 'his aiming photo had overshot by 1,000 yards'. On the assumption that 'the camera never lies' and that there was no mix-up with the films, perhaps this was a matter of seeing-is-believing while over-excited in the heat of the battle. For anyone wanting to digest 'the full story', *The Peenemunde Raid* is commended.

**Chapter 10: Pathway to Romance**

1 For his own books Martin Middlebrook has had the opportunity for in-depth research specific to the series of attacks on Berlin. During the second half of November 1943, he indicates in *The Berlin Raids* that RAF bombers, in total, dropped over 7,000 tons of explosives on four nights. In *The Bomber Command War Diaries* (co-authored with Chris Everitt) he states that the main part of the offensive against Berlin was from 18/19 November 1943 to the end of January 1944 during which Bomber Command lost 384 aircraft – a rate of some five per cent.

2 The Cranswick family were living at No. 2, Polstead Road. Among its previous occupants were the Lawrences and their five sons, the second oldest the legendary T. E. Lawrence – 'Lawrence of Arabia' – who was aged about 8 at the time he arrived there. A subsequent Blue Plaque records that this was his home for twenty-five years until 1921. It was a period that included his first-class degree in Modern History from Jesus College, Oxford, his travels in the Middle East as an archaeologist and his leadership of the Arabian revolt during the First World War – all of which was before he decided to change his name, to join the RAF and unsuccessfully to seek obscurity. Lawrence died in 1935, aged 46, the result of a motorcycle accident near his then home in Dorset, an isolated cottage at Clouds Hill (since owned by the National Trust), where he wrote some of his book *The Seven Pillars of Wisdom.*

3 No. 109 Squadron was a key player in the creation, development and introduction of *Oboe*, the blind-bombing system, and, until joined by No. 105 Squadron in June 1943, its crews were alone in using the two-seater, twin-engined Mosquito on *Oboe*-directed target-marking and bombing sorties during its operational lifetime from 20 December 1942 to 5 May 1945. Compared with the 'heavies', these Mosquitos generally functioned closer to home and were higher flying as well as faster – advantages that arguably reduced the operational risks facing their crews. Path Finder Force commander Don Bennett took the comparison further: he judged the fatigue on an *Oboe* operation to be less, as well as putting the risk element lower, when, in correspondence with 'Bomber' Harris, he suggested an *Oboe* op counted as three-quarters of an op on 'heavies'.

4 For his fourth tour, Cranswick would have a mix of fresh and seasoned flyers. Navigator Reg Kille, coming to the squadron on 19 March straight from training, would be in the crew for their first op on 19/20 May (as would flight engineer Charles Erickson); second air bomber Mike Gibson Taylor, newcomer on the seventh, would come with operational experience gained with 'C' Flight during January and February.

5 Cranswick's 100th op was against Aachen on 24/25 May, the next against a flying-bomb site at Mardick (28/29 May) and then four the following month, against targets in the Forêt de Cerisy (7/8 June), an airfield at Rennes (9/10 June) and flying-bomb sites at Coubronne (23/24 June) and Rimeux (24/25 June).

**Chapter 11: The Last Command**

1 In fact one or more crew members in each of the two Lancasters belonging to No. 35 Squadron managed to escape by parachute; as became known later, although Wilfred Horner was the only person to do so in Cranswick's crew, four in Lambert's crew parachuted to safety, all five becoming prisoners of war.

2 Recalling the series of air attacks on the railway system at Villeneuve-St.-Georges by the Americans with their Flying Fortresses and Liberators in daylight and by the RAF during the night, led by Path Finder Force, one resident of Villecresnes wrote – in a letter post-war seen by the author – that it was possible, in Villecresnes, some 5 miles from the target, to 'read a newspaper in the light of the flares to mark- out the target before the bombing'.

3 Research in France on behalf of the author pointed to Réau as the crash site; in fact *J-Johnnie*, barely out of the target area, came down in the commune of Villecresnes.

4 There were two Lancasters of No. 35 Squadron reported missing as a result of the air operations carried out during the night of 4–5 July 1944, the two captains being Squadron Leaders Cranswick and Lambert, both aircraft going down shortly after heading back for

home. Pilots in the same Luftwaffe night-fighter units each claimed the destruction of one of those two Lancasters, which occurred within the space of four minutes. A detailed account appears in the Appendix, in the section entitled 'End of a Life – End of a Riddle'.

5   This photograph of the remains of Cranswick's Lancaster was a last-minute 'find' that owes its appearance in *Pathfinder Cranswick* to Claude Archambault, who is one of the foremost photo-journalists in France specializing in Second World War aviation. He holds the copyright for this unique photograph, which came into his possession while pursuing an ongoing interest in crash sites where aircraft fell on French soil – this was then the 1,523rd such site that he had logged for potential research, though now the numbered files have since passed 10,000. In the summer of 1987, Jean Marson, who was still living in the locality where the Lancaster came down, responded to an appeal for information by Claude Archambault in the Villecresnes municipal magazine, explaining in a letter that he took the picture on what he described as a '6 x 9 camera', though without indicating how he had been able to do so, literally beneath the eyes of uniformed representatives of the occupying forces surveying the wreckage. When the author was in contact with Claude Archambault, he kindly agreed immediately to send a copy of the crash-site photograph for inclusion in this 50th Anniversary Edition.

### Appendix 2. A Dummy Airfield and a Near-fatal Crash

1   Source is TNA: PRO AIR 15/320, Encl 74A.

2   For their help in pinpointing sources of information about the Crostwick decoy aerodrome and other aspects of Britain's deception strategy in the Second World War, the assistance so readily given by Jan Allen and Edwin Rose of the Norfolk Museums & Archaeology Service as well as by Dave Wood (Military Structures Database website) and Guy Jefferson (British Military Airfield Histories website) is gratefully acknowledged.

### Appendix 3. Remembering Fallen Comrades: No. 35 Squadron and Path Finder Force

1   Though the end of hostilities saw the end of Path Finder Force, No. 35 Squadron remained active – but with a chequered existence. Successive re-equipping saw the Lancasters giving way to Lincolns, to Washingtons and then to Canberras, the latter aircraft being detached from the squadron's UK base to Cyprus in October 1956 during the Suez crisis. On 1 December 1962 came the last truly memorable event in its history, No. 35 Squadron becoming part of the V-bomber force, flying Vulcan B.2s. When the squadron disbanded on 28 February 1982, it was for a third and final time since the end of the Second World War.

2   As well as remembering RAF aircrew who lost their lives with Cranswick, the memorial at Villecresnes remembers the five crew members who lost their lives when a US Army Air Force B-17 crashed on 3 September 1943.

3   At one minute after noon on 3 September 1939, a Blenheim piloted by Flying Officer A. McPherson took off on a reconnaissance mission to Wilhelmshaven. The aircraft returned safely 4 hours 49 minutes later. On the night of 2–3 May 1945, Wyton aircraft took part in the last Bomber Command raid on Germany, attacking Kiel, later repatriating prisoners of war and providing 'Cooks Tours' facilities to enable ground personnel to have an aerial view of the destruction caused to German cities.

### Appendix 4. End of a Life – End of a Riddle

1   Among Main Force squadrons engaged in the raid on Villeneuve-St.-Georges that night, Nos 419 and 433 each lost three Lancasters and three Halifaxes respectively, with Nos 424 and 427 each losing one Halifax and No. 428 losing one Lancaster.

2   Steve Darlow, whose books have entailed considerable research into German military documentation, kindly pointed the author in the right direction when discussing the possibility of confirming the manner in which Alec Cranswick's Lancaster was hit and set afire 'by enemy shells' – to use the term that was put to the biographer in the late 1950s and onwards.

It appeared to be common ground that anti-aircraft fire – flak – brought him down, rather than a night-fighter's guns. With RAF records indicating greater activity from the aerial defences that night than there was from the ground defences, the starting point became Tony Wood's *Combat Claims* and *Casualties Lists* (specifically *OKL Fighter Claims by JaFü 11, Jagdkorps/Lfl.3*), these opening the way to clarification, elaboration and confirmation using very many sources, among them web forums and such much-used facilities as *The Nachtjagd War Diaries* by Dr Theo Boiten, the Aircrew Remembrance Society and Tom Kracker's *Luftwaffe Pilot Archive*, all gratefully acknowledged here and certainly appreciated by this author.

### Appendix 5. Assessment

1  Squadron Leader Bob Palmer lost his life on 23 December 1944, in a raid on the Gremberg railway yards – an action for which he was awarded the Victoria Cross – while Master Bomber flying an *Oboe*-equipped Lancaster. It was his 111th op. The author is aware of four pilots and twelve navigators who flew *Oboe* sorties with No. 109 Squadron or No. 105 Squadron and reached the 'magic' 100 when combined with ops on bomber squadrons in pre-PFF service. Squadron Leaders John Burt, pilot, and Ron Curtis, navigator, members of No. 109 Squadron, both exceeded that figure on *Oboe* ops alone (104 apiece, neither flying with anyone else) to amass totals of 129 and 139 respectively when, on 6 March 1945, Path Finder Force commander Don Bennett withdrew them permanently from operational duties. Both wanted to continue, pressing hard to be allowed to do so, but Bennett was having none of it – if he were to agree, he told them, 'there would be questions asked in Parliament!' (See *Beam Bombers, The Secret War of No. 109 Squadron*, by Michael Cumming, published in 1998). Burt's 129 ops as a pilot remained unbeaten, the 145 ops credited to navigator Squadron Leader E. R. Benson earning him the distinction of having completed more ops than anyone else who served on an *Oboe* squadron. Coincidentally, this 'top trio' of Benson, Burt and Curtis each gained a Bar to the DFC (a second DFC) on the same day in November 1944.

   Seven members of No. 109 Squadron were each 'gazetted' on 8 December 1944 with a Bar to the DFC – Squadron Leader Sooby, Acting Squadron Leaders Esler and Jefferson, Flight Lieutenants Emmerson, Palmer and Turnbull and Acting Flight Lieutenant Burnett – with four members of No. 105 Squadron similarly honoured – Acting Squadron Leaders Gilbert and Helmore, Flight Lieutenant Spencer and Flying Officer Poll. The Distinguished Flying Cross recognised courage or devotion to duty while flying in active service against the enemy; the Distinguished Service Order recognised distinguished service, normally in positions of command but also – less frequently – individual acts of gallantry.

# Index